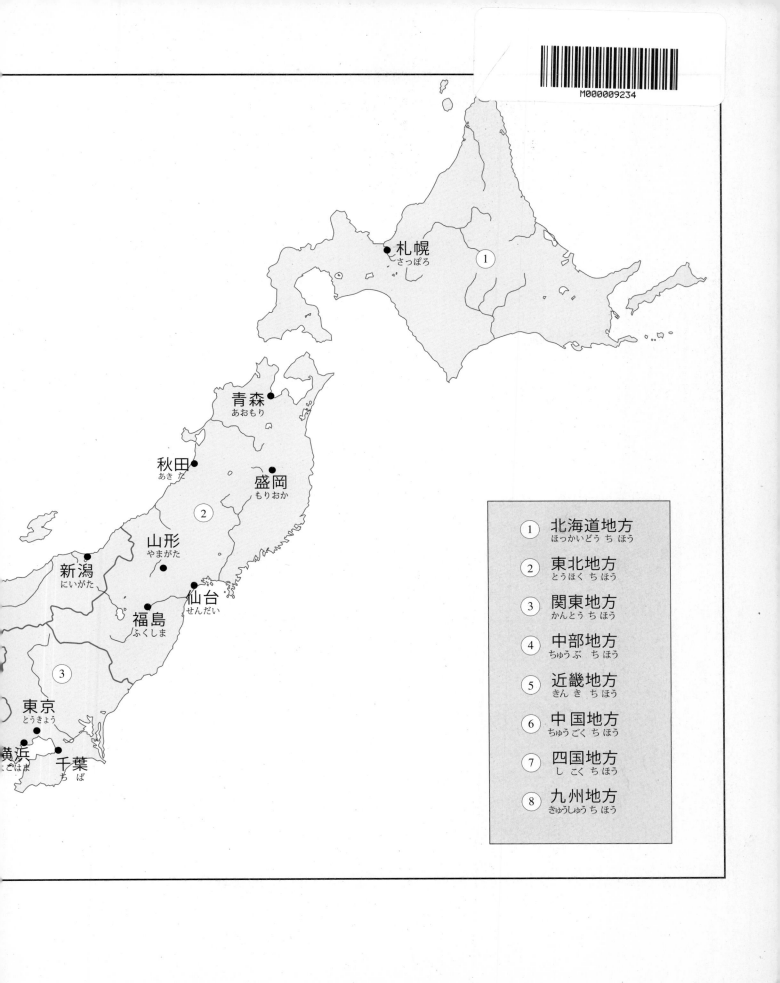

札幌
さっぽろ

① 北海道地方
ほっかいどう ち ほう

青森
あおもり

秋田
あき た

盛岡
もりおか

② 東北地方
とうほく ち ほう

③ 関東地方
かんとう ち ほう

山形
やまがた

新潟
にいがた

仙台
せんだい

福島
ふくしま

④ 中部地方
ちゅうぶ ち ほう

⑤ 近畿地方
きん き ち ほう

⑥ 中国地方
ちゅうごく ち ほう

⑦ 四国地方
し こく ち ほう

⑧ 九州地方
きゅうしゅう ち ほう

東京
とうきょう

横浜
よこはま

千葉
ち ば

②

③

NAKAMA 1b

INTRODUCTORY JAPANESE: *COMMUNICATION, CULTURE, CONTEXT*

Second Edition

Yukiko Abe Hatasa
Hiroshima University

Kazumi Hatasa
Purdue University
The Japanese School, Middlebury College

Seiichi Makino
Princeton University

HEINLE
CENGAGE Learning™

HEINLE
CENGAGE Learning™

Publisher: Rolando Hernández
Senior Sponsoring Editor: Glenn A. Wilson
Executive Marketing Director:
   Eileen Bernadette Moran
Discipline Product Manager: Giuseppina Daniel
Senior Development Editor: Judith Bach
Development Editor: Kim Beuttler
Senior Project Editor: Margaret Park Bridges
Senior Media Producer: Mona Singh
Senior Content Manager: Janet Edmonds
Cover Design Director: Tony Saizon
Senior Photo Editor: Jennifer Meyer Dare
Senior Composition Buyer: Chuck Dutton
Senior New Title Project Manager: Pat O'Neill
Marketing Assistant: Lorreen Ruth Pelletier

Cover image: Harold Burch, New York City

Photographs unless otherwise noted
courtesy of the authors.
Page b-15: © Hugh Threlfall/Alamy
Page b-46: © D. Hurst/Alamy
Page b-46: © Hugh Threlfall/Alamy
Page b-46: © Hugh Threlfall/Alamy
Page b-46: © D. Hurst/Alamy
Page b-46: © Bloomimage/Corbis
Page b-46: © Lew Robertson/Corbis
Page b-47: © Kenneth Hamm/Photo Japan
Page b-60: © Kenneth Hamm/Photo Japan
Page b-60: © Kenneth Hamm/Photo Japan
Page b-102: © Kenneth Hamm/Photo Japan
Page b-102: © Kenneth Hamm/Photo Japan
Page b-133: © Kenneth Hamm/Photo Japan
Page b-148: © Joeri DeRocker/Photo Japan
Page b-148: © Chad Ehlers/Alamy
Page b-165: © Stefan Zaklin/epa/Corbis
Page b-175: Handout/Getty Images
Page b-190: © Kenneth Hamm/Photo Japan
Page b-190: © Kenneth Hamm/Photo Japan
Page b-191: © Kenneth Hamm/Photo Japan
Page b-223: © Barry Lewis/Alamy
Page b-239: © Kenneth Hamm/Photo Japan

For product information and technolog assistance, contact us at
Cengage Learning Customer & Sales Support, 1-800-354-9706

For permission to use material from this text or product, submit all requests online at **cengage.com/permissions**
Further permissions questions can be emailed to
permissionsrequest@cengage.com

Library of Congress Control Number: 2007926500

Instructor's Annotated Edition
   ISBN-10: 0-547-20842-1
   ISBN-13: 978-0-547-20842-8

For orders, use student text ISBNs
   ISBN-10: 0-547-20840-5
   ISBN-13: 978-0-547-20840-4

Heinle
20 Channel Center
Boston, MA 02210
USA

Cengage Learning is a leading provider of customized learning solutions with office locations around the globe, including Singapore, the United Kingdom, Australia, Mexico, Brazil, and Japan. Locate your local office at:
international.cengage.com/region

Cengage Learning products are represented in Canada by Nelson Education, Ltd.

For your course and learning solutions, visit
academic.cengage.com

Purchase any of our products at your local college store or at our preferred online store **www.ichapters.com**

Printed in the United States of America

5 6 7 8 9-RRJ-12 11 10

ABOUT THE AUTHORS

Professor Yukiko Abe Hatasa received her Ph.D. in linguistics in 1992 from the University of Illinois at Urbana-Champaign. She is known nationwide as one of the premier Japanese methodologists in the United States and as an experienced coordinator of large teacher training programs. She has served as the coordinator of the Japanese language program at the University of Iowa and is currently a professor at Hiroshima University, where her primary responsibilities are teacher training and SLA research.

Professor Kazumi Hatasa received his Ph.D. in education in 1989 from the University of Illinois at Urbana-Champaign. He is currently a professor at Purdue University and Director of the Japanese School at Middlebury College. He is recognized internationally for his work in software development for the Japanese language and distributes most of his work as freeware over the Internet.

Professor Seiichi Makino received his Ph.D. in linguistics in 1968 from the University of Illinois at Urbana-Champaign. He is an internationally prominent Japanese linguist and scholar who is recognized throughout the world for his scholarship and for his many publications. Before beginning his tenure at Princeton University in 1991, he taught Japanese language, linguistics and culture at the University of Illinois while training lower division language coordinators. He is an experienced ACTFL oral proficiency trainer in Japanese and frequently trains Japanese instructors internationally in proficiency-oriented instruction and in the administration of the Oral Proficiency Interview. Professor Makino has been the Academic Director of the Japanese Pedagogy M.A. Summer Program at Columbia University since 1996. He also directs the Princeton-in-Ishikawa Summer Program.

CONTENTS

CHAPTER 9: RESTAURANTS AND INVITATIONS

CHAPTER 10: MY FAMILY

TO THE STUDENT

Nakama 1 is based on the principle that learning another language means acquiring new skills, not just facts and information—that we learn by doing. To achieve this goal, *Nakama 1* systematically involves you in many activities that incorporate the language skills of listening, speaking, reading, and writing. We believe that culture is an integral component of language, too. To help you become familiar with Japanese culture, your text includes high-interest culture notes and relevant communication strategies. New to this edition, an appealing story line video, featuring a Japanese-American exchange student in Tokyo, bring chapter dialogues to life.

ORGANIZATION OF THE TEXTBOOK

Nakama 1 consists of twelve chapters in two parts. *Nakama 1a* contains Chapters 1–6; *Nakama 1b* contains Chapters 7–12. In Chapter 1, you will learn the sounds of the Japanese language and a set of Japanese syllabary symbols called **hiragana**. You will also learn basic greetings and classroom instructions. A second Japanese syllabary called **katakana** is presented after Chapter 2. Chapters 2 through 12 each focus on a common communicative situation and contain the following features:

- Chapter Opener: Each chapter opens with a theme-setting photograph and chapter contents by section. Keeping in mind the objectives listed at the top of the opener will help you focus on achieving your learning goals.

- Vocabulary: The vocabulary is presented in thematic groups, each followed by a variety of communicative activities and activities in context. Supplemental vocabulary is also provided throughout the chapter, but you are not expected to retain it. All active vocabulary is listed by function at the beginning of each chapter, except for Chapter 1, where the list appears last, after you've learned to read **hiragana**.

- Dialogue: The lively dialogues center on Alice Ueda, a Japanese-American college student, who is spending two years studying in Japan. Through the dialogue and accompanying video, you will get to know a series of characters and follow them through typical events in their lives. The video, related activities, and interactive online practice will all reinforce your understanding of the content, discourse organization, and use of formal and casual Japanese speech styles.

- Japanese Culture: Up-to-date culture notes in English explore social, economic, and historical aspects of Japanese life that are essential to effective communication.

- Grammar: Clear, easy-to-understand grammar explanations are accompanied by sample sentences and notes that help you understand how to use the grammar appropriately. In-class pair and group activities let you practice immediately what you've learned. As there is a high correlation between successful communication and grammar accuracy, this section is especially important.

- Listening: Useful strategies and pre-listening activities for general comprehension precede the section's main listening practice. Post-listening activities concentrate on more detailed comprehension and apply what you have learned to other communicative purposes.

- Communication: This section will provide you with knowledge and practice of basic strategies to accelerate your ability to communicate in Japanese.

- **Kanji:** Chapters 4 through 12 introduce a total of 127 **kanji** (Chinese characters). The section begins with useful information such as the composition of individual characters, word formation, and how to use Japanese dictionaries. The presentation of each character includes stroke order to help you master correct stroke orders when writing in Japanese and to prepare you for the reading section.

- Reading: Each reading passage begins with a reading strategy, and includes pre- and post-reading activities designed to help you become a successful reader of Japanese. From Chapter 2, the text is written in all three scripts: **hiragana, katakana,** and **kanji. Hiragana** subscripts (**furigana**) are provided for **katakana** through Chapter 3, and for unfamiliar **kanji** throughout the textbook. The readings include a small number of unknown words to help you develop strategies for understanding authentic texts.

- Integration: Integrated practice wraps up every chapter using discussion, interviewing, and role-play activities that interweave all the skills you've learned in the current and previous chapters.

STUDENT COMPONENTS

- Student Text: Your Student Text contains all the information and activities you need for in-class use. It is divided into two parts encompassing twelve chapters plus a special chapter following Chapter 2 that introduces **katakana.** Each regular chapter contains vocabulary presentations and activities, a thematic dialogue and practice, grammar presentations and activities, cultural information, reading selections, writing practice, and ample communicative practice. Valuable reference sections at the back of the book include verb charts, a **kanji** list, and Japanese-English and English-Japanese glossaries.

- In-Text Audio CD: The In-Text Audio CD contains recordings of all the listening activities in the text as well as all active chapter vocabulary. The audio activity clips are also available as MP3 files and the vocabulary pronunciations can be found in the flashcards on the student website. These audio materials are designed to maximize your exposure to the sounds of natural spoken Japanese and to help you practice pronunciation.

- Student Activities Manual (SAM): The Student Activities Manual (SAM) includes out-of-class practice of the material presented in the Student Text. Each chapter of the SAM includes a workbook section, which focuses on written vocabulary, grammar, **kanji** and writing practice, and a lab section, which focuses on pronunciation and listening comprehension, including Dict-a-Conversation dictation activities.

- SAM Audio Program: The SAM Audio Program corresponds to the audio portion of the SAM and reinforces your pronunciation and listening skills. You may listen to this material in the lab or on CD. The audio is also available as MP3 files from the passkey-protected area of the student website.

- DVD: New for the second edition, the two-tiered Nakama video program includes a story line video, where the experiences of a Japanese-American exchange student, Alice Ueda, featured in the chapter dialogues are brought to life. A series of cultural segments that depict everyday situations are tied to the theme of each chapter. You will be able to view the video in class, on DVD, on the student website as MP4 files, or while working on video comprehension activities found on the passkey-protected area of the site.

• Student companion site: You will find a variety of resources on the student website. A wealth of interactive exercises and games give you further practice with chapter topics. Vocabulary and grammar quizzes, audio flashcards for vocabulary, and **kanji** and pronunciation review help you monitor and assess your progress. MP3 files for the text listening activities can also be downloaded from the site. The website is accessible at college.cengage.com/PIC/nakamaone2e.

ACKNOWLEDGMENTS

The authors and publisher thank the following people for their recommendations regarding the content of *Nakama 1*. Their comments and suggestions were invaluable during the development of this publication.

Noriko Akatsuka
Aloysius Chang
Len Grzanka
Hiroko Harada
Masako Hamada
Janet Ikeda
Mieko Ishibashi
Noriko Iwasaki
Kimberly Jones
Sarachie Karasawa
Hiroko Kataoka
Yukio Kataoka
Michiya Kawai
Chisato Kitagawa
Lisa Kobuke
Chiyo Konishi
Junko Kumamoto-Healey
Yukari Kunisue
Yasumi Kuriya
John Mertz
Masahiko Minami
Akira Miura
Shigeru Miyagawa
Seigo Nakao
Hiroshi Nara
Machiko Netsu
Catherine Oshida
Yoko Pusavat
Yoshiko Saito-Abbott
Haruko Sakakibara
Kitty Shek
Ritsuko Shigeyama
Satoru Shinagawa
Zenryu Shirakawa
Shizuka Tatsuzawa
Miyo Uchida
Alexander Vovin
Paul Warnick
Yasuko Ito Watt
Kikuko Yamashita

The authors and publisher also thank the following people for field-testing *Nakama 1*. Their comments contributed greatly to the accuracy of this publication.

Nobuko Chikamatsu
Fusae Ekida
Junko Hino
Satoru Ishikawa
Yoshiko Jo
Sayuri Kubota
Yasumi Kuriya
Izumi Matsuda
Junko Mori
Fumiko Nazikian
Mayumi Oka
Amy Snyder Ohta
Mayumi Steinmetz
Keiko Yamaguchi

The authors are also grateful to the following people at Cengage Learning for their valuable assistance during the development of this project: Rolando Hernández, Glenn Wilson, Eileen Bernadette Moran, Lorreen Pelletier, Judith Bach, Kim Beuttler, Charline Lake, and Margaret Bridges.

They are especially grateful to Yoshiko Jo and Margaret Hines for copyediting, to Satoru Ishikawa, Bill Weaver, and Yoshiko Jo for proofreading, and to Michael Kelsey of Inari Information Services, Inc. Finally, profound thanks go to Noriko Hanabusa for her work on the Student Activities Manual and to Kazuko Yokoi for her work on the illustrations in this edition.

Chapter 7

第
七
課
<ruby>第<rt>だい</rt></ruby><ruby>七<rt>なな</rt></ruby><ruby>課<rt>か</rt></ruby>

好きなものと 好きなこと
<ruby>好<rt>す</rt></ruby>きなものと <ruby>好<rt>す</rt></ruby>きなこと
Favorite Things and Activities

Objectives	Describing likes, dislikes, and preferences
Vocabulary	Food, beverages, sports, music, leisure activities
Dialogue	上田さんと リーさんのしゅみ *Ms. Ueda's and Mr. Li's Hobbies*
Japanese Culture	Popular leisure activities and consumer goods in Japan
Grammar	I. Expressing likes or dislikes using 好き or きらい and the particle や
	II. Forming noun phrases using の and plain present affirmative verbs (dictionary form)
	III. Making contrasts using the particle は, and expressing *but* using が
	IV. Making comparisons using 一番 and 〜（の）方が 〜より, and 〜も〜も and expressing lack of preference
	V. Giving reasons using the plain form + ので
Listening	Identifying conversation fillers
Communication	Giving positive feedback with も; making contrasts with は
Kanji	時 間 分 半 毎 年 好 語 高 番 方 新 古 安 友
Reading	Understanding word formation

単語
たん ご
Vocabulary

Nouns

うた	歌	song
エアロビクス		aerobics
おちゃ	お茶	tea, green tea
オレンジ		orange
カラオケ		Karaoke, sing-along
くだもの	果物	fruit
クラシック		classical music
こうちゃ	紅茶	black tea
コーラ		cola
こと		thing (intangible)
ゴルフ		golf
さかな	魚	fish
ジャズ		jazz
ジュース		juice
しゅみ	趣味	hobby
しょくじ	食事	dining しょくじする dine
スキー		skiing
スポーツ		sports
たべもの	食べ物	food
たまご	卵／玉子	egg
つり	釣り	fishing
トマト		tomato
ドライブ		driving (for pleasure)
にく	肉	meat

にんじん		carrot
のみもの	飲み物	beverage, drink
ハイキング		hiking
バスケットボール		basketball (abbreviated as バスケット or バスケ)
バナナ		banana
ヒップホップ		hip-hop music
ビール		beer
フットボール		(American) football (アメフト)
ポップス		pop music
みず	水	water
ミルク		milk
やきゅう	野球	baseball
やさい	野菜	vegetable
ラップ		rap music
りょこう	旅行	traveling りょこうする to travel
りんご		apple
レタス		lettuce
ロック		rock and roll
ワイン		wine

う -verbs

うたう	歌う	to sing
おわる	終わる	(for something) to end えいがが　おわる the movie is over.
つくる	作る	to make
とる	撮る	to take (a photograph) しゃしんを　とる
はじまる	始まる	(for something) to begin じゅぎょうが　はじまる the class begins

い -adjectives

おいしい		delicious, good, tasty
たかい	高い	expensive (Chapter 4: high, tall)
やすい	安い	inexpensive

な -adjectives

きらい (な)	嫌い (な)	dislike, hate
すき (な)	好き (な)	like

Question words

どうして	why

Adverbs

もっと	more

Particles

や	and (when listing examples)
	おちゃや　コーヒー tea, coffee, and so on

Prefixes

だい	大	very much, 大すき like very much

Conjunctions

それから		and, in addition, then
たとえば	例えば	for example
でも		but

Expressions

すきでもきらいでもありません	好きでも嫌いでもありません	I neither like nor dislike it.
〜 (は) どうですか		How about 〜 ?

単語の練習 Vocabulary Practice
たんご　れんしゅう

A. たべもの　　Food

Name each item in the picture.

1. さかな　　　　fish
2. にく　　　　　meat
3. たまご　　　　egg
4. やさい　　　　vegetable
5. くだもの　　　fruit
6. レタス　　　　lettuce
7. にんじん　　　carrots
8. トマト　　　　tomato
9. バナナ　　　　banana
10. オレンジ　　　orange
11. りんご　　　　apple

Activity 1

しつもんに　　日本語で　　こたえて下さい。　　Answer these questions in Japanese.
　　　　　ご

1. にくを　　よく　　たべますか。さかなは　　どうですか。
2. スーパーで　よく　何を　かいますか。　　（かいます *to buy*)
3. 何を　あまり　たべませんか。
4. 今　どんなものが　高いですか。
　　　　　　　　　　　　たか

★ Ask your instructor the word for any other food that you want to know how to say in Japanese.

Supplementary Vocabulary: Food

えび	海老	shrimp
キャベツ		cabbage
ぎゅうにく	牛肉	beef
きゅうり		cucumber
たまねぎ	玉ねぎ	onion
とりにく	鳥肉	chicken
ねぎ		green onion
ぶたにく	豚肉	pork
ほうれんそう		spinach
ピーマン		green pepper
みかん		tangerine
メロン		melon
いちご	苺	strawberry
ぶどう		grape

B. のみもの   Beverages

Look at the pictures below and read each word in Japanese.

おちゃ
tea, green tea

ジュース
juice

ミルク
milk

（お）さけ
rice wine / alcoholic beverage

コーヒー
coffee

こうちゃ
black tea

コーラ
cola

ワイン
wine

ビール
beer

水
みず
water

NOTES

- お in おちゃ is a polite prefix for the noun ちゃ, but it is rather rare to use ちゃ alone. Most people say おちゃ to refer either to green tea or tea as a general category of beverages.
- お in おさけ is also a polite prefix for the noun さけ. Although people say both おさけ and さけ, the latter tends to sound more masculine. （お）さけ can mean either Japanese rice wine or alcoholic beverages in general.

Activity 2

しつもんに　日本語で　こたえて下さい。Answer these questions in Japanese.

1. おさけを　のみますか。のみませんか。
2. どんなおさけを　のみますか。
3. よく　おちゃを　のみますか。のみませんか。
4. どんなおちゃを　のみますか。
5. どんなのみものを　よく　のみますか。どんなのみものは
   あまり　のみませんか。
6. 学食には　どんなのみものが　ありますか。
7. スーパーには　どんなのみものが　ありますか。

C. スポーツ　　Sports

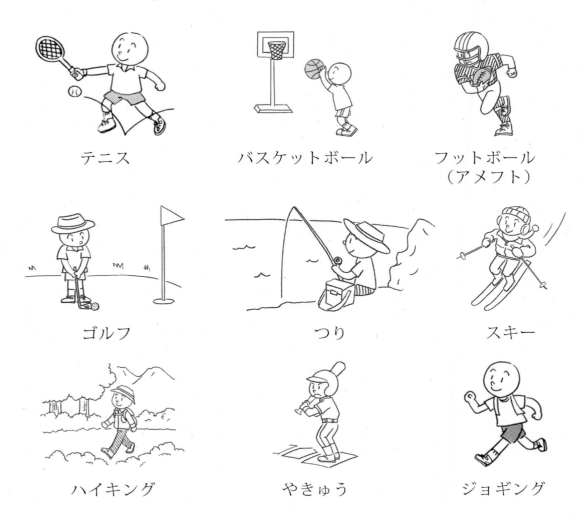

テニス　　　　　　　　バスケットボール　　　　フットボール
　　　　　　　　　　　　　　　　　　　　　　　　（アメフト）

ゴルフ　　　　　　　　　　つり　　　　　　　　　スキー

ハイキング　　　　　　　やきゅう　　　　　　　ジョギング

Activity 3

Match the Japanese words with their English equivalents in the above list.

_____1. エアロビクス   a. golf

_____2. バスケットボール   b. football

_____3. フットボール   c. jogging

_____4. ゴルフ   d. fishing

_____5. つり   e. hiking

_____6. スキー   f. skiing

_____7. ハイキング   g. aerobics

_____8. やきゅう   h. basketball

_____9. ジョギング   i. baseball

Activity 4

しつもんに　日本語で　こたえて下さい。　Answer these questions in Japanese.

1. どのスポーツを　よく　しますか。

2. どのスポーツを　よく　みますか。

3. 〜さんの友達は　どのスポーツを　よくみますか。

Supplementary Vocabulary: Sports

からて	空手	karate
サッカー		soccer
じゅうどう	柔道	judo
すいえい	水泳	swimming
スケート		skating
ソフトボール		softball
たいそう	体操	calisthenics, gymnastics
バレーボール		volleyball
ボーリング		bowling

D. おんがく Music

クラシック   ジャズ   ロック
classical   jazz   rock and roll

ポップス
pop music

ラップ、ヒップホップ
rap, hip-hop

Activity 5

Find the above words in the grid and circle them.

ク	ラ	シ	ラ	ク	ズ	ロ	ッ	プ
ジ	ク	ッ	ギ	タ	シ	ポ	ラ	ク
ポ	プ	ラ	ピ	ャ	ア	ッ	ジ	ズ
ッ	ズ	ッ	シ	ポ	ャ	プ	ポ	ロ
ノ	ノ	プ	ア	ッ	ズ	ス	ッ	ッ
シ	ラ	プ	ジ	ノ	ク	ラ	ク	ズ
ズ	ロ	ッ	ク	ス	ッ	ジ	ャ	ク
ク	ギ	シ	ッ	ク	ポ	ジ	ラ	プ
ジ	ロ	プ	ス	ラ	ッ	ス	ズ	ク

E. レジャーと しゅみ   Hobbies and leisure activities

Starting with this chapter, verbs are presented in dictionary form (plain present affirmative form).

りょこうする／
りょこうに いく
to travel

ドライブに いく／
ドライブを する
to go for a drive

うたを うたう
to sing songs

えを かく
to draw

りょうりを する／つくる
to cook

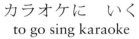

カラオケに　いく
to go sing karaoke

しゃしんを　とる
to take pictures

そとで　しょくじする
to dine out

Activity 6

Charades. Work in groups of three or four. Take turns acting out one of the activities listed above while the rest of the group tries to guess what it is in Japanese.

Activity 7

Say as many leisure activities as you can, using the following review expressions.

コンサート、おんがく、レストラン、かいもの、ビデオ、でんわ、テレビ、ゲーム、パーティ、およぐ（およぎます）、さんぽ、こうえん、あそびます（あそぶ）、メール

Supplementary Vocabulary: Hobbies and Leisure activities

いけばなを　する	生け花をする	to do **ikebana** (Japanese flower arrangement)
おどりに　いく	踊りに行く	(to) go dancing
ギターを　ひく	ギターを弾く	(to) play guitar
きってを　あつめる	切手を集める	(to) collect stamps
サイクリングに　いく	サイクリングに行く	(to) cycle, bike
せいじについて　はなす	政治について話す	(to) talk about politics
ガーデニングを　たのしむ	ガーデニングを楽しむ	(to) enjoy gardening
ピクニックに　いく	ピクニックに行く	(to) go on a picnic
ブログを　かく	ブログを書く	(to) write a blog
ペットと　あそぶ	ペットと遊ぶ	(to) play with a pet
ボランティアかつどうに　さんかする	ボランティア活動に　参加する	(to) participate in a volunteer activity

ダイアローグ
Dialogue

はじめに　Warm-up

しつもんに　日本語で　こたえて下さい。　Answer these questions in Japanese.

1. しゅみは　何ですか。
2. よく　スポーツを　しますか。
3. よく　スポーツばんぐみ (program) を　みますか。
4. どんなおんがくを　ききますか。

上田さんと　リーさんのしゅみ　*Ms. Ueda's and Mr. Li's Hobbies*

上田：　リーさんのしゅみは　何ですか。

リー：　そうですね。スポーツと　おんがくが　好きですね。

上田：　そうですか。どんなスポーツが　好きですか。

リー：　やきゅうや　バスケットボールが　好きですね。上田さんは？

上田：　私は　すいえいが　一番　好きです。でも、バスケットも
　　　　好きですよ。

リー：　そうですか。バスケットは　よく　しますか。

上田：　いいえ、バスケットは　するより　みる方が　好きですね。
　　　　リーさんは　バスケットを　よく　しますか。

リー： ええ、バスケットは　みるのも　するのも　大好きです。

上田： そうですか。いいですね。

リー： ところで、上田さんは　おんがくが　好きですか。

上田： ええ、好きですよ。

リー： そうですか。どんなおんがくが　好きですか。

上田： しずかなおんがくが　好きなので、ジャズを　よく　ききます。

リー： そうですか。ぼくも　ジャズが　大好きです。

上田： そうですか。じゃあ、クラシックは　どうですか。

リー： ざんねんですが、　クラシックは　あまり。ぼくには　ちょっと　むずかしくて。

DIALOGUE PHRASE NOTES

- ところで means *by the way*.
- ぼくには means *to me*.
- When used before 好き , 大 does not mean *big*, but *very*.
- すいえい means *swimming* and it is used to indicate a catagory of sport rather than the act of swimming.

ダイアローグの後で　Comprehension
<ruby>後<rt>あと</rt></ruby>

A.　Circle はい if the following statement is true, and circle いいえ if it is false.

1. はい　　いいえ　　　リーさんは　やきゅうが　好きです。
<ruby>好<rt>す</rt></ruby>

2. はい　　いいえ　　　上田さんと　リーさんは　バスケットが
　　　　　　　　　　　　好きです。
<ruby>好<rt>す</rt></ruby>

3. はい　　いいえ　　　上田さんは　バスケットを　するのが
　　　　　　　　　　　　好きです。
<ruby>好<rt>す</rt></ruby>

4. はい　　いいえ　　　上田さんは　ジャズが　好きです。
<ruby>好<rt>す</rt></ruby>

5. はい　　いいえ　　　リーさんは　クラシックの方が　ジャズより
　　　　　　　　　　　　好きです。
<ruby>方<rt>ほう</rt></ruby>
<ruby>好<rt>す</rt></ruby>

B.　Complete the following passage by filling in an appropriate word in each blank.

リーさんは　よく＿＿＿＿＿＿＿＿＿＿＿＿＿＿＿＿＿＿します。

上田さんは＿＿＿＿＿＿が　好きです。＿＿＿＿＿も　好きです。
<ruby>好<rt>す</rt></ruby>
<ruby>好<rt>す</rt></ruby>

日本の文化
ぶんか
Japanese Culture

Popular leisure actvities

A recent survey indicates that the following are the most popular leisure activities among Japanese between 18 and 30. The ranking of activities is based on the number of people who participated in the activities, not on frequency of participation.

おとこの人	おんなの人
1. ドライブに　いく	1. ドライブに　いく
2. おさけを　のみに　いく	2. そとで　しょくじを　する
3. インターネットを　する	3. おんがくを　きく
4. カラオケで　うたう	4. カラオケで　うたう
5. そとで　しょくじを　する	5. ビデオを　みる

Japanese ideas about sports have evolved in recent years. Where people once saw sports as a leisure activity they now see them as a lifestyle. Sports are no longer only to watch, but are for participation. A survey conducted by Hakouhodo, Inc., in 2006 found that 76.9 percent of the people surveyed had participated in some sort of sport over the past year, and that 65.7 percent hope to participate in the future.

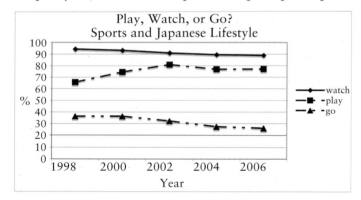

The same survey found that yoga and aerobics are the most popular sports, followed by jogging and track.

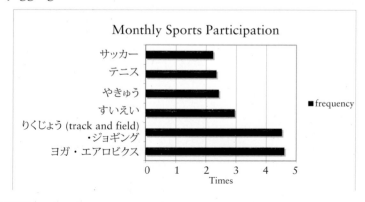

Traditional arts such as いけばな (flower arrangement), さどう (tea ceremony), and しょどう (calligraphy) ranked very low in terms of the number of participants.

Popular Consumer Goods

Cellular phones are extremely popular among Japanese. Young Japanese frequently use them to exchange e-mail, photos, and video clips. Cell phones are also used to download music, surf the Internet, play games, watch TV, and read books. Some phones can even be used like a debit card to make purchases in retail stores. As a result of such widespread cell-phone use, the number of public phones has greatly diminished, and it can be difficult to travel in Japan without a cell phone. Both Japanese travel agencies and phone companies with airport locations in Japan offer cell phone rentals to visitors.

Another well-known obsession of the Japanese, particularly among women, is their love of luxury goods by such designers as Gucci, Chanel, and Prada. Most major Japanese department stores have designer goods sections. Wherever you walk in Japan, you will see women carrying designer handbags and wearing expensive scarves and belts.

This popularity has continued for more than three decades and does not seem to be affected by economic conditions in Japan. For example, in the middle of

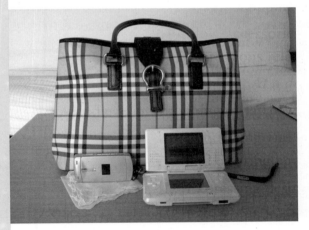

an economic depression in 2002, Louis Vuitton sold over one billion dollars' worth of merchandise in Japan—a 15% increase in profit over the previous year, and about half of the company's total sales for that year.

Why do the Japanese love brand-name items so much? One explanation is that Japanese people traditionally place a high value on quality. After the Meiji Restoration (1868–1912), many expensive foreign goods were imported from Europe, creating the association between quality and European luxury items. Today, brand names imply high quality, impeccable service, luxury, and status. Unlike a house or even furniture, these items are still within reach of the average consumer. Owning them gives some people the satisfaction of possessing something valuable and unique. At the same time, many others consider a preoccupation with brand names to be shallow.

文法
ぶんぽう
Grammar

> ### I.   Expressing likes or dislikes using 好き or きらい and the particle や
> す

In Japanese, 好き (like) and きらい (dislike, hate) are used to express one's likes and
す
dislikes. In English, *like*, *dislike*, and *hate* are verbs, but in Japanese 好き and
す
きらい are な - adjectives. Therefore, the negative form is じゃありません or
す
じゃないです. The object of 好き and きらい cannot be indicated by を because
す
they are not verbs. Instead, use が to mark the object.

Topic (person, animal)		Noun (thing that s/he likes)	Particle	
私の友達 ともだち	は	テニス	が	好きです。 す

My friend likes tennis.

To list two or more items you like or dislike, use the particle と (and) as introduced
in Chapter 5. However, と indicates that you like only the specific items you
mentioned. For more items that you like or dislike, and for which you wish to show
an example, use the particle や.

> 私は りんごと オレンジが 好きです。
> す
> *I like apples and oranges (but nothing else).*

> 私は りんごや オレンジが 好きです。
> す
> *I like apples and oranges (and other food).*

> スミスさんは にんじんと たまごが きらいです。
> *Mr. Smith dislikes carrots and eggs.*

> スミスさんは にんじんや たまごが きらいです。
> *Mr. Smith dislikes carrots and eggs (and other things).*

> キム： はやしさんは どんなのみものが 好きですか。
> す
> *What kinds of drinks do you like, Ms. Hayashi?*

> はやし： そうですね。私は こうちゃや 日本のおちゃが
> 大好きですね。
> だいす
> *Well, I love black tea and Japanese tea (and so on).*

> キム： じゃあ、おさけは どうですか。
> *How about alcoholic beverages?*

> はやし： おさけは ちょっと。
> *Alcohol is a bit . . . (= I don't like alcoholic beverages very much.)*

NOTES

- 好き and きらい can also be used before nouns. In this case, 好き means *favorite* and きらいな is the opposite of favorite.

  <u>私の好きな</u> くだものは りんごです。
  My favorite fruit is the apple.

  <u>私のきらいな くだもの</u>は バナナです。
  The fruit that I don't like is the banana.

- You might want to avoid using きらい in an answer to a question because it has a strong negative connotation. You can use expressions such as 〜は　ちょっと (〜 is a bit) and あまり.

- In Chapters 2 through 5, 〜は　どうですか meant "How is 〜?" Another meaning of 〜は　どうですか is "How about 〜?"

  大木： 私は ワインが 好きです。
  I like wine.

  水田： じゃあ、 ビールは どうですか。
  Well, how about beer?

  大木： ビールも 好きですよ。
  I like beer, too.

- The prefix 大 is commonly used with 好き and きらい. 大好き means *love* or *really like*, and 大きらい means *hate* or *really don't like*. 大好き and 大きらい are more commonly used than とても 好き or とても　きらい.

- If you don't like or dislike something, use 好きでも　きらいでも ありません or 好きでも　きらいでも ないです. (*I neither like nor dislike it.*)

話してみましょう   Conversation Practice

Activity 1

The following chart indicates what Mr. Yamada and Ms. Brown like and dislike. Express what they like or dislike, using 好き, きらい. Use the particles と or や wherever appropriate.

Example: 山田さんは　りんごが　好きです。

	山田さん		ブラウンさん	
	好き	きらい	好き	きらい
たべもの	apples	carrots and eggs	meat, fish, etc.	vegetables, fruit, etc.
のみもの	juice and coffee	milk	wine, beer, etc.	juice, black tea, etc.
スポーツ	golf, tennis, etc.	football	football	golf, jogging, etc.
おんがく	pop, jazz, etc.	classical music	rap and rock	classical music

Activity 2

Ask a partner what types of food, drinks, sports, and music he/she likes and dislikes. Your partner will give you examples using や.

Example:　A: 〜さんは　どんなたべものが　好きですか。
　　　　　　B: りんごや　オレンジが　好きです。
　　　　　　A: そうですか。

	私	パートナー
たべもの		
のみもの		
スポーツ		
おんがく		

Activity 3

Now work with the class. Ask your classmates what kinds of food, drinks, sports, and music they like and dislike. See if you can determine the most popular item in each category.

Example:　A: 〜さんは　どんなたべものが　好きですか。
　　　　　　B: 〜が　好きです。
　　　　　　A: そうですか。じゃあ、どんなたべものが　きらいですか。
　　　　　　B: 〜は　あまり　好きじゃありません。

	好き	きらい
たべもの		
のみもの		
スポーツ		
おんがく		

II. Forming noun phrases using の and plain present affirmative verbs (dictionary form)

The plain present affirmative form of a verb is also called the dictionary form because this is the form used for dictionary entries. This form also appears in time expressions, relative clauses, gerunds, and other structures. It is used in casual conversation, newspapers, expository writing, and other contexts. Learning when to use it appropriately can take some time.

   In this section, you will learn to use the plain present affirmative form with の to convert verb phrases into noun phrases. This use of の is different from the pronoun の (one) and from the particle の in the structure Noun の Noun.

A. Plain present affirmative verbs (dictionary form)

The charts below show how to create the dictionary forms of verbs from their polite forms.

う -verbs

Remove ます from the polite verb form and change the vowel sound of the last letter to **u**.

ます -form	Plain present affirmative (dictionary) form		
よみます (*read*)	yomi + masu →	yomu	よむ
かきます (*write*)	kaki + masu →	kaku	かく
あいます (*meet*)	ai + masu →	au	あう
はなします (*talk*)	hanashi + masu →	hanasu	はなす
のみます (*drink*)	nomi + masu →	nomu	のむ

る -verbs

Change ます to る.

ます -form	Plain present affirmative (dictionary) form
たべます (*eat*)	→ たべる
ねます (*sleep*)	→ ねる
います (*be, exist*)	→ いる
おきます (*get up*)	→ おきる

Irregular verbs

ます -form	Plain present affirmative (dictionary) form
します (*do*)	→ する
きます (*come*)	→ くる

Once you know the plain affirmative form, it is relatively easy to identify the group to which it belongs (う-verb, る-verb, or irregular verb) by using the following three steps:

1. Remember that する and くる are the only irregular verbs.
2. If a dictionary form ends in -**Xiru** or -**Xeru** (*X* represents any consonant here), it is a る-verb. For example, since たべる ends in **beru** and おきる ends in **kiru**, they are る-verbs. However, つくる, おわる, and はじまる are not る-verbs, because they end in -**Kuru**, -**Waru**, and -**Maru**, and not -**Xiru** or -**Xeru**.
3. The rest are all う-verbs. There are some exceptions to this rule. Among them, the ones you have learned are かえる (*return*) and はいる (*enter*). These are う-verbs.

B. The plain present affirmative form + のが　好きです・きらい です (like/dislike doing 〜)

The plain present affirmative form (dictionary form) + のが　好きです／きらい です is used to express one's likes or dislikes in terms of doing something. In English, the gerund (-ing) form of a verb and the infinitive (*to* + verb) may be used as nouns, as in examples such as *seeing is believing* or *to play a musical instrument is fun*. In a similar manner, Japanese adds の to the plain present affirmative form to create a noun phrase.

		Noun phrase			
		Verb (dictionary form)		Particle	
私は	本を	よむ	の	が	好きです。

I like reading books.

Here are some more examples.

私は えいがを みるのが 好きです。
I like watching movies.

えいがを みるのは おもしろいです。
Watching movies is fun.

スミス： 田中さんは 何を するのが 好きですか。
What do you like to do, Ms. Tanaka?

田中： そうですね。私は インターネットで あそぶのが 好きですね。スミスさんは どうですか。
Let's see. I like to surf the Internet. How about you, Mr. Smith?

スミス： ぼくは クラシックおんがくを きくのが 好きです。
I like to listen to classical music.

話してみましょう　Conversation Practice
はな

Activity 1

Create questions using the following expressions and 　〜のが　好きですか.
　　　　　　　　　　　　　　　　　　　　　　　　　　　　　　　　　　　　　　す

Example:　てがみを　かきます
　　　　　てがみを　かくのが　好きですか。
　　　　　　　　　　　　　　　　す

1. 友達のしゃしんを　とります　　　　6. ごはんを　つくります
　 ともだち
2. そとで　しょくじを　します　　　　7. えを　かきます
3. ジョギングを　します　　　　　　　8. 日本語を　はなします
　　　　　　　　　　　　　　　　　　　　　　ご
4. カラオケに　いきます　　　　　　　9. おふろに　はいります
5. うたを　うたいます　　　　　　　 10. およぎます

Activity 2

Work with a partner. Using the questions you created in Activity 1, ask your
partner which activities he/she likes to do.

Example:　たべます
　　　　　A:　たべるのが　好きですか。
　　　　　　　　　　　　　　す
　　　　　B:　ええ、大好きです。
　　　　　　　　　だい　す
　　or　いいえ、あまり　好きじゃないですか／好きじゃありません。
　　　　　　　　　　　　　す　　　　　　　　　　す

Activity 3

The following pictures illustrate activities that Kimura-san likes to do. Describe
them using 〜のが　好きです.

Example:　木村さんは　テニスを　するのが　好きです。

Activity 4

Ask a partner what he/she likes to do during school breaks.

Example:　A:　〜さんは　やすみの日に　何を　するのが　好きですか。
　　　　　　B:　そうですね。ねるのが　好きですね。

III. Making contrasts using the particle は, and expressing *but* using が

A. Using は for contrast

Besides indicating a topic, は can indicate a contrast between two items. In both of the following sentences, the second は in the example puts りょうり and そうじ in contrast.

私は よく りょうりを します。でも、そうじは あまり しません。
I cook often but I don't do the cleaning very often.

キムさんは りょうりが 好きです。でも、そうじは 好きじゃ ありません。
Mr. Kim likes cooking but he does not like cleaning.

The particle は for contrast is often used in sentences ending with negative forms. Often, there is no explicit item of contrast in this case.

田中：　明日も きますか。　　　　　*Are you coming tomorrow?*

スミス：　いいえ、明日は きません。　*No, I am not coming tomorrow.*
　　　　　　　　　　　　　　　　　　　(but I may come some other time).

The use of は for contrast may appear in more than one sentence or clause to make the contrast explicit. In the following example sentences, the topic of the first sentence is 私, so it is marked with the topic marker は. And although this first sentence does not end in a negative form, コーヒー also takes は, because it is in contrast with コーラ in the second sentence.

私は コーヒーは 好きです。 でも、コーラは あまり 好き じゃありません。
I like coffee. But I don't like cola very much.

は for contrast can be used with any type of noun as well. Like は for topic, and も for similarity, は replaces を (direct object) or が (subject), but it is usually added to another particle, as in the examples below. Some particles, such as に (point of time) and に・へ (goal) may be deleted if they can be easily understood from context.

よく としょかんで べんきょうします。でも、学生会館では しません。
I often study in the library. But, I don't (study) in the student union.

ここに ねこが います。 あそこには いません。
There is a cat here. It's not over there.

山田さんは 今日は きません。でも、土曜日 (に) は きます。
Mr. Yamada does not come today. But, he will come tomorrow.

B. Expressing *but* using が

The particle が can be used to connect two sentences or clauses that oppose each other. が is attached at the end of the first sentence.

Clause	Particle (but)	Clause
こうちゃは　好きです	が、	おちゃは　あまり 好きじゃないです。

I like black tea but I don't like green tea very much.

Since が often connects two clauses in a contrasting or negative relationship, the contrast marker は is often used with が as well. For example:

ゴルフを　するのは　好きですが、みるのは　あまり　好き じゃありません。
I like playing golf but I don't like watching it.

あさは　ごはんを　たべませんでしたが、ひるは　たべました。
I did not eat breakfast but I did eat lunch.

そうじは　しましたが、せんたくは　しませんでした。
I did the cleaning but I didn't do laundry.

友達と　えいがは　みませんでしたが、テレビは　みましたよ。
I didn't watch a movie with my friends, but we did watch TV.

ゆうびんきょくには　いきませんでしたが、ぎんこうには いきました。
I didn't go to the post office, but I did go to the bank.

NOTE

- が can also be used to open a conversation, or to introduce a topic of conversation. This is called a "weak but." It does not introduce a strong negative relation, and it is similar to the use of *but* in English as in: "Excuse me, <u>but</u> could you turn on the TV?"

  あのう　すみませんが、今　何時ですか。
  Excuse me, but what time is it?

  私のうちは　あれですが、田中さんのは　どれですか。
  My house is that one over there, but which one is Ms. Tanaka's?

話してみましょう   Conversation Practice
<small>はな</small>

◢ **Activity 1**

Look at the drawings below and describe what Yamada-san likes, doesn't like very much, and positively dislikes. Use は to contrast his likes and dislikes.

Example: 山田さんは　りんごが　好きですが、トマトは　あまり
<small>す</small>
　　　　　好きじゃありません。
<small>す</small>

好きです　　　　　　　　あまり　　　　　　　　きらいです
<small>す</small>　　　　　　　　好きじゃありません
　　　　　　　　　　　<small>す</small>

◢ **Activity 2**

Work with a partner. Referring to the items in the table below, ask questions to determine your partner's preferences. Try to use both particles も and は correctly in your follow-up questions.

Example: A: ～さんは　どんなたべものが　好きですか。
<small>す</small>

　　　　　B: レタスが　好きです。
<small>す</small>

　　　　　Follow-up questions:

　　　　　A: そうですか。にんじん<u>も</u>　好きですか。
<small>す</small>

　　　　　B: いいえ、にんじん<u>は</u>　あまり　好きじゃありません。
<small>す</small>

　　　　　A: じゃあ、トマト<u>は</u>　どうですか。

　　　　　B: はい、トマト<u>は</u>　好きです。
<small>す</small>

Categories	Items
たべもの	トマト　にんじん　レタス　バナナ　オレンジ
どうぶつ	いぬ　ねこ　さかな　くま (bear)　とり (bird)　さる (monkey)
のみもの	ビール　ワイン　コーラ　こうちゃ　コーヒー　ミルク　ジュース　水_{みず}
スポーツ	エアロビクス　ハイキング　テニス　フットボール　ゴルフ
おんがく	クラシック　ジャズ　ポップス　ロック　ラップ　ヒップホップ

Activity 3

For each statement below, create two sentences. One should express a similarity with the statement; the other should express a contrast.

Example:　私は　あさごはんを　たべます。

　　　　　ばんごはんも　たべます。でも、ひるごはんは　たべません。

1. 私は　よく　テレビを　みます。
2. 月曜日に　アルバイトを　します。
3. 昨日　山本さんに　メールを　かきました。
4. スミスさんは　先生に　しつもんしました。
5. 山本さんの友達は　週末　よく　おんがくを　ききます。
6. 毎日　りょうりを　します。

Activity 4

Describe what each person likes and does not like to do.

Example:　山田さんは　パーティに　いくのが　好_すきですが、

　　　　　パーティを　するのは　あまり　好_すきじゃありません。

山田	パーティに　いきます	パーティを　します
小川 おがわ	あそびます	べんきょうします
山本	そとで　しょくじを　します	うちで　たべます
大川	えいがを　みます	ゲームを　します
金田 かねだ	コンサートに　いきます	うたを　うたいます
田中	しゃしんを　とります	えを　かきます

IV. Making comparisons using 一番(いちばん) and 〜（の）方(ほう)が 〜より, and 〜も〜も and expressing lack of preference

In English, preference can be expressed by changing the form of an adjective into a superlative (e.g., *the best, the prettiest, the nicest, the most wonderful*) or a comparative (e.g., *better, prettier, nicer, more wonderful*). Japanese has a similar set of expressions, but the adjective forms do not change. Instead, preference is expressed in other parts of the sentence. This chapter introduces the superlative with the adverb 一番(いちばん), the comparative with 〜の方(ほう)が　〜より, and lack of preference using 〜も〜も.

A. Superlatives using 一番(いちばん)

一番(いちばん) means *number one* or *first*, and it is used to form a superlative, such as the *nicest person, prettiest house, the best movie,* and *I like X the best.* 一番(いちばん) must be followed by an adjective or adverb. For example, *the best movie* should be expressed as 一番(いちばん) いい えいが. 一番(いちばん) えいが is a common mistake that native English speakers make.

としょかんは　一番(いちばん)　大きい　たてものです。
The library is the <u>biggest building</u>.

このたまごが　一番(いちばん)　安(やす)いです。
These eggs are the <u>cheapest</u>.

ジャズが　一番(いちばん)　好(す)きです。
I <u>like</u> jazz <u>the best</u>.

山本さんが　一番(いちばん)　よく　べんきょうします。
Ms. Yamamoto studies <u>the hardest</u>.

私の一番(いちばん) 好(す)きな　たべものは　バナナです。
My <u>most favorite</u> food is bananas.

To indicate the scope of a preference, use the phrase 〜の中で.

<u>スポーツの中で</u>　何が　一番(いちばん)　おもしろいですか。
Which sport is the most interesting among sports?

<u>くだものの中で</u>　何を　一番(いちばん)　よく　たべますか。
Which fruits do you eat most?

<u>のみものの中で</u>　コーヒーが　一番(いちばん)　好(す)きです。
Coffee is the beverage I like best.

If the preceding noun is a place noun, 中 is omitted:

<u>このクラスで</u> 山田さんが 一番 よく べんきょうします。

Mr. Yamada studies the hardest in this class.

富士山は <u>日本で</u> 一番 高い 山です。

Mt. Fuji is the highest mountain in Japan.

田中： このクラスで どの人が 一番 よくべんきょうしますか。

Which person studies the most in this class?

石田： 山田さんが 一番 よく べんきょうします。

／山田さんです。

Mr. Yamada studies the hardest. / It's Mr. Yamada.

スミス： たべものの中で 何が 一番 好きですか。

Which type of food do you like best?

大田： さかなが 一番 好きです。

I like fish the best.

B. Comparatives using ～（の）方が ～より

The expression ～（の）方が ～より is used to compare two items. The item preceding ～（の）方が is emphasized or preferred over the item that precedes ～より. These items can be either noun phrases or verb phrases ending in the dictionary form.

Noun (Preferred)	Particle	Noun	Particle	Noun (Less preferred)	Particle	
きょうと	の	方	が	（とうきょう	より）	きれいです。

Kyoto is prettier than Tokyo.

とうきょうの方が ニューヨークより 大きいです。

Tokyo is larger than New York.

このさかなの方が にくより 安いです。

This fish is cheaper than meat.

りょうりは つくる方が たべるより 好きです。

I like cooking more than eating.

やきゅうは みるより する方が たのしいです。

Playing baseball is more fun than watching it.

In order to ask one's preference between two items, use 〜と〜と どちらの方が.

Noun (Choice A)	Particle	Noun (Choice B)	Particle	Question word	Particle	Noun	Particle	
とうきょう	と	きょうと	と	どちら	の	方	が	きれいですか。

Which is prettier, Tokyo or Kyoto?

とうきょうと ニューヨークと どちらの方が 大きいですか。
Which is larger, Tokyo or New York?

さかなと にくと どちらの方が 安いですか。
Which is cheaper, fish or meat?

To ask about two actions, use the dictionary form + の. This の is the same one used in 〜のが 好きです.

テニスを みるのと するのと どちらの方が 好きですか。

Which do you like better, watching tennis or playing it?

ここに いるのと でかけるのと どちらの方が いいですか。
Which is better, staying here or going out?

リー： 大川さんと 山本さんと どちらの方が よく りょうりを しますか。

Who cooks more often, Mr. Okawa or Ms. Yamamoto?

上田： 山本さんの方が よく りょうりを します。

Ms. Yamamoto cooks more often.

リー： 上田さんは どうですか。
How about you, Ms. Ueda?

上田： そうですね。私は りょうりを するより たべる方が いいですね。
Well, eating is better than cooking in my case.

When you want to compare the preference between two actions, use the dictionary form of verb + 方が.

NOTES

- If 〜より is obvious from the context, then it can be omitted, as in the above example conversation between Mr. Li and Ms. Ueda.
- The adverb もっと is used with adjectives or verbs, and it means *more* or *even more*.

  もっと たべませんか。   *Why don't you eat more?*
  私のいぬは もっと 大きいです。   *My dog is bigger.*

C. Expressing lack of preference (comparisons of equality)

If you do not have preference for one item over another, use 〜も 〜も. Items can be two noun phrases or two verb phases ending with の.

Noun A	Particle	Noun B	Particle	
とうきょう	も	きょうと	も	好きです。

I like both Tokyo and Kyoto.

Noun A	Particle	Noun B	Particle	
とうきょう	も	きょうと	も	好きじゃありません。／ 好きじゃないです。

I don't like either Tokyo or Kyoto.

田中： ペプシと コカコーラと どちらの方が おいしいですか。
Which is more delicious, Pepsi or Coca-Cola?

中山： ペプシも コカコーラも おいしいです。
Both Pepsi and Coca-Cola are delicious.

でも、私は ペプシの方が 好きです。
But I like Pepsi better.

ペギー： うちで たべるのと そとで しょくじするのと どちらの方が 好きですか。
Which do you like better, eating at home or dining out?

あやか： そうですね。うちで たべるのも そとで しょくじするのも 好きですが、
Well, I like both eating at home and dining out.

たいてい うちで たべます。
But I usually eat at home.

NOTE

- 〜も 〜も can be used in either a positive or negative statement. A も B も+ affirmative statement means *both A and B.* A も B も + negative statement (or in a negative statement) means *neither A nor B.*

やきゅうも バスケットも 好きです。
I like both baseball and basketball.

ロックも ジャズも 好きじゃありません。
I don't like either rock or jazz very much.

話してみましょう　Conversation Practice
はな

Activity 1

Answer the questions.

Example: おんがくの中で　何が　一番　好きですか。
　　　　　　　　　　　　　いちばん　す

　　　　　ジャズが　一番　好きです。
　　　　　　　　いちばん　す

1. スポーツの中で　何が　一番　好きですか。
　　　　　　　　　　　いちばん　す

2. たべものの中で　何が　一番　きらいですか。
　　　　　　　　　　　いちばん

3. のみものの中で　何を　一番　よく　のみますか。
　　　　　　　　　　　いちばん

4. どんなおんがくを　一番　よく　ききますか。
　　　　　　　　　　いちばん

5. このクラスで　だれが　一番　よく　日本語を　はなしますか。
　　　　　　　　　　　　いちばん　　　　ご

Activity 2

Ask a partner about places and things that have the most in some attribute, using the nouns and adjectives provided. Follow the example.

Example: アメリカ／川／大きい

　　　　　A: アメリカでは　どの川が　一番　大きいですか。
　　　　　　　　　　　　　　　いちばん

　　　　　B: ミシシッピー川が　一番　大きいです。
　　　　　　　　　　がわ　　いちばん

1. アメリカ／まち／古い　　　　4. キャンパス／たてもの／新しい
　　　　　　　　ふる　　　　　　　　　　　　　　　あたら

2. 日本／山／高い　　　　　　　5. アメリカ／しゅう (state) ／小さい
　　　　　たか

3. せかい (world) ／まち／きれい　6. アメリカ／たべもの／おいしい

Activity 3

First determine the order of the two items in parentheses using the adjectives provided. Then form a comparative sentence.

Examples: 好き　（こうちゃ／コーヒー）
　　　　　す

　　　　　こうちゃの方が　コーヒーより　好きです。
　　　　　　　　　ほう　　　　　　　　す

　　　　　むずかしい（日本語で　かく／はなす）

　　　　　日本語で　かく方が　はなすより　むずかしいです。
　　　　　　ご　　　ほう

1. いい（いぬ／ねこ）
2. しずか（としょかん／ラボ）
3. いそがしい（先生／学生）
4. 好き（たべる／ねる）
　 す
5. 大きい（ニューヨーク／とうきょう）
6. むずかしい（日本語／スペイン語）
　 　 　 　 　 　 　 ご　　　　　　　　 ご
7. きらい
　 （りょうりをする／そうじを　する）
8. 大変
　 たいへん
　 （べんきょうする／しごとを　する）

Activity 4

Work with a partner. Using the items in Activity 3, taking turns asking each other three comparative questions.

Example:　好き　（ こうちゃ／コーヒー ）
　　　　　 す
　　　　　 A: こうちゃと　コーヒーと　どちらの方が　好きですか。
　　　　　 　　　　　　　　　　　　　　　　　 ほう　　 す
　　　　　 B: コーヒーの方が　好きです。
　　　　　 　　　　 ほう　　 す

　　　　　 A: 日本語で　かくのと　はなすのと　どちらの方が
　　　　　 　　 ご　　　　　　　　　　　　　　　　　　 ほう
　　　　　 　　むずかしいですか。
　　　　　 B: かく方が　はなすより　むずかしいです。
　　　　　 　　　 ほう

Activity 5

Work with a partner. Ask your partner about at least two things he/she likes, and then ask him/her to rank them. If he/she likes both equally, write both words in Column 1.

Example:　A: どんなくだものが　好きですか。
　　　　　 　　　　　　　　　　　　 す
　　　　　 B: りんごや　オレンジが　好きです。
　　　　　 　　　　　　　　　　　　　 す
　　　　　 A: じゃあ、りんごと　オレンジと　どちらの方が　好きですか。
　　　　　 　　　　　　　　　　　　　　　　　　　 ほう　　 す
　　　　　 B: そうですね。オレンジの方が　好きです。
　　　　　 　　　　　　　　　　　 ほう　　 す
　　　　　 or　りんごも　オレンジも　好きです。
　　　　　 　　　　　　　　　　　　　 す

Category	1	2
くだもの	りんご	オレンジ
のみもの		
スポーツ		
おんがく		

V. Giving reasons using the plain form + ので

The conjunction ので indicates a reason, and it is attached to the end of the clause that expresses the reason. If a sentence contains both a reason and result, the clause for the reason must come before the clause indicating the result. For example, in the sentence 来週から　テストが　はじまるので、今週はよく　べんきょうします。
らい
(*I will study hard this week because exams begin next week.*), the reason is stated at the beginning of the sentence and it ends with ので ; the cause is mentioned in the latter half of the sentence.

Clause (reason)	Particle (reason)	Clause (result)
いちごが　好きな す	ので、	よく　かいます。

I like strawberries, so I often buy some.

しごとが　もうすぐ　おわるので、ここで　まって下さい。
My job will be finished soon, so please wait here.

J－ポップが　好きなので、よく　J－ポップのうたを　うたいます。
す
I like J-pop (Japanese pop music), so I often sing J-pop songs.

The 〜ので construction is preceded by a clause ending with the plain form of a verb or adjective. The following charts show the plain affirmative and negative forms of verbs and adjectives. In these charts, *I*, *it*, *he*, and *she* are given as subjects in English, but these forms can also be used to indicate *you*, *we*, and *they*, depending on context.

Plain form + ので / noun or な-adjective + な + ので

な -adjectives

In the case of な-adjectives, the affirmative is expressed by using the stem + ので.

Dictionary form	Prenominal form	Plain negative	〜ので (because 〜)	
			Affirmative (Plain)	Negative (Plain)
きれい *pretty*	きれいな （もの） *pretty thing*	きれい じゃない （もの） *not pretty thing*	きれいなので *because it is pretty*	きれいじゃない ので *because it is not pretty*

Noun + です (copula verb)

Noun + な expresses the affirmative.

Dictionary form	Noun + な	Plain negative form	〜ので (because 〜)	
			Affirmative (Plain)	Negative (Plain)
日本人 *Japanese*	日本人<u>な</u> *be Japanese*	日本人<u>じゃない</u> *not Japanese*	日本人<u>な</u>ので *because he/she is Japanese*	日本人 <u>じゃない</u>ので *because he/she is not Japanese*

い -adjectives

The plain affirmative form of an い-adjective is the same as its dictionary form. The plain negative form is created by deleting です from the polite version.

Dictionary form / Plain affirmative form	Plain negative form	〜ので (because 〜)	
		Affirmative (Plain)	Negative (Plain)
うれしい *happy, be happy*	うれし<u>くない</u> *not happy*	うれしいので *because he/she is happy*	うれし<u>くない</u>ので *because he/she is not happy*

う -verbs

To form the negative of a う-verb, delete ます from the ます-form, change the vowel sound of the last letter [i] to [a], and add ない.

ます -form	Dictionary form / Plain affirmative form	Plain negative form	〜ので	
			Affirmative (Plain)	Negative (Plain)
よみます /yom/+/<u>i</u>/+/masu/ *read*	よむ /yom/+/u/ *read*	よ<u>ま</u>ない /yom/+/a/+/nai/ *not read*	よむので *because he/she reads*	よまないので *because he/she does not read*
かきます /kak/+/<u>i</u>/+/masu/ *write*	かく /kak/+/<u>u</u>/ *write*	か<u>か</u>ない /kak/+/a/+/nai/ *not write*	かくので *because he/she writes*	かかないので *because he/she does not write*
はなします /hanash/+/<u>i</u>/+ /masu/ *talk*	はなす /hanas/+/u/ *talk*	はな<u>さ</u>ない /hanas/ +/<u>a</u>/+ /nai/ *not talk*	はなすので *because he/she talks*	はなさない ので *because he/she does not talk*
おわります /owar/+/<u>i</u>/+/masu/ *end*	おわる /owar/+/<u>u</u>/ *end*	おわ<u>ら</u>ない /owar/+/a/+/nai/ *not end*	おわるので *because it ends*	おわらない ので *because it does not end*

If there is no consonant before the [i] sound of the ます-form, as in あいます, change [i] to [wa] instead of [a]. The plain present negative form of あります is <u>ない</u>.

ます -form	Dictionary form/ Plain affirmative form	Plain negative form	〜ので	
			Affirmative (Plain)	Negative (Plain)
あいます /a<u>i</u> /+ /masu/ *meet*	あ<u>う</u> *meet*	あ<u>わ</u>ない /a<u>wa</u>/ +/nai/ *not meet*	あうので *because he/she meets*	あわないので *because he/she does not meet*
あります /ari/+ /masu/ *be, exist**	ある *be, exist*	<u>ない</u> /nai/ *not be, exist*	あるので *because there is 〜*	ないので *because there isn't 〜*

*Remember that あります is used only for inanimate objects or events.

る -verbs

Change ます to ない to form the plain negative form.

ます -form	Dictionary form/ Plain affirmative form	Plain negative form	〜ので	
			Affirmative (Plain)	Negative (Plain)
たべます *eat*	たべる *eat*	たべ<u>ない</u> *not eat*	たべるので *because he/she eats*	たべないので *because he/she does not eat*
ねます *sleep*	ねる *sleep*	ね<u>ない</u> *not sleep*	ねるので *because he/she sleeps*	ねないので *because he/she does not sleep*
います *be, exist**	いる *be, exist*	い<u>ない</u> *not be, exist*	いるので *because there is 〜*	いないので *because there isn't 〜*

*Remember that います is used only for live beings such as people and animals.

Irregular verbs

ます -form	Dictionary form/ Plain affirmative form	Plain negative form	〜ので	
			Affirmative (Plain)	Negative (Plain)
します *do*	する *do*	し<u>ない</u> *not do*	するので *because he/she does*	しないので *because he/she does not do*
きます *come*	くる *come*	<u>こ</u>ない *not come*	くるので *because he/she comes*	こないので *because he/she does not come*

話してみましょう Conversation Practice
はな

Activity 1

Combine the following pairs of sentences using 〜ので . Make sure to start with the sentence that expresses a reason and is followed by ので.

Example: にくを たべます。さかなは きらいです。
さかなは きらいなので、にくを たべます。

1. 毎日 しごとを します。いそがしいです。
   まい
2. よく デパートに いきます。かいものが 好きです。
3. 七時に おきます。八時に じゅぎょうが はじまります。
   しち じ   はち じ   す
4. トマトが たくさん あります。トマトで りょうりを します。
5. うちで ゆっくりします。今日は いそがしくありません。
6. 今日は じゅぎょうが ありません。ひるまで ねます。

Activity 2

Work with a partner. The following table shows what Mr. Tanaka dislikes and why. Create a conversation using the table and the dialogue model below. Note that もの refers to a tangible object such as food, drinks, and places and こと refers to an intangible thing like an activity and event.

Example: A: 私の きらいな ものは さかなです。
B: え、どうしてですか。
A: ほね (bone) が あるので、きらいです。
B: そうですか。

きらいなもの・きらいなこと		りゆう (reason)
Example:	さかな	ほね (bone) が あります
1	レストランに いきます。	高いです
2	パーティ	人と はなすのが 好きじゃありません。
3	大きいまち	しずかな ところが 好きです。
4	カラオケに いきます。	うたを うたうのが きらいです。
5	ハイキングを します。	あるくのが 好きじゃありません。

Activity 3

Work with a partner. Invite your partner to do an activity together. He/She will refuse the invitation and give a reason using ので.

Example: A: 来週の水曜日に　コンサートに　いきませんか。
らい

B: ありがとうございます。でも、水曜日は、りょうしんが
あいに　くるので。

A: あ、そうですか。ざんねんですね。

B: すみません。あの、また　さそってくれませんか。
(さそう *to invite*)

A: いいですよ。じゃあ、また、今度。
ど

聞く練習
きくれんしゅう
Listening

上手な聞き方   Listening Strategy
じょうず きかた

Identifying conversation fillers

In conversations in English, you hear many empty words and expressions such as *hmm*, *uh*, and *well*. Their approximate equivalents in Japanese are えーと, あのう, and そうですね. These words are referred to as conversation fillers. While the words themselves have little meaning, they are used to keep the conversation flowing when the person speaking does not know what to say.

練習   Practice
れんしゅう

Listen to the following statements and short conversations. Circle the fillers you hear.

1. あのう　　えーと　　そうですね
2. あのう　　えーと　　そうですね
3. あのう　　えーと　　そうですね
4. あのう　　えーと　　そうですね

日本人学生に きく   Interviews with Japanese students

Listen to the interviews between a reporter for a student newspaper and four Japanese students who are visiting the college campus. Fill in the chart with their names and what each one likes to do.

	なまえ	好き す
Interview 1		
Interview 2		
Interview 3		
Interview 4		

聞き上手 話し上手
きじょうずはなじょうず
Communication

上手な話し方 Communication Strategy
じょうずはなかた

Giving positive feedback with も; making contrasts with は

Like そうですか and そうですね, the particles も (similarity) and は (contrast) can be used to carry on a conversation more smoothly. If a person mentions something that you have in common, use も to give that person positive feedback.

中田： 大川さんは どんなスポーツが 好きですか。
す

大川： やきゅうが 好きですね。
す

中田： ああ、そうですか。私も やきゅうが 大好きですよ。
だい す

By establishing that you both like baseball, the conversation can now progress to subtopics, such as which teams you do like. In cases where you do not share common interests, you can use は to mark a contrast.

スミス： 高山さんは どんなスポーツが 好きですか。
たかやま　　　　　　　　　　　　す

高山： そうですね。やきゅうが 好きですね。
たかやま　　　　　　　　　　　す

スミス： ああ、そうですか。私は テニスが 大好きです。
だい す

Be careful not to focus too much on your differences, however, since this may become disruptive or seem unfriendly. Instead, you might want to follow up with other questions to find something you do have in common.

上田： リーさんは どんなスポーツが 好きですか。
す

リー： そうですね。やきゅうや ゴルフが 好きですね。
す

上田： そうですか。じゃあ、サッカーも 好きですか。
す

or サッカーは どうですか。

リー： ええ、サッカーも よく みますよ。

or そうですね、サッカーは ちょっと。

Carrying on a conversation in any language is like playing catch. You must take turns speaking and listening while sustaining common topics. It is especially important to be aware of these strategies while trying to speak a second language. Being a good listener is key to participating successfully in a conversation.

練習 Practice
れんしゅう

With a partner, choose a topic below or one of your own. Discuss your individual preferences, incorporating the communicative strategies you have learned.

1. leisure activities   3. sports   5. food
2. music   4. movies   6. books

漢字
かんじ
Kanji

History of the Japanese Writing System

Historically Chinese characters are classified into the following six categories called 六書 . The first four categories are based on structural composition and the last two
りくしょ
are based on usage. The distinction among them is not clear-cut because some belong to more than one category and the definitions are not always clear.

象形文字 (Pictographs) are based on pictures of objects they represent, as
しょうけいもじ
explained in Chapter 5. For example, 大 in Chapter 4, 人 , 山 , 川 , 田 in chapter 5, and 月 , 火 , 水 , 木 , 金 , 土 , and 日 are all in this category. Some of them are very different from the original illustration, and are often hard to see the origin. The number of **kanji** in this category is only a few hundreds.

指事文字 (Logograms or ideographs) are originated from simple graphic
しじもじ
representation of an abstract concept. The number of **kanji** in this category is extremely limited as they are primarily used for direction 上 and 下 and numbers 一 , 二 , 三 , 四 , 八 , 十 , and 百 . Others include 本 and 末 .

会意文字 (compound ideographs or ideographs) are a combination of
かいいもじ
pictographs and logograms to repent an overall meaning. For example, the combination of 人 (*person*) and 木 (*tree*), becomes 休 (*to rest*), and the combination of 日 and 月 becomes 明 (*bright*). Other examples are 学 and 先 .

形声文字 (semantic-phonetic characters, phonetic-ideographic characters) are
けいせいもじ
by far the largest **kanji** category, including kanji such common as 曜 , 時 , and 週 . The proportion of kanji varies depending on the total number of **kanji** considered, but it is usually estimated as between 80 to 90 percent of characters. They usually consist of phonetic component, which indicates on-reading of the **kanji,** and the semantic component, which indicates the categorical meaning of the **kanji**. For example, the left side of 語 , 言 means *to say*, indicating 語 has something to do with speech or language. The right side 吾 provides pronunciation /go/ for this **kanji**. The combination of the two indicates that 語 refers to language and it is pronounced as ご . Other semantically related words such as 話 (/wa/ story, talking) 読 (/doku/ reading), 訳 (/yaku/ translation) and 説 (/setsu/ explanation) all have 言 but have different pronunciation.

転注文字 (delivative characters) is not a well-defined category and thus is rather
てんちゅうもじ
problematic. It refers refer to **kanji** where the original meaning has become extended from its original usage. For example, 楽 (*music, comfort, ease*) is thought by some to have began as a picture of a drum, and by others to have represented bells on a plank of wood. The number of **kanji** in this category is extremely limited.

仮借文字 (phonetic loan characters) are characters from pronunciation in
かしゃもじ
Chinese is imported into Japanese but not the meaning. For example, 来 was a

pictograph that meant *wheat* in the ancient Chinese. When this **kanji** was imported, its pronunciation /rai/ was adopted but the meaning was not. Since one of the meanings of /rai/ is *to come* in Japanese, 来 is used to indicated to come and has the **on**-reading /rai/. Other common characters in its category are 今 , 五 , 六 , and 七 but the number in this category is also very limited.

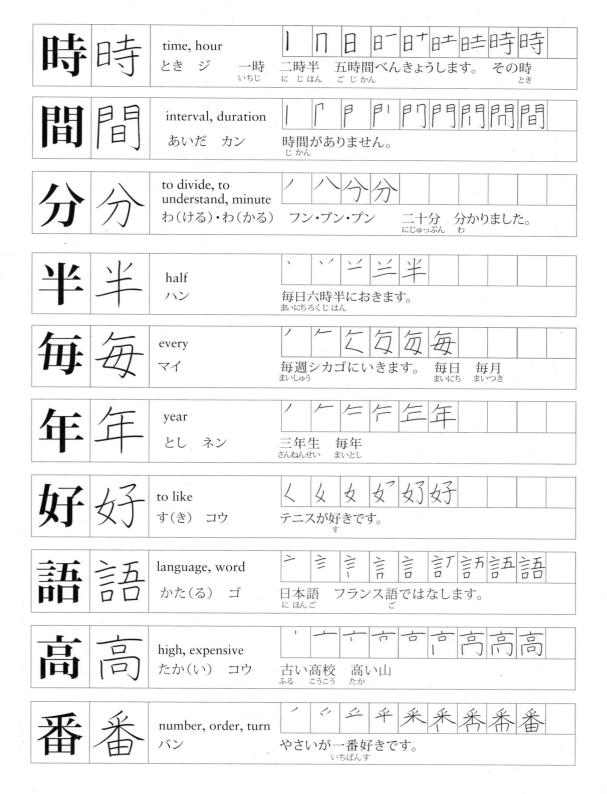

時 時	time, hour とき ジ	一時 いちじ　二時半　五時間べんきょうします。　その時 にじはん　ごじかん　　　　　　　　とき	
間 間	interval, duration あいだ カン	時間がありません。 じかん	
分 分	to divide, to understand, minute わ（ける）・わ（かる）　フン・ブン・プン	二十分　分かりました。 にじゅっぷん　わ	
半 半	half ハン	毎日六時半におきます。 まいにちろくじはん	
毎 毎	every マイ	毎週シカゴにいきます。　毎日　毎月 まいしゅう　　　　　　　　まいにち　まいつき	
年 年	year とし ネン	三年生　毎年 さんねんせい　まいとし	
好 好	to like す（き） コウ	テニスが好きです。 す	
語 語	language, word かた（る） ゴ	日本語　フランス語ではなします。 にほんご　　　　ご	
高 高	high, expensive たか（い） コウ	古い高校　高い山 ふる　こうこう　たか	
番 番	number, order, turn バン	やさいが一番好きです。 いちばんす	

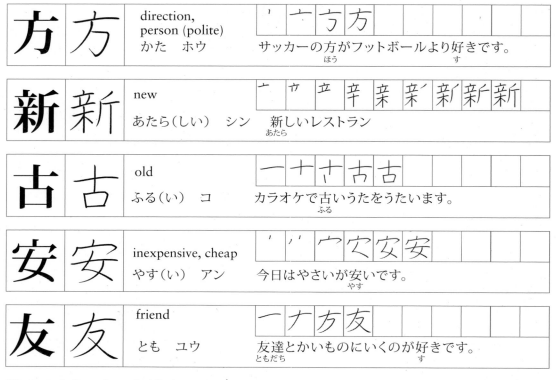

方方	direction, person (polite) かた　ホウ	＇　一　方　方
		サッカーの方がフットボールより好きです。 ほう　　　　　　　　　　　　　　　す

新新	new あたら（しい）　シン	一　ウ　立　辛　亲　亲＇　新　新　新
		新しいレストラン あたら

古古	old ふる（い）　コ	一　十　十　古　古
		カラオケで古いうたをうたいます。 ふる

安安	inexpensive, cheap やす（い）　アン	＇　＇　宀　宀　安　安
		今日はやさいが安いです。 やす

友友	friend とも　ユウ	一　ナ　方　友
		友達とかいものにいくのが好きです。 ともだち　　　　　　　　　　　　す

読めるようになった漢字 (Kanji and compounds you can now read)
よ　　　　　　　　　　　　　　かん　じ

一時　八時半　時々　時計　三時間　二週間　三十分　分かりました
　　　はち　　　ときどき　とけい　さん　　　　に　　　さんじゅっ

毎日毎朝　毎晩　毎週　毎年　毎月　来年　好き　大好き　日本語
　　あさ　　ばん　　　　　　　　　　らい

英語中国語　高い　高校　一番　新しい　新聞　古い　安い　友達　水
えい　ちゅうごく　　　　　　　　いち　　　　　　しんぶん　　　　　　　だち　みず

日本人のなまえ：高山　古山　大木　大田　金田　中山　水田　石田
　　　　　　　たかやま　ふるやま　おおき　おおた　かねだ　なかやま　みずた　いしだ

練習　Practice
れんしゅう

Read the following sentences written in **hiragana**, **katakana**, and **kanji**.

1. 私の友達は毎日5時半におきます。
　　　だち

2. 小川さんは古いきっさてんも新しいカフェも大好きです。

3. 大川さんは毎週テニスを二時間します。
　　　　　　　　　　　　　に

4. 本田：「安いワインと高いワインとどちらの方が好きですか。」
　　金田：「安いワインや高いワインより、おいしいワインが一番
　　　　　　　　　　　　　　　　　　　　　　　　　　　　いち
　　　　　好きです。」

5. スミスさんは日本の高校で一年間べんきょうしました。その時、
　　　　　　　　　　　　　いち
　　日本語もべんきょうしました。

6. 古山：「今、何時ですか。」
　　高田：「8時15分です。」

読む練習
よ れんしゅう
Reading

上手な読み方   Reading Strategy
じょうず よ かた

Understanding word formation

Many words are made up of one or more words as well as prefixes and suffixes. It is important to examine the components of a word to guess its meaning and increase your vocabulary. For example, the suffix ～や indicates a *store* or a *shop* in Japanese, and さかな means *fish*. So what does さかなや mean? How about にくや and くだものや?

読む前に   Pre-reading
よ まえ

Take apart the following words and give their meanings. Follow the example.

Example: 大学院生
              いんせい

大学院 and 生, graduate school + student = graduate student
いん

1. フランス人	4. 大学生	7. のみもの
2. しょくじする	5. 三年生	8. 大好き
3. そうじする	6. 毎日	

本田さんのしゅみ

言葉のリスト
ことば

おそい	slow
モーツァルト	Mozart
ベートーベン	Beethoven
時間がかかる	to take time

私の趣味はスポーツと音楽です。スポーツの中ではテニスが一番好きです。それから、エアロビクスとスキーも大好きです。でも、野球やゴルフは時間がかかるので、あまり好きじゃないのです。バスケットボールは見るのは好きですが、するのはあまり好きじゃありません。

音楽はにぎやかな音楽の方が好きなので、クラシックよりポップスやロックをよく聞きます。クラシックは好きなのもありますが、きらいなのもあります。たとえば、モーツァルトはよく聞きますが、ベートーベンはあまり好きじゃないので、聞きません。

読んだ後で　Comprehension

A. しつもんに　日本語で　こたえて下さい。Answer these questions in Japanese.

1. 本田さんのしゅみは　何ですか。
2. 本田さんは　スキーと　バスケットと　どちらの方が　好きですか。
3. 本田さんは　どんなスポーツが　きらいですか。
4. 本田さんは　どんなおんがくを　よく　ききますか。
5. 本田さんは　だれのおんがくを　ききますか。

B. Underline the following transitional words in the text, and observe how they help indicate relationships between sentences.

それから　　in addition, also, and
でも　　　　but
たとえば　　for example

C. Write a short paragraph about your hobbies. Describe at least two hobbies and provide details such as where, when, how often, and with whom you do them.

総合練習
そうごうれんしゅう
Integration

A. Work with a partner. You need to pick out a birthday present for your partner from a mail-order catalogue. In order to do so, you want to find out his/her hobbies, favorite things, and things that he/she wants. Ask your partner questions to come up with as many options as you can.

Example:　A:　～さんの しゅみは　何ですか。

　　　　　B:　そうですね。私は　しゃしんを　とるのが　好きですね。

　　　　　A:　そうですか。しゃしんですか。いいですね。

　　　　　　　ほかにも (*In addition*)　しゅみが　ありますか。

　　　　　B:　ええ、スポーツが　好きですよ。

　　　　　A:　どんなスポーツが　好きなんですか

　　　　　B:　ハイキングや　ゴルフが　好きですね。

　　　　　A:　そうですか。たべものは　どうですか。

　　　　　B:　たべものですか。ケーキ (*cake*)や　くだものが　好きですね。

B. Work with a new partner. Look at the following items in a mail-order catalogue. Ask each other about each person's previous partner's hobbies and favorite things. Then discuss and decide on what to buy for the previous partner. Compare at least two items.

Example:　A:　～さん (previous partner) は　何が　好きですか。

　　　　　B:　そうですね。しゃしんを　とるのが　好きです。そして、
　　　　　　　ゴルフと　ハイキングも　好きです。

　　　　　A:　たべものは　どうですか。

　　　　　B:　ケーキ (*cake*) や　くだものが　好きです。

　　　　　A:　そうですか。じゃあ、誕生日 (*birthday*) には
　　　　　　　たんじょう び
　　　　　　　どんなものが　いいですか。

　　　　　B:　そうですね。このフォトフレーム (*photo frame*) は　どうですか。

　　　　　A:　いいですね。でも、新しいデジカメも　ありますよ。

　　　　　B:　そうですね、でも、フォトフレームの方が　デジカメより
　　　　　　　安いので、フォトフレームの方が　いいです。

　　　　　A:　じゃあ、このフォトフレームは　どうですか。
　　　　　　　一番安いですよ。

　　　　　B:　そうですね。いいですね。

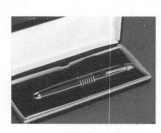

ピクチャーカラー
フォトフレームS
定価 700 円

パーカー クラシック
GT ボールペン
定価 4,000 円

ミ ラ ッ ク ス デ ジ タ ル
カメラ
ウルトラミニ５０万画素
定価 25,000 円

マグカップ 200
定価 750 円

おまかせフラワー
アレンジ
定価 4,000 円

トラベル キャリーケース
定価 3,000 円

ロールプレイ

1. Work with a partner. Using the dialogue as a model conversation, create a new conversation in which you ask your partner about his/her favorite things and hobbies.
2. You are at a party. Introduce yourself to someone and start a conversation. Find out whether he/she shares some of your interests.
3. You are planning a blind date for a friend. Find out what kind of person she/he likes.
4. You are looking for an apartment. Tell your real estate agent what kind of place you'd like. Mention your preferences for size, rooms, location, and other details that are important to you.

Chapter 8

第八課
（だいはちか）

買い物
（か）　　（もの）
Shopping

Objectives	Making requests, expressing quantities and numbers, talking about prices, shopping
Vocabulary	Clothing, accessories and departments; numbers 100 and above, expressions related to merchandise, prices, and activities in a store
Dialogue	デパートで　*At a department store*
Japanese Culture	Shopping in Japan, Japanese department stores, payment practices
Grammar	I.　Requesting and giving explanations or additional information, and creating harmony and shared atmosphere using 〜んです
	II.　Expressing desire using ほしい・ほしがっている and 〜たい・〜たがっている
	III.　Expressing quantities with numbers and the counters まい, 本, ひき, and さつ
	IV.　Expressing quantities using Japanese-origin numbers
	V.　Talking about prices using 円（えん）; indicating floor levels with かい
Listening	Recognizing the characteristics of speech
Communication	Asking for paraphrases and repetition
Kanji	Using **kanji** for numbers
	一　二　三　四　五　六　七　八　九　十　百　千　万　円　店
Reading	Scanning

単語
たん
Vocabulary

Nouns

アクセサリー		accessories
アクセサリーうりば	アクセサリー売り場	accessory department
イヤリング		earring
うでどけい	腕時計	wristwatch
うりば	売り場	department, section (of a store)
CD/DVD うりば	CD/DVD 売り場	CD/DVD section
かさ	傘	umbrella
くつ	靴	shoes
くつした	靴下	socks
コート		coat
ジーンズ		jeans
ジャケット		jacket
シャツ		shirt
しょくひん	食品	food
しょくひんうりば	食品売り場	food department
しんしふく	紳士服	menswear
しんしふくうりば	紳士服売り場	menswear department
スーツ		suit
スカート		skirt
ストッキング		stockings, pantyhose
ズボン		(primarily men's) trousers
セーター		sweater
セール		sale
たんじょうび	誕生日	birthday

ちか	地下	basement	ちかいっかい　　B1
Tシャツ		T-shirt	
ドレス		dress	
ネクタイ		tie	
ネックレス		necklace	
はこ	箱	box	
パンツ		(primarily women's) trousers, shorts	
ハンドバッグ		handbag	
ふく	服	clothing	
ふじんふく	婦人服	woman's clothing	
ふじんふくうりば	婦人服売り場	women's clothing section	
ブラウス		blouse	
ぶんぼうぐ	文房具	stationery	
ぶんぼうぐうりば	文房具売り場	stationery section	
ベルト		belt	
ぼうし	帽子	hat, cap	
みせ	店	store, shop	
ゆびわ	指輪	ring	

う -verbs

かう	買う	to buy
とる	取る	to take

取る is a general equivalent for *to take*, but 撮る is used when one takes a picture, records a video, or makes a copy.

る -verbs

いれる	入れる	to put　　はこに　いれる to put in a box
みせる	見せる	to show

Adverbs

すこし	少し	a little, a few
たくさん		a lot, many, much

ちょっと		a little, a few (more casual than すこし)
もう		〜 more, another 〜
もう　すこし	もう少し	a little more
もう　ちょっと		a little more

Counters

〜えん	〜円	counter for Japanese currency
〜かい	〜階	counter for floors of a building
〜つ		general counter (Japanese origin number)
〜ひき	〜匹	counter for fish and small four-legged animals
〜ほん	〜本	counter for long, cylindrical objects (e.g., bottles, films, pens, pencils)
〜まい	〜枚	counter for thin objects (e.g., film, paper, plates, shirts)
〜さつ	〜冊	counter for bound objects (e.g., books, magazines)

Question words

いかが		how (polite form of どう)
いくつ		how many
いくら		how much (money)

Expressions

いらっしゃいませ		Welcome
ぜんぶで	全部で	all together
〜は　ありませんか		Do you have 〜 ? Do you carry 〜 ? (literally, *Isn't there* 〜 *?*)
〜を　ください	〜を下さい	Please give me 〜
やさしい　ことばで　いってください	やさしい言葉で言って下さい	Please say it in easier words

単語の練習 Vocabulary Practice
たん　　れんしゅう

A. ふくとアクセサリー　Clothing and accessories

シャツ
shirt

T- シャツ
T-shirt

セーター
sweater

ブラウス
blouse

ジャケット
jacket

ドレス
dress

コート
coat

パンツ・ズボン
pants

ジーンズ
jeans

スカート
skirt

スーツ
suit

ネクタイ
tie

ベルト
belt

靴下
くつした
sock

ストッキング
stockings, pantyhose

くつ
shoes

かばん
bag, luggage

ハンドバッグ
handbag

ぼうし
hat/cap

腕時計
うで　どけい
wristwatch

ネックレス
necklace

イヤリング
earrings

ゆびわ
ring

かさ
umbrella

Activity 1

Name the clothing that the following people are wearing.

チェイス   ジョーダン   山田   ブラウン

大木   リー   キム   フォード

Activity 2

Work with a partner. Name the clothing and accessories that your partner is wearing and list them.

Activity 3

しつもんに　日本語で　こたえて下さい。　Answer the questions in Japanese.

1. さいきん (recently) どんなふくを　かいましたか。
2. さいきん (recently) どんなアクセサリーを　かいましたか。
3. アクセサリーの中で　何が　一番好きですか。
4. ふくの中で　何が　一番好きですか。

Supplementary Vocabulary: clothing

あさ	麻	linen
ウール		wool
きもの	着物	kimono (traditional Japanese clothing)
サンダル		sandal
したぎ	下着	underwear
スーツ		suit
シルク		silk
スカーフ		scarf
スニーカー		sneaker(s)
ブーツ		boot(s)
ブレスレット		bracelets
コットン		cotton

B. うりば   Store Departments

ふじんふくうりば	women's clothing section
しんしふくうりば	mensware section
かばんうりば	luggage section
アクセサリーうりば	accessory section
しょくひんうりば	food section
ぶんぼうぐうりば	stationery section
CD ／ DVD うりば	CD/DVD section

Activity 4

Imagine where various sections of a large department store in your country might be located in the store. Then jot down a few items that you would find in each section.

Example: A: 一かいに　何が　ありますか。
いっ

B: アクセサリーうりばが　あります。

A: そうですか。アクセサリーうりばには　どんなものが　ありますか。

B: ハンドバッグやネックレスが　あります。

Floor	うりば	Items
ろっかい　（6F）		
ごかい　（5F）		
よんかい　（4F）		
さんがい　（3F）		
にかい　（2F）		
いっかい　（1F）		

C. 100 から上の数字   Numbers above 100
すう じ

100	ひゃく	1,000	せん	10,000	いちまん
200	にひゃく	2,000	にせん	20,000	にまん
300	さんびゃく	3,000	さんぜん	30,000	さんまん
400	よんひゃく	4,000	よんせん	40,000	よんまん
500	ごひゃく	5,000	ごせん	50,000	ごまん
600	ろっぴゃく	6,000	ろくせん	60,000	ろくまん
700	ななひゃく	7,000	ななせん	70,000	ななまん
800	はっぴゃく	8,000	はっせん	80,000	はちまん
900	きゅうひゃく	9,000	きゅうせん	90,000	きゅうまん

Notes

- Like ふん (*minute*), ひゃく (*hundred*) and せん (*thousand*) change their pronunciation with some numbers.
- Numbers like 346, 995, and 6,126 are formed by combining the thousands digit, hundreds digit, tens digit, and ones digit.

346	さんびゃくよんじゅうろく
995	きゅうひゃくきゅうじゅうご
6,126	ろくせんひゃくにじゅうろく

- For numbers 10,000 or larger, まん becomes the base unit.

10,000	いちまん
100,000	じゅうまん
1,000,000	ひゃくまん
20,000	にまん
200,000	にじゅうまん
2,000,000	にひゃくまん
35,000	さんまんごせん
350,000	さんじゅうごまん
3,500,000	さんびゃくごじゅうまん

Activity 5

Say the following numbers in Japanese.

Example: 100ひゃく

1. 200	5. 600	9. 1,000	13. 88,666
2. 300	6. 700	10. 2,100	14. 142,918
3. 400	7. 800	11. 3,333	15. 153,000
4. 500	8. 900	12. 20,600	

Activity 6

Write the following mathematical problems in Japanese. The plus sign (+) is pronounced たす, and the minus sign (-) is pronounced ひく. The topic marker は is used for the equal sign (=).

Example: 100+200=300   ひゃく　たす　にひゃくは　さんびゃくです。

1. 300 + 9,500 =	5. 45,000 - 870 =
2. 660 - 40 =	6. 3,210 + 28 =
3. 12,350 + 45 =	7. 7,600 - 283 =
4. 3,900 + 700 =	

Activity 7

Work with a partner. Your partner will write a three-digit number on your back. Say the number.

Example: Your partner writes 100 on your back. You say: ひゃく.

Activity 8

Work in groups of three or four. Each member writes five-digit numbers on two different cards. Show one card to the other members of the group, and have them read it aloud as quickly as they can. Give the card to the winner.

Activity 9

Work in groups of three or four. One person writes a number between 100 and 90,000 on a sheet of paper. The rest of the group guess the number using comparative expressions.

Example: A: そのすうじ (number)は　百より　大きいですか。小さいですか。
　　　　　　　　　　　　　　　　ひゃく

　　　　　　 B: 大きいです。

　　　　　　 C: じゃあ、二百より　大きいですか。小さいですか。
　　　　　　　　　　　　に ひゃく

　　　　　　 B: 小さいです。

　　　　　　 D: 百五十より　大きいですか。小さいですか。
　　　　　　　　ひゃく ご じゅう

　　　　　　 E: 大きいです。

D. 店で　つかう　ことば　　Useful expressions in a store
　　みせ

～を　みせて下さい	Please show me ～　（みせる to show）
～を　とって下さい	Please get, pick up ～　（とる to pick up）
～を　はこに　いれて下さい	Please put ～ in a box（いれる to put）
～は　ありませんか	Do you have ～ ?
～を　下さい	Please give me ～
セール	sale
Money/time します	It costs/takes ～　（する to cost/to take）

Activity 10

Work with a partner. Take turns asking questions or making requests using one of the expressions from the table. Your partner either acts out or responds to the question.

かさを　とる	本を　かばんに　いれる	シャツを　みせる
セールが　ある	ジャケットを　みせる	腕時計を　とる うでどけい
10ドル　する	ネックレスを　はこに　いれる	靴下を　みせる くつした

Activity 11

Work with a partner. Take turns playing the roles of customer and store clerk. Each of you should make at least two requests.

Example: あのコートを　とって下さい。
           Your partner pretends to get a coat for you.

E. サイズ、りょう、ねだん Size, quantity, and price

たくさん	a lot
もっと　たくさん	more quantity
もっと　高い	more expensive
もっと　安い	less expensive
もっと　大きい	larger
もっと　小さい	smaller
すこし／ちょっと	a little, less
	（すこし and ちょっと are interchangeable.）
もう　すこし／もう　ちょっと	a little more
もう　すこし　大きい／もう　ちょっと　大きい	a little bigger
もう　すこし　小さい／もう　ちょっと　小さい	a little smaller

Activity 12

Work with a partner. Complete the following conversation using the appropriate quantity and size expressions. There may be more than one possible answer.

Example: A: コーヒーを　のみますか。

           B: ええ、大好きなので、<u>たくさん</u>　のみます。

1. A: このセーターは　いかがですか。
   B: 小さいですね。　_____のは　ありませんか。
2. A: このシャツは　いかがですか。
   B: すこし　高いですね。　_____のは　ありませんか。
3. A: このくつは　いかがですか。
   B: ちょっと　大きいです。　_____のを　みせて下さい。
4. A: このストッキングは　あまり　よく　ありませんね。
   B: じゃあ、_____ですが、こちらは　いかがですか。

ダイアローグ

はじめに　Warm-up

しつもんに日本語でこたえて下さい。Answer these questions in Japanese.
1. よく　デパートに　いきますか。
2. デパートで　何を　よく　かいますか。
3. アメリカのデパートには　どんなものが　ありますか。
4. よく　どんな店に　かいものに　いきますか。
　　　　みせ

デパートで　*At a department store*

今日は　石田さんの誕生日 (birthday) です。上田さんは　デパートに
　　　　いし　たんじょう び
いきました。

あんないがかり (*information assistant*)：　いらっしゃいませ。

　　　　上田：　すみません。しょくひんうりばは　どこに　ありますか。

あんないがかり：　しょくひんうりばは　地下一かいで　ございます。
　　　　　　　　　　　　　　　　　　ち か いっ
(Clerk at information desk)

　　　　上田：　そうですか。じゃあ、しんしふくうりばは　何かい
　　　　　　　　ですか。

あんないがかり：　しんしふくうりばは　三かいで　ございます。

上田さんは　しょくひんうりばに　いきました。

店の人 (sales clerk)：　いらっしゃいませ。

　　　　上田：　あのう、このりんごを　三つ　下さい。それから

　　　　　　　そのオレンジを　五つ　下さい。

　　　店の人：　はい。　りんごを　三つと　オレンジ　五つですね。

　　　　　　　ぜんぶで 863 円に　なります。

上田さんは　しんしふくうりばに　います。

　　　店の人：　いらっしゃいませ。

　　　　上田：　あのう、　そのネクタイを　みせて下さい。

　　　店の人：　これですか。　どうぞ。

　　　　上田：　いくらですか。

　　　店の人：　一万円です。

　　　　上田：　そうですか。もうすこし　安いのは　ありませんか。

　　　店の人：　じゃ、こちらは　いかがでしょうか。

　　　　上田：　これは　いくらですか。

　　　店の人：　四千円です。

　　　　上田：　いいですね。じゃあ、これ　下さい。

　　　店の人：　かしこまりました。では、一万円　おあずかりします。

　　　　　　　おくりもので　ございますか。

　　　　上田：　はい、そうです。

店の人は　ネクタイを　はこに　いれました。

　　　店の人：　六千円の　おかえしで　ございます。どうも

　　　　　　　ありがとうございました。

DIALOGUE PHRASE NOTES

- 〜で　ございますis a polite form of 〜です.
- 〜に　なります is commonly used by store clerks instead of です.
- いかがでしょうか。is a polite expression for どうですか.
- おあずかりしますis a polite expression for あずかる, which means *to keep* or *to hold temporarily*.
- おくりもの means *present* or *gift*.
- おかえし is a polite expression for *change* (money returned).

ダイアローグの後で　Comprehension
_{あと}

A.　Fill in the blanks with the appropriate words.

上田さんは＿＿＿＿＿に　いきました。＿＿＿＿＿＿＿で

りんごと＿＿＿＿を　かって、＿＿＿＿＿で　＿＿＿＿を

かいました。ぜんぶで＿＿＿＿＿＿＿円でした。
_{えん}

B. Circle はい if the a statement is true and いいえ if it is false.

1. はい　いいえ　　上田さんは　オレンジを　三つ　かいました。
_{みっ}

2. はい　いいえ　　しんしふくうりばは　三かいに　あります。
_{さん}

3. はい　いいえ　　上田さんは　一万円の　ネクタイを　かいました。
_{いちまんえん}

4. はい　いいえ　　しょくひんうりばは　地下に　あります。
_{ち　か}

日本の文化
ぶん か
Japanese Culture

買い物   Shopping
か もの

In addition to high-tech goods and high-fashion apparel, Japan is famous for its sheer silks, top-quality pearls, fine ceramics, lacquerware, colorful and historic

woodblock prints, handcrafted bamboo ware, and other crafts. Although the cost of living in Japan is high, there are many places to shop inexpensively. The Akihabara District in Tokyo, for example, is full of discount stores specializing in electronics, household appliances, CDs, DVDs, and anime merchandise. There are also many 百円ショップ
ひゃくえん
(100-yen shops) around Japan, where you can purchase inexpensive household gadgets. Shopping hours in Japan are usually from 10 or 11 a.m. to 7 or 8 p.m., and most retail stores are open on weekends and holidays.

デパート   Department Stores

Japanese department stores are fun places to shop. They carry the latest fashions, traditional Japanese goods, gourmet foods, books, CDs, DVDs, and other merchandise. Some of the large department stores contain restaurants, spas, beauty salons, and amusements for children. Semiannual store sales are usually held in July and August, and December and January.

To ask where something is sold, simply add the word うりば to the item you are looking for. For example, *food* is しょくひん in Japanese, so the *food section* would be しょくひんうりば.

Visit the *Nakama 1* student website to learn more about Japanese department stores.

Customer Service

As in other countries, customer service is very important in Japan. Some department stores even have uniformed elevator operators who announce each floor as well as sales and special events. Salespeople are trained to use very polite Japanese when speaking to customers. Here are some commonly used phrases :

いらっしゃいませ。 — *Welcome, good of you to come.*

何か おさがしでしょうか。 — *May I help you? (literally, Are you looking for something?)*

何〜／いくつ さしあげましょうか。 — *How many 〜 do you need? (literally, Shall I give you?)*

〜は いかがですか。 — *How about/is 〜 ? (polite form of 〜は どうですか)*

このセーターは いかがですか。 — *How about this sweater?*

〜で ございます。 — a polite form of 〜です

このコートは 一万円で ございます。
いちまんえん — *This coat is 10,000 yen.*

はい、かしこまりました。 — *Yes, I shall do as you say.*

しょうしょう おまち下さい。 — *Please wait a moment.*

Methods of payment

For retail transactions, cash is still the most common method of payment, although many stores do accept credit cards. A 5% consumption tax is applied throughout Japan. Some stores give discounts for cash payments. Personal checks are not used. There are also prepaid rechargeable contact-less smart cards, which are similar to debit cards and can be used at participating stores, vending machines, and websites. Payment by smart card works just like cash.

Some cell phones can be used just like a smart card. Charges to smart-card accounts can also be made online using a cell phone.

文法
ぶんぽう
Grammar

> ## I. Requesting and giving explanations or additional information, and creating harmony and shared atmosphere using 〜んです

The structure 〜んです is frequently used in conversation instead of 〜ます. The use of 〜んです helps to establish or maintain rapport with the listener. By using 〜んです the speaker treats the addressee as a member of his/her own social group rather than as an outsider. On the other hand, 〜ます merely conveys a fact as it is observed, so statements with 〜ます sound more neutral or impersonal in tone. Japanese people often use 〜んです to sound friendly and show concern for each other, as a way to be polite. The charts below show how 〜んです can be used.

Comment

	Verb (plain form)		
あまり	たべない	んですね。	

You don't eat much.

Response

Topic		Adjective (plain form)	
にくは	あまり	好きじゃない	んですよ。

I don't like meat very much.

Although 〜んです is used in many different situations, there are a few situations where 〜んです is most commonly used. First, 〜んです is used to invite additional information or explanations beyond the simple answer. For example, おんがくが 好きなんですか indicates that the speaker not only wants to know whether the addressee likes music but also wants to learn more about it. On the other hand, おんがくが 好きですか merely asks the listener's likes and dislikes about music. This use of 〜んです can express the speaker's interest to the addressee and friendliness. If overused, however, it sounds nosy or imposing.

水本：　あの シャツ いいですね。
みずもと
That shirt's nice.

田中：　ええ、とても 好きなんですが、ちょっと　高いんですよ。
I really like it, but it's a bit expensive.

水本：　そうですか。いくらぐらいですか。
みずもと
Really? How much is it?

田中：　セールで 二万円です。
にまんえん
It's 20,000 yen on sale.

水本：　二万円！　それは　高いですね。
みずもと　　に まんえん
20,000 yen! That's really expensive.

NOTES

- 〜んです can be also used to make an excuse or to explain the reasons for a situation without indicating it explicitly. In the following example, Mr. Kim gives a vague excuse when Ms. Smith approaches him.

  スミス：　あのう、すみませんが。
  Excuse me.

  キム：　すみません。今　ちょっと　いそがしいんです。
  Sorry, I'm tied up now.

- The 〜んです structure is also used for confirming the speaker's assumption, or giving and requesting an explanation or reason. For example, if the speaker assumes that the listener is going home, he/she would likely use かえるんですか instead of かえりますか.

- In addition, 〜んです can a imply surprise or irritation. In the following example, Ms. Lopez expresses her surprise by using 〜んですか in her second utterance.

  ロペス：　どこに　いくんですか。
  Where are you going?

  山田：　びょういんです。
  To the hospital.

  ロペス：　えっ、びょういんへ　いくんですか。
  What? Are you going to the hospital?

- The structure 〜のです・のだ is used in writing instead of 〜んです. In casual speech, 〜んです becomes の in a question or statement. A male speaker may use 〜んだ・のだ in a statement as well.

  ロペス：　どこに　いくの？
  Where are you going?

  山田：　びょういんに　いくの。
  　　　　びょういんに　いくんだ。
  To the hospital.

- The question word どうして (*why*) is frequently used with 〜んです, implying that an explanation is being asked for. The answer to such a question will also be given with 〜んです as well as ので indicating that the explanation is being given. どうしてですか means *why is that?* どうして tends to imply surprise about someone's response or behavior and the demand for an explanation, so it can sound rather aggressive or accusatory.

話してみましょう   Conversation Practice
はな

Activity 1

You have heard various things about different people. Ask questions to confirm whether your understanding is correct.

Example: 大田さんは　新しいかれし (*boyfriend*) が　います。

えっ、かれしが　いるんですか。

1. 高山さんは　やさいを　たべません。
2. 古田さんの店は　山の中に　あります。
   ふる た   みせ
3. 山本さんは　パンツ／ズボンが　好きです。
4. 友田さんは　ぜんぜん　りょうりをしません。
   とも だ
5. 大川さんのジーンズは　五万円します。([money] +する means *to cost*.)
                        ご まんえん
6. 高田さんのジーンズは　古いです。
7. 上田さんは　スカートが　好きじゃありません。

Activity 2

Work with a classmate. Extend an invitation for this weekend. Your partner will refuse the invitation. Follow up by asking 何か　あるんですか。 (*Do you have something to do?*) Find out why your invitation was refused.

Example: A: 今週の週末に　あそびに　きませんか。

B: ありがとう。でも、ちょっと　つごうがわるくて。

A: そうなんですか。何か (*something*)　あるんですか。

B: ええ、月曜日に　テストが　あるんですよ。

A: そうですか。それは　大変ですね。
                    たいへん

Activity 3

Work with a partner. You bump into each other on the street. Both of you are going shopping today. First decide the place, the item, and/or your reason for shopping. Then ask each other about your plans.

Example: A: おでかけですか (*Are you going out?*)

B: ええ、ちょっと　友達と　デパートまで。
                  だち
A: そうですか。　おかいものですか。
    （おかいもの is a polite form of かいもの）

B: ええ、今日は　セールが　あるんですよ。

II. Expressing desire using ほしい・ほしがっている and 〜たい・〜たがっている

Japanese has two ways to indicate desire. ほしい means *I want* something, and たい means *I want to do* something. ほしい and たい express only what you (the speaker) want. To talk about what someone else wants, ほしい and たい are attached to other expressions such as 〜がっている (*showing a sign that* 〜), 〜んです (*it is the case that* 〜), and 〜そうです (*I heard that* 〜).

A. ほしい   I want (something)

ほしい is an adjective that indicates the speaker wants something (a physical object). The subject of ほしい must be the speaker in a statement and either the speaker or the listener in a question. The object of ほしい takes the particle が.

Question

Topic (subject)		Noun (object)	Particle	い -adjective	
スミスさん	は	何	が	ほしいです	か。

What do you want, Ms. Smith?

Answer

Noun (object)	Particle	い -adjective
ジャケット	が	ほしいです。

I want a jacket.

おきゃくさん (customer)：　あのう、しろいブラウスが　ほしいんですが。
　　　　　　　　　　　　　Excuse me, I want a white blouse.

店の人：　はい、こちらに　ございますが。
みせ
　　　　　　Yes, here it is.

As shown in the chart, ほしい is an い-adjective and takes が to mark the object, though が is often replaced by the contrastive marker は in negative form.

くろいきれいな　ストッキング<u>が</u>　ほしいです。
I want pretty black pantyhose.

ストッキングは　ほしくありません。／ほしくないです。
I don't want pantyhose.

B. ほしがっている　Someone else wants (something)

To express what someone else wants, ほしい is often followed by the suffix
〜がっている (*he/she is showing signs of 〜*). When the suffix 〜がっている is
used, the object is marked by the particle を.

Topic (subject)		Noun (object)	Particle	い -adjective (stem)	Auxiliary verb
スミスさん	は	ジャケット	を	ほし	がっています。

Ms. Smith wants a jacket.

私の友達は　誕生日に　腕時計を　ほしがっている。
　だち　　たんじょう び　　うでどけい

My friend wants a wristwatch for his birthday.

This 〜がっている form is used because the Japanese language considers that one's
emotional state is known only by that person. Others can only guess about another
person's feelings. For this reason, expressions of emotive states, such as 〜ほしい
and 〜たい, are reserved for the speaker. To talk about other people's emotions,
always use expressions that imply an understanding or a guess on the part of the
speaker, such as 〜がっている (*showing a sign of*), 〜んです (*it is the case that 〜*),
and そうです (*I heard*) (see chapter 12, grammar IV, for a detailed explanation).
Note that with 〜んです and そうです, the direct object particle remains が,
because the phrase 〜が ほしい is part of a clause embedded in the main clause
with 〜んです and そうです.

山本さんは　しろいドレスが　ほしいそうです。

I heard that Ms. Yamamoto wants a white dress.

鈴木さんは　くろいコートが　ほしいんですよ。
すず

It is the case that Mr. Suzuki wants a black coat.

C. 〜たい　I want (to do something)

Unlike ほしい, 〜たい indicates the speaker's wish to do something (an action).
This is conveyed using verb-masu stem + たい. Compare these two examples.

このケーキが　ほしい。

I want this cake .

このケーキが／を　たべたい。

I want to eat this cake.

Topic (subject)		Direct object	Particle	Verb (stem)	Auxiliary (い -adjective)
私	は	コーヒー	が／を	のみ	たいです。

I want to drink some coffee.

山田：　日本で　何が　したいですか。
What do you want to do in Japan?

トム：　そうですね、富士山が　みたいですね。
　　　　　ふ　じ さん
Well, I want to see Mt. Fuji.

それから、きょうとにも　いきたいですね。
I want to go to Kyoto, too.

NOTES

- With たいです, the direct object marker を can be replaced with が. The first two sentences below are identical in meaning. Other particle usages remain unchanged.

  私は　そのくつを　かいたいです。
  I want to buy those shoes .

  私は　そのくつが　かいたいです。
  I want to buy those shoes.

  私は　おふろに　はいりたいです。
  I want to take a bath.

  私は　ここで　まちたいです。
  I want to wait here.

- It is impolite to use 〜たいですか to your superior when asking if a superior wants to do something. Use 〜ますか or 〜いかが ですか instead.

  ごはんを　たべますか。
  Would you like to eat (rice/a meal)?

  ケーキは　いかがですか。
  Would you like some cake?

As with ほしい, add 〜たがっている to express what someone else wants to do, and use を for the direct object marker.

Topic (subject)		Direct object	Particle	Verb (stem)	たがっている (る -verb)
山田さん	は	スーツ	を	かい	たがっています。

Mr. Yamada wants to buy a suit.

キム：　ジョンソンさんは　四月に　日本に　いくんですか。
　　　　　　　　　　　　　　　し がつ
Is Ms. Johnson going to Japan in April?

高子：　ええ、日本で　日本語を　べんきょうしたがっているので。
たか こ
Yes, because she wants to study Japanese in Japan.

You can also use 〜たいんです and 〜たいそうです. The direct object particle can be が or を.

田中さんは その本が／を かいたいんです。
It is that Mr. Tanaka wants to buy the book.

田中さんは その本が／を かいたいそうです。
I heard that Mr. Tanaka wants to buy the book.

話してみましょう   Conversation Practice
はな

Activity 1

Each of the following people wants certain gifts for certain occasions. Assume the identity of each person to tell others what you would like. Use ほしい.

Example: Assume you are Mr./Ms. Smith.

私は 誕生日に いぬが ほしいです。
たんじょう び

	スミス	リー	ジョーンズ	キム
誕生日 たんじょう び	いぬ	腕時計 うでどけい	じてんしゃ	ジャケット
クリスマス／ ハヌカ (Hanukkah)	ハンドバック	ネックレス	ぼうし	スーツ
バレンタインデー	イヤリング	ベルト	ネクタイ	ゆびわ

Activity 2

Now look at the chart again and use ほしがっている and/or ほしいんです to say what each person wants for the various occasions.

Example: スミスさんは 誕生日に いぬを ほしがっています。
たんじょう び
スミスさんは 誕生日に いぬが ほしいんです。
たんじょう び

Activity 3

Work with a partner. You are a customer and your partner is a salesperson in a clothing department in a department store. First think about a few clothing items you want. Then ask for his/her assistance.

Example:　おきゃくさん：あのう、すみません。ジャケットが　ほしいんですが。

店の人：ジャケットですか。じゃあ、こちらは　いかがですか。

おきゃくさん：ああ、いいですね。

Or ちょっと　小さいですね。もっと　大きいのが
ほしいんですが。

店の人：じゃあ、こちらは　いかがですか。

おきゃくさん：ああ、いいですね。

Activity 4

Conjugate the verbs using the phrases 私は　〜たいです and スミスさん
は　〜たがっています.

Example:　うちに　かえる

私は　うちに　かえりたいです。スミスさんは　うちに
かえりたがっています。

1. りょこうに　いく　　　4. 日本で　べんきょうする
2. 新しいふくを　かう　　5. ゲームを　する
3. おちゃを　のむ　　　　6. おふろに　はいる

Activity 5

In pairs, say what you want to do in each of the following situations. Note that
だったら means if 〜 is 〜.

Example:　A: お金持ち (rich person) だったら、何が　したいですか。

B: そうですね。大きい　うちを　かいたいですね。

1. 大学の先生だったら、何が　したいですか。
2. おとこ (male) だったら／おんな (female) だったら、何が　したいですか。
3. 日本人だったら、何が　したいですか。
4. 有名人 (celebrity) だったら、何が　したいですか。
5. 明日　休みだったら、何が　したいですか。

Activity 6

Work with the class. Ask your classmates what they want and what activities they want to do on their birthdays. Then decide which items or activities are most popular and which is the most unusual.

Example: A:　～さんは　誕生日に　どんなことが　したいですか。

B:　そうですね。うちで　パーティが　したいですね。

A:　そうですか。いいですね。

　　じゃあ、プレゼントは　どんなものが　いいですか。

B:　そうですね。新しいくつが　ほしいですね。

なまえ	したいこと	ほしいもの

III. Expressing quantities with numbers and the counters まい, 本, ひき, and さつ

You have already learned some expressions with numbers such as 〜時, 〜時間, and 〜分. These are called counter expressions. In this chapter, you will learn more of them and how they work. In counting things, and even people, a counter must be attached to the number. Some English equivalents of Japanese counters are expressions such as "two *cups* of coffee" or "three *sheets* of paper." Japanese uses a number of different counters. The type, shape, and size of an object determines which counter should be used.

Counter	Object Type	Examples
〜まい	thin objects	paper, plates, T-shirts, CDs, DVDs
〜ひき	fish, small four-legged animals	dogs, cats, mice
〜本	long cylindrical objects	pencils, pens, bottles, cans, belts, ties, trousers, movies/films
〜さつ	bound objects	books, dictionaries, magazines

The following chart illustrates how to combine numbers with counters. As you have seen in 分, 百, and 千, combining counters with numbers sometimes changes the pronunciation of both the numbers and the counters themselves. The underlined expressions in the chart are examples of these changes. Pronunciation changes for 本 and ひき follow the same pattern.

		Thin, flat objects 〜まい	Cylindrical objects 〜ほん（本）	Fish, animals 〜ひき	Bound objects 〜さつ
?	何	なんまい	※なんぼん	※なんびき	なんさつ
1	一	いちまい	※いっぽん	※いっぴき	※いっさつ
2	二	にまい	にほん	にひき	にさつ
3	三	さんまい	※さんぼん	※さんびき	さんさつ
4	四	よんまい	よんほん	よんひき	よんさつ
5	五	ごまい	ごほん	ごひき	ごさつ
6	六	ろくまい	※ろっぽん	※ろっぴき	ろくさつ
7	七	ななまい	ななほん	ななひき	ななさつ
8	八	はちまい	※はっぽん	※はっぴき	※はっさつ
9	九	きゅうまい	きゅうほん	きゅうひき	きゅうさつ
10	十	じゅうまい	※じゅっぽん	※じゅっぴき	※じゅっさつ

The counter expressions come immediately after the object and its particle.

Noun + Particle	Number + Counter	Verb	
セーターを	一まい いち	かいました。	*I bought one sweater.*
水を	四本 よんほん	のみました。	*I drank four bottles of water.*
ねこが	十ぴき じゅっ	います。	*There are ten cats.*
そのざっしを	二さつ に	下さい。	*Give me two magazines.*
ベルトを	何本 ぼん	かいますか。	*How many belts will you buy?*
本は	何さつ	ありますか。	*How many books are there?*

山田： このTシャツを 三まい 下さい。
　　　　　　　　　　　さん
Please give me these three T-shirts.

店の人： 三まいですね。かしこまりました。
みせ　　さん
Three of them. Certainly, sir.

田中： そこに えんぴつが 何本 ありますか。
　　　　　　　　　　　　ぼん
How many pencils are there?

スミス： 六本 あります。
　　　ろっぽん
There are six.

山田： ねこを 何びき みましたか。
How many cats did you see?

山本： 二ひき みました。
　　　に
I saw two.

上田： としょかんには 日本語の本が たくさん ありますか。
Are there a lot of Japanese books in the library?

川口： ええ。四千さつぐらい ありますよ。
　　　　　よんせん
Yes, there are about four thousand.

When talking about multiple items in a single sentence, the particle と comes after the counter expression.

大きいノートを 三さつと、小さいのを 二さつ 下さい。
　　　　　　　さん　　　　　　　　　に
Please give me three large notebooks and two small ones.

そのシャツ 二まいと、ベルトを はこに いれて下さい。
　　　　　に
Please put two shirts and a belt in the box.

話してみましょう　Conversation Practice
はな

Activity 1

Describe each picture using an appropriate counter expression.

Example: ネクタイが　一本　あります。
いっぽん

1.　　　　2.　　　　3.　　　　4.　　　　5.

6.　　　　7.　　　　8.　　　　9.　　　　10.

Activity 2

Work in groups of three or four. Ask your classmates how many of the following items they own. Find out who owns the most of each item. Then write down the name of the person and the quantity.

Example:　A: ～さんは　セーターが　何まい　ありますか。

　　　　　B: そうですね。十まいぐらい　ありますね。
　　　　　　　　　　じゅう

なまえ	私（　　　）			
セーター				
日本語の本				
ペット (いぬ／ねこ／ other)				
ベルト				

Activity 3

Work with a partner. Ask what kind of clothing and how many items your partner would have if he/she were a famous movie star. Note that おもちですか is a polite expression that means *to own*. Take turns.

Example:　A: あのう、どんなふくを　おもちですか 。

　　　　　B: そうですね。パンツ／ズボンが　六十本と　シャツが
　　　　　　　百まいぐらい　ありますね。
　　　　　　　ひゃく　　　　　　　　ろくじゅっぽん

　　　　　A: すごいですね。(*Wow!*).

IV. Expressing quantities using Japanese-origin numbers

Numbers such as いち, に, and さん are Chinese-origin numbers. There is another series of numbers called *Japanese-origin numbers*. These numbers do not require counter expressions and are usually used for round, discrete objects, such as apples, oranges, or pebbles, or for objects that do not fit any specific category. Japanese-origin numbers only go up to ten. For numbers larger than ten, Chinese-origin numbers are used. The corresponding question word is いくつ.

		Japanese-origin numbers
1	一	ひとつ
2	二	ふたつ
3	三	みっつ
4	四	よっつ
5	五	いつつ
6	六	むっつ
7	七	ななつ
8	八	やっつ
9	九	ここのつ
10	十	とお

		Chinese-origin numbers
11	十一	じゅういち
12	十二	じゅうに
13	十三	じゅうさん
·	·	·
·	·	·
·	·	·
·	·	·
·	·	·
·	·	·
20	二十	にじゅう

		Chinese-origin numbers
30	三十	さんじゅう
45	四十五	よんじゅうご
100	百	ひゃく

タン：　ぼうしは　いくつ　ありますか。
How many hats are there?

モリル：　十二 あります。
　　　　 じゅう に
There are twelve.

店の人：　いらっしゃいませ。
みせ
Welcome.

リー：　あのう　りんごを　五つと　バナナを　五本 下さい。
　　　　　　　　　　 いつ　　　　　　 ご ほん
Could you give me five apples and five bananas.

店の人：　りんごを　五つと　バナナを　五本ですね。はい。
みせ　　　　　　　 いつ　　　　　　 ご ほん
Five apples and five bananas. Here they are.

話してみましょう   Conversation Practice
はな

Activity 1

Describe the following pictures using the appropriate counter expression.

Example: ゆびわが 一つ あります。
ひと

1.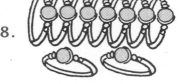

2.

3.

4.

5.

6.

7.

8.

9.

10.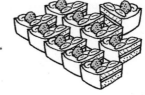

11.

12.

> **Activity 2**

Classify the following words using the appropriate counter. Then make a sentence for each item with the counter.

えんぴつ、かばん、CD、きょうかしょ、けしゴム、じしょ、ノート、ペン、ボールペン、本、木、ねこ、いぬ、ざっし、コーラ、さかな、たまご、トマト、にんじん、セーター、バナナ、ビール、りんご、レタス、ワイン

Example: えんぴつ   えんぴつを 十本 下さい。
じゅっぽん

Counter	Item
まい	
さつ	
本	えんぴつ
ひき	
Japanese-origin numbers	

> **Activity 3**

Work with a partner. You are going shopping and your partner is the clerk at each of the stores in the table below. First make out a shopping list. Then go to each store and ask for the items on your list. Your partner will ask how many you need of each item and write down your purchases.

Example: A: いらっしゃいませ。

B: あのう、りんごを 下さい。

A: いくつ さしあげましょうか。

B: 一つ 下さい。
ひと

スーパー	デパート	コンビニ

> **Activity 4**

Work with a different partner. Say what you have bought in Activity 3, and compare your purchases. Follow the example.

Example: 私は スーパーで りんごを 二つ かいました。
ふた
〜さんは りんごを 二つ かいました。
ふた

V. Talking about prices using 円; indicating floor levels with かい
えん

A. Asking about and stating prices with 円
えん

You are probably familiar with the ¥ symbol for Japanese currency. *Yen* can also be written as 円. Numbers that precede 円 are pronounced in the same way as with the counter まい, except that four yen becomes よえん. The question word for price is いくら.
えん   えん

1（一）	いちえん	6（六）	ろくえん
2（二）	にえん	7（七）	ななえん
3（三）	さんえん	8（八）	はちえん
4（四）	＊よえん	9（九）	きゅうえん
5（五）	ごえん	10（十）	じゅうえん

上田： これは いくらですか。
How much is this?

店の人： 百五十円です。
みせ　　　ひゃく ご じゅうえん
It is 150 yen.

スミス： きれいなイヤリングですね。
You have pretty earrings on.

田中： ありがとう。でも 安かったんですよ。
Thanks, but they were inexpensive.

スミス： そうですか。いくらだったんですか。
Really? How much were they?

田中： 二千円です。
に せんえん
2000 yen.

スミス： それは いい かいものですね。
That's a good buy!

B. Indicating floor levels with かい

Numbers before the counter かい are pronounced in the same way as with the counter 本. Both さんかい (*third floor*) and なんかい (*what floor?*) can be
ほん
pronounced as さんがい and なんがい, respectively. Use 地下～ (*underground*)
ちか
to indicate a basement floor. (地下いっかい = B1)
ちか

?	なんかい なんがい		
1（一）	いっかい	6（六）	ろっかい
2（二）	にかい	7（七）	ななかい
3（三）	さんかい さんがい	8（八）	はちかい
4（四）	よんかい	9（九）	きゅうかい
5（五）	ごかい	10（十）	じゅっかい

Because floor levels indicate location, かい is used with a variety of location particles, such as に (*place of existence*), に (*goal*), で (*place of action*) , まで (*to*), and から (*from*).

リー：　アクセサリーうりばは　何かいに　ありますか。
Which floor is the accessory department on?

店の人：　一かいに　ございます。
　みせ　　　　いっ
It's on the first floor.

山本：　すみません。ぶんぼうぐうりばは　どこですか。
Excuse me. Where is the stationery section?

店の人：　六かいに　ございます。
　みせ　　　　ろっ
It's on the sixth floor.

二かいまで　あるいていきます。
　に
I will walk up to the second floor.

三がいで　あいませんか。
　さん
Why don't we meet on the third floor?

話してみましょう   Conversation Practice
はな

Activity 1

Look at the following pictures of Japanese currency and say how many yen each one is worth.

Example: 一円
いちえん

1.   2.   3.   4.   5.

6.    7.

8.

Activity 2

Look at the following items and say how much each one costs.

Example:  25円

えんぴつは 二十五円です。
に じゅう ご えん

1. 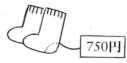 750円   2.  50円   3.  3400円

4.  8700円   5.  19800円   6.  4600円

7. 1290円   8.  2800円

Activity 3

Work with a partner. You want to buy items in the chart and your budget is 20,000 yen. Your partner is a salesperson, and he/she decides on the price of each item. Ask your partner how much each item costs and say whether you will buy it. Make sure to stay within your budget!

Example:　A: すみません、この靴下は　いくらですか。

　　　　　　B: 〜円です。

　　　　　　A: じゃ、これを　下さい。(*if buying*)

　　　　　or　そうですか。じゃ、また　きます。(*if not buying*)

	〜円	かう?
靴下		
シャツ		
ジーンズ		
ジャケット		
ベルト		

Activity 4

Look at the floor directory below, and answer the following questions using 〜かい.

Example:　くつうりばは　何がいに　ありますか。
　　　　　　一かいに　あります。

おくじょう (R)	ゆうえんち (*amusement center*)
8F	レストラン
7F	ぶんぼうぐ　本　CD ／ DVD　おもちゃ (*toys*)
6F	でんきせいひん　(*electrical appliances*)
5F	かぐ (*furniture*)　しょっき　(*tableware*) だいどころようひん (*kitchenware*)
4F	こうげいひん (*traditional Japanese crafts and giftware*) きもの (*kimonos*)
3F	ふじんふく
2F	しんしふく
1F	ハンドバッグ (*handbags*)　くつ　ネクタイ　かばん アクセサリー　けしょうひん (*cosmetics*)
B1	しょくひん

1. レストランは　何がいに　ありますか。
2. どこで　つくえを　かいますか。
3. どこで　パンツ／ズボンを　かいますか。
4. ぶんぼうぐうりばは　どこに　ありますか。
5. どこで　スカートを　かいますか。
6. 何がいで　にくを　かいますか。

Activity 5

Work with a partner. You are the customer and your partner works at the information desk on the first floor of a department store. Your partner will make a floor directory. Ask where the following sections or facilities are and write the information in the chart below.

Example:　A:　いらっしゃいませ。

　　　　　B:　すみませんが、かばんうりばは　どこですか。

　　　　　A:　かばんうりばは　一かいに　ございます。
　　　　　　　　　　　　　　いっ

　　　　　A:　一かいですね。どうも　ありがとう。
　　　　　　　いっ

1. かばんうりば
2. トイレ
3. CD うりば
4. レストラン
5. ふじんふくうりば
6. しんしふくうりば
7. しょくひんうりば
8. アクセサリーうりば

8F	
7F	
6F	
5F	
4F	
3F	
2F	
1F	
B1F	

聞く練習
き　　れんしゅう
Listening Practice

上手な聞き方　Listening Strategy
じょうず　き　かた

Recognizing the characteristics of speech

Being aware of the characteristics of spoken language will help you to understand it better. Spoken language is highly redundant; that is, it repeats the same information more than once. It also contains hesitations, false starts, incomplete sentences, interruptions, and over-talk. These are all integral parts of authentic speech.

練習
れんしゅう

A. Listen to two conversations. For each one, write in English whether the customer is willing to buy the items. Then try to identify which characteristics of speech indicate the customer's intent.

1. _____

2. _____

B. 何を　かいましたか。

You will hear three conversations. Listen to each one and list in Japanese the items the customer bought and the quantity of each item. Then write the total amount the customer paid.

	何	ねだん (price per item)	いくつ	ぜんぶで いくら
1				
2				
3				

聞き上手 話し上手
き　　じょうず　はな　　じょうず
Communication

上手な話し方   Communication Strategy
じょうず　はな　かた

Asking for paraphrase and repetition

So far, you have learned some strategies for providing feedback to indicate that you are listening to the speaker and understanding what is being said. For example, you nod your head and say はい or ええ. There will be times when you find yourself in situations where you don't understand what the speaker is saying and can't respond, because you don't know the words used or you didn't hear what was said. In these cases it is important to know how to ask for repetition or paraphrasing, and how to ask someone to speak more loudly or more slowly. Chapter 1 introduced these phrases using おねがいします, but you can also use 〜てくれませんか (Chapter 6) to articulate your request even more clearly. The following is a list of some useful expressions to employ in these situations.

Asking for repetition:

もう一度 いってくれませんか。
　　　いちど
Please say it again.

Asking for paraphrasing:

やさしいことばで いってくれませんか。
Please say it in easier words.

Asking someone to speak slowly:

ゆっくり いってくれませんか。
ゆっくり はなしてくれませんか。
Please say it / speak slowly.

Asking someone to speak more loudly:

大きいこえで いってくれませんか。
大きいこえで はなしてくれませんか。
Please say it / speak more loudly.

Also remember that it is a good strategy to add conversation fillers and phrases like あのう and すみませんが before making a request. These phrases not only soften a request—an essential part of communicating in Japanese—but give you time to think of your next phrases.

練習
れんしゅう

Work with a partner. Imagine that you are a store clerk. Find polite expressions used by sales staff in this chapter. Say those expressions to your partner and have your partner respond with the expressions above.

漢字
かん じ
Kanji

Using kanji for numbers

Although you can write any number in **kanji**, you don't normally see numbers written in a long string of kanji, such as 六万三千五百二十二円 (¥63,522). In general, relatively simple numerical expressions are written in **kanji**, while long expressions are written in Arabic numerals.

The following are some common examples:

Prices with simple numbers such as 100, 100, 2000, etc.:　百円　千円　二千円
ひゃくえん　せんえん　に せんえん

Counter expressions with single- or double-digit numbers:　三本　四　八階
さんぼん　よん　はっかい

Dates:　六月二十五日　　十二月三十日
ろくがつ に じゅう ご にち　じゅう に がつさんじゅうにち

Times:　一時　三時二十分
いち じ　さん じ　に じゅっぷん

Pronunciation changes for kanji with numbers

Pronunciations of **kanji** sometimes change slightly. For example, 一（いち）is pronounced いっ when it is used in the word 一本. 本（ほん）in this example is
いっぽん
pronounced ぽん.

えんぴつを　一本　下さい。
いっぽん

えんぴつを　二本　下さい。
に ほん

When you read a sentence, you don't see any markings indicating such changes, because the reader makes the adjustment automatically. By the same token, you don't add any markings when you write them. (Note that the **furigana** accompanying new **kanji** is intended as a learning aid here.)

一	一	one ひと(つ)　イチ	一つ　一本　いぬが一匹います。 ひと　いっぽん　　いっぴき
二	二	two ふた(つ)　ニ	りんごが二つあります。　二さつ　二本 ふた　　　　　に　　にほん
三	三	three みっ(つ)　サン	けしゴムを三つかいました。　三本 みっ　　　　　　さんぼん

| 四 | 四 | four | | 一 | 冂 | 冂 | 四 | 四 | | | | |
| | | よ・よん・よっ（つ）　シ | | | | 四つ　四時　ビールが四本あります。 | | | | | | |

| 五 | 五 | five | | 一 | 丁 | 五 | 五 | | | | | |
| | | いつ（つ）　ゴ | | | | 五つ　ベルトが五本あります。 | | | | | | |

| 六 | 六 | six | | ' | 亠 | 六 | 六 | | | | | |
| | | むっ（つ）　ロク・ロッ | | | | 六つ　六時　えんぴつが六本あります。 | | | | | | |

| 七 | 七 | seven | | 一 | 七 | | | | | | | |
| | | なな（つ）　シチ | | | | 七時　七本　オレンジが七つあります。 | | | | | | |

| 八 | 八 | eight | | ノ | 八 | | | | | | | |
| | | やっ（つ）　ハチ・ハツ | | | | 八つ　八時　ペンが八本あります。 | | | | | | |

| 九 | 九 | nine | | ノ | 九 | | | | | | | |
| | | ここの（つ）　キュウ・ク | | | | 九つ　九時　バナナが九本あります。 | | | | | | |

| 十 | 十 | ten | | 一 | 十 | | | | | | | |
| | | とお　ジュウ・ジュッ | | | | 靴下が十あります。　十本　十時 | | | | | | |

| 百 | 百 | hundred | | 一 | 丆 | 丆 | 百 | 百 | 百 | | | |
| | | ヒャク・ビャク・ピャク | | | | 二百　三百　六百 | | | | | | |

| 千 | 千 | thousand | | ノ | 一 | 千 | | | | | | |
| | | セン・ゼン | | | | 二千　三千　八千　千円 | | | | | | |

| 万 | 万 | ten thousand | | 一 | 丆 | 万 | | | | | | |
| | | マン | | | | 一万円　百万円 | | | | | | |

| 円 | 円 | yen (Japanese currency) | | 丨 | 冂 | 冂 | 円 | | | | | |
| | | エン | | | | 五十円　このセーターは、七千八百円です。 | | | | | | |

| 店 | 店 | store, shop | | ' | 亠 | 广 | 广 | 庐 | 店 | 店 | 店 | |
| | | みせ　テン | | | | 大きい店　店の人 | | | | | | |

読めるようになった漢字 (Kanji and compounds you can now read)

一時　一本　一つ　一緒に　もう一度　二時　二本　二つ　三時

三本　三つ　四時　四本　四つ　五時　五本　五つ　六時　六本

六つ　七時　七本　七つ　八時　八本　八つ　九時　九本　九つ

十時　十本　十　百円　千円　一万円　店の人　喫茶店　腕時計

靴下　誕生日　地下　婦人服

日本人のなまえ：川口　友田　古田　水本

練習

Read the following sentences with numerical kanji.

1. 田中さんは十一時三十分に学生会館にきます。
2. としょかんには日本の本が四千五百さつぐらいあります。
3. 山川さんのつくえの上に二万八千円あります。
4. 私は六時にごはんをたべます。そして、七時に大学にいきます。
5. そこに小さい店があります。

読む練習
よ　　れんしゅう
Reading Practice

上手な読み方　Reading Strategy
じょうず　よ　かた

Scanning

It is not always necessary to read an entire text when you are looking for specific information. For example, when you want to find out which floor of a department store sells food, you do not read the entire floor directory. You would look for a specific character such as the kanji 食 (*eat*). By employing this strategy, you will be able to find the information you need more quickly.

The same is true when you read a text looking for particular information. You can skip through the passage to find the specific information you need. This method of reading is called scanning.

練習
れんしゅう

Read the following advertisements and find out what is being sold in each ad.

1.

ふとんばさみ （4個組）
天気がいい日は、ふとんをほす日。
きれいなふとんで、ぐっすり快眠。

ふところが深く、
しっかりはさめます。
バネを中心部に内蔵しているので、
ふとんを汚さずにはさめます。

4個組 **680**円

●サイズ／約27X15.5X厚 3cm●材質／本体：ポリプロピレン、バネ：鋼
●重量／約140g(1 個)●耐熱温度／約 100℃●中国製

2.
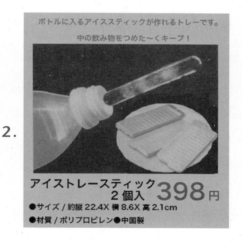

ボトルに入るアイススティックが作れるトレーです。
中の飲み物をつめた〜くキープ！

アイストレースティック
2 個入 **398**円

●サイズ／約縦 22.4X 横 8.6X 高 2.1cm
●材質／ポリプロピレン●中国製

3.

つくって、たのしんで、たべる。
そば打ち5点セット
おいしい「おそば」がつくれます。
うどんもつくれます。

ねる　のばす

6,500円

●セット内容／のし板、こね鉢、めん棒、こま板、麺きり包丁
●包丁・こね板／日本製、のし板・めん棒・こま板／中国製

4.

リントクリーナー
セーターの毛玉をきれいにカットしてリメイク。
ふるいセーターも、
あたらしいセーターみたい！
ソックス、ジャージ、ニット、
カーペットの毛玉もとれます。
おそうじブラシ付

1,480円

●サイズ／約 8X14X12cm●材質／ポリスチレン、
ABC 樹脂、ステンレス鋼●電池／単 2 電池 X2(別売)
●台湾製

きんじょのスーパー   Neighborhood supermarket

言葉の　リスト
ことば

タオル	towel
スリッパ	slippers
洗剤 せんざい	soap

私の家の近くに大きいスーパーがあります。そのスーパーの地下
うち　ちか　　　　　　　　　　　　　　　　　　　　　　　　　ち
一階には食品売り場があります。高いものはありませんが、私
かい　　しょくひんう　　ば
はそこでよく野菜や魚を買います。二階は日用品売り場です。
や さい　さかな　か　　　　　　かい　　にちようひんう　ば
タオルやスリッパやシャンプーや洗剤があります。　三階には本や
せんざい　　　　　　　かい
文房具があります。昨日、私はこのスーパーでノートを三冊と
ぶんぼうぐ　　　　　　きのう　　　　　　　　　　　　　　　　さつ
ボールペンを五本買いました。
か

読んだ後で   Comprehension
あと

A. しつもんに　日本語で　こたえて下さい。Answer these questions in Japanese.

1. この人は　このスーパーで　何を　よく　かいますか。
2. このスーパーの　三階に　何が　ありますか。
かい
3. 三階に　何が　ありますか。
かい
4. 魚は　何階に　ありますか。
さかな　　かい
5. 日用品って　何ですか。
にちようひん
6. 昨日　この人は　何を　かいましたか。それは　どこに　ありましたか。
きのう

B. Write a short passage about a department store you know. Use the following
questions as a guide for what information to include.

1. デパートは　どこに　ありますか。
2. デパートは　大きいですか。小さいですか。
3. いいデパートですか。
4. デパートに　どんなうりばが　ありますか。
6. いりぐち (entrance) のちかくに　何が　ありますか。
7. そのデパートで　何を　よく　かいますか。どうしてですか。

総合練習
そうごうれんしゅう
Integration

A. デパートのうりば   **Department Store Sections**

The following is the floor directory of a full-scale department store in Tokyo. Work with a partner to describe the types of items available on different floors. Try to guess the meanings of the words written in **katakana**. Next, your instructor will give you a list of specific items to purchase. Figure out where each item would be located.

東館(ひがしかん)		西館(にしかん)	
R/8 学生服(がくせいふく)/商品券(しょうひんけん) サービス/介護用品(かいごようひん)		屋上遊園(おくじょうゆうえん) 金魚(きんぎょ)・熱帯魚(ねったいぎょ) **R**	
7 呉服(ごふく)/宝飾品(ほうしょくひん) 時計(とけい)・メガネ・文具(ぶんぐ) レストラン		レストラン/催事場(さいじじょう) **7**	
6 催事場(さいじじょう)/婦人服(ふじんふく) [Lサイズ]		こども服(ふく)・ベビー用品 (ようひん)/おもちゃ **6**	
5 婦人服(ふじんふく) [プレタポルテ&エレガンス]		リビング用品(ようひん)/タオル/ 寝具(しんぐ)/家具(かぐ) インテリア/美術画廊(びじゅつがろう) **5**	
4 婦人服(ふじんふく) [デザイナーズブティック&カジュアル] 婦人肌着(ふじんはだぎ)		リビング/和洋食器(わようしょっき)/ 調理(ちょうり)・日用品(ようひん)/ ギフトサロン **4**	
3 婦人服(ふじんふく) [インポートブティック]		紳士服(しんしふく)/紳士用品(しんし ようひん)/紳士靴(しんしぐつ) **3**	
2 婦人服(ふじんふく) [キャリアブティック]		紳士服(しんしふく)/紳士用品(しんし ようひん)/ゴルフウェア/カバン **2**	
1 ハンドバッグ/婦人靴(ふじんぐつ) 婦人小物(ふじんこもの)/アクセサリー/ 化粧品(けしょうひん)		ファッション雑貨(ざっか) **1**	
B1 食品(しょくひん) [和洋菓子(わようがし)/のり/茶(ちゃ)/ 和洋酒(わようしゅ)・缶詰(かんづめ)] 地下鉄連絡口(ちかてつれんらくぐち)		食品(しょくひん)[鮮魚(せんぎょ) 精肉(せいにく)・野菜(やさい) 和洋中華惣菜(わようちゅうかそうざい)] **B1**	
		レストラン/喫茶(きっさ) 書籍(しょせき) **B2**	

ロールプレイ

1. Work in a group of six. You and one other person are customers in a department store with 50,000 yen each to spend. The other classmates of the group are salesclerks in different departments, and your instructor will give them a price list of items for their department. Go to as many departments as you can, and make one or more purchases. Before leaving each department, note what you have bought and how much you paid. You must buy at least four different items. Try to spend all your money. Whoever is left with the smallest amount of change wins.

Examples:

店の人：　いらっしゃいませ。

おきゃくさん (*Customer*)：　あのう、あかいハンドバッグが　ほしいんですが。

Or　そのあかいハンドバッグを　みせて下さい。

店の人：　はい、どうぞ。

おきゃくさん：　ちょっと小さいですね。もっと大きいのは　ありますか。

店の人：　じゃあ、こちらはいかがですか。

おきゃくさん：　ああ、いいですね。いくらですか。

店の人：　四万円です。

おきゃくさん：　ああ、ちょっと高いですね。

店の人：　いらっしゃいませ。

おきゃくさん：　しろいシャツが　ほしいんですが。

店の人：　こちらは　いかがですか。

おきゃくさん：　いいですね。

Or　ちょっと高いですね。もうすこし　安いのは　ありますか。

2. You have run out of fruits and vegetables. Go to a market and buy the following items.

Item	Amount
レタス	1
トマト	3
にんじん	5
たまご	12
バナナ	6

Chapter 9

第九課
(だい)(く)(か)

レストランとしょうたい
Restaurants and Invitations

Objectives	Extending invitations, ordering at a restaurant
Vocabulary	Dishes, types of cuisine, food expressions
Dialogue	レストランで *At a restaurant*
Japanese Culture	Eating habits in Japan, Japanese restaurants
Grammar	I. Indicating choices using 〜にします; making requests using 〜をおねがいします
	II. Eliciting and making proposals using 〜ましょうか and 〜ましょう
	III. Using question word + か + (particle) + affirmative and question word + (particle) + も + negative
	IV. Giving reasons using から; expressing opposition or hesitation using けど
	V. Making inferences based on direct observation using verb and adjective stems + そうだ
Listening	Using context
Communication	Introducing a new topic
Kanji	Creating inflectional endings with **okurigana**
	行 来 帰 食 飲 見 聞 読 書 話 出 会 買 起 寝 作 入
Reading	Understanding Japanese e-mail formats

単語
たん

Nouns

アイスクリーム		ice cream
あぶら	油 (oil) ／脂 (fat)	oil あぶらが　おおい　fatty, oily
イタリア		Italy
		イタリアりょうり　Italian cuisine
うどん		Japanese wheat noodles
ランチ		lunch, lunch set　A ランチ　Lunch A
カレーライス		Japanese curry and rice dish
		(abbreviation: カレー)
カロリー		calorie
クッキー		cookie
ケーキ		cake
(お)さしみ	御刺身	sashimi (fillet of fresh raw fish,
		usually preceded by お)
サラダ		salad
サンドイッチ		sandwich
スープ		soup
(お)すし	御寿司／鮨	sushi (usually preceded by お)
ステーキ		steak
スパゲティ		spaghetti
セット		a Western-style fixed menu,
		ハンバーガーセット　hamburger set
そば	蕎麦	Japanese buckwheat noodles
チーズ		cheese
チキン		chicken
チャーハン		Chinese-style fried rice
ちゅうかりょうり	中華料理	Chinese cuisine
ちゅうもん	注文	order ちゅうもんする　to order

チョコレート		chocolate
ていしょく	定食	a Japanese or Asian-style dish set, さしみていしょく　sashimi set
デザート		dessert
てんぷら	天ぷら / 天麩羅	tempura (fish, shrimp, and vegetables battered and deep-fried)
トースト		toast
ハンバーガー		hamburger
パン		bread
ビーフ		beef
ピザ		pizza
フライドチキン		fried chicken
ポーク		pork
ようしょく	洋食	Western-style cuisine
ライス		rice
		ライス　is served on a plate, not in a bowl. ごはん　is a generic term for cooked rice.
ラーメン		ramen (Chinese-style noodles in broth)
ランチ		lunch
		A ランチ　lunch set A
わしょく	和食	Japanese cuisine (also 日本りょうり)

う -verbs

いる	要る	to need something ソースがいる　(It needs sauce.)

い -adjectives

あたたかい	温かい	warm
あつい	熱い	hot
あまい	甘い	sweet
おおい	多い	a lot, much
かたい	固い	hard, tough

からい	辛い	spicy
しょっぱい		salty
すくない	少ない	little (in number), few
すっぱい	酸っぱい	sour
つめたい	冷たい	cold
にがい	苦い	bitter
ひくい	低い	low, カロリーがひくい low in calories
やわらかい	柔らかい	soft

Prefixes

| ご～ | 御～ | polite prefix　ごちゅうもん |

Expressions

| ～に　します | | to decide on ～ |
| ～を　おねがいします | ～をお願いします | I would like to have ～ |

単語の練習
たん　　　れんしゅう

A. りょうり Types of food

（お）すし
sushi

（お）さしみ
sashimi

てんぷら
tempura

うどん
udon noodles

そば
buckwheat noodles

ラーメン
Chinese noodles

チャーハン
Chinese fried rice

カレーライス
Japanese curry and rice

スパゲティ
spaghetti

ステーキ
steak

サラダ
salad

フライドチキン
fried chicken

ハンバーガー
hamburger

サンドイッチ
sandwich

スープ
soup

チーズ
cheese

Aランチ
Lunch A (Western-style)

さしみ定食
ていしょく
sashimi set (Japanese or Asian style)

デザート
dessert

アイスクリーム
ice cream

クッキー
cookies

ケーキ
cake

おぼえていますか   **Do you remember these words?**

さかな、にく、たまご、やさい、くだもの、レタス、トマト、にんじん、バナナ、オレンジ、りんご、おちゃ、ジュース、ミルク、（お）さけ、コーヒー、こうちゃ、ワイン、ビール、水、コーラ

Activity 1

しつもんに日本語でこたえて下さい。

1. レストランでよく何をちゅうもんしますか。
2. あさは、よく何を食べますか。よく何を飲みますか。
3. おひるごはんには、よく何を食べますか。よく何を飲みますか。
4. ばんごはんはどうですか。
5. どんなりょうりを　よく作りますか。
6. 今何が食べたいですか。
7. あなたのくにには (*in your country*) どんなランチセットや定食がありますか。

B. りょうりのタイプ   Types of cuisine

Country names are often, but not always, used to identify types of dishes, as shown in the table below. スペインりょうり、メキシコりょうり、かんこくりょうり、インド (Indian) りょうり are commonly used terms in Japanese, but Japanese has no specific terms for "American" or "Canadian" cuisine.

Activity 2

In the table below, write the names of some dishes that belong to each category and say them aloud.

タイプ	りょうり
和食／日本りょうり *Japanese cuisine*	
中華りょうり *Chinese cuisine*	
イタリアりょうり *Italian cuisine*	
フランスりょうり *French cuisine*	
そのほかの (*other*) 洋食	

Activity 3

しつもんに日本語でこたえて下さい。

Example: A: おさしみは何りょうりですか。

B: 和食です。
わしょく

1. どのくに (country) のりょうりが好きですか。
2. 何りょうりのレストランによく行きますか。
3. どのくに (country) のりょうりは好きじゃないですか。
い
4. ちかくにどんなレストランがありますか。

C. 食べ物をせつめいすることば   Food expressions
た　　もの

あまい	sweet	あつい	hot (temperature)
からい	spicy	つめたい	cold
しょっぱい	salty	あたたかい	(comfortably) warm
すっぱい	sour	かたい	hard, tough
にがい	bitter	やわらかい	soft
あぶらがおおい	oily, fatty	あぶらがすくない	not oily
カロリーが高い	high-calorie	カロリーがひくい	low-calorie

おぼえていますか。　　おいしい

Activity 4

Work in groups of four. Discuss the dishes of the countries listed in the table, then fill in the right-hand column with the adjectives or expressions that you feel best describe the cuisine of each one.

〜のりょうり	どんなりょうりですか。
日本	
中国 ごく	
かんこく	
イギリス	
フランス	
メキシコ	
アメリカ	
イタリア	

Activity 5

Ask a partner about his/her food preferences.

Example:　あまい／からい

A:　あまいものとからいものと、どちらの方が好きですか。

B:　あまいものの方が好きです。

1. あまいもの／からいもの
2. あぶらが　おおいもの／あぶらが　すくないもの
3. つめたいスープ／あたたかいスープ
4. あついコーヒー／つめたいコーヒー
5. かたいりんご／やわらかいりんご
6. からいカレー／あまいカレー
7. すっぱいもの／からいもの
8. すこししょっぱいチップス (chips)/ すこしにがいチョコレート
9. カロリーが高いもの／カロリーがひくいもの

ダイアローグ

はじめに　**Warm-up**

A. しつもんに日本語でこたえて下さい。

1. 週末に友達と何をよくしますか。
2. 和食のレストランにはどんなものがありますか。
3. 中華りょうりのレストランにはどんなものがありますか。
4. どんな洋食が好きですか。

B. Make a phone call inviting a partner out to eat somewhere. Remember to use 〜ませんか　and the expressions you've learned to identify yourself when calling and responding to a caller.

レストランで　*At a restaurant*

今日は土曜日です。石田さんと上田さんと山本さんはしぶやにあそびに来ました。

　　　石田：　あのう、上田さん、山本さん。
上田と山本：　はい。
　　　石田：　そろそろ十二時ですから、何か食べませんか。
　　　山本：　いいですね。じゃあ、あそこはどうですか。
　　　上田：　イタリアりょうりですね。いいですよ。

石田：　じゃあ、あそこへ行きましょう。

石田さんと上田さんと山本さんはレストランでメニューを見ています。

上田：　何にしましょうか。

石田：　そうですね。このピザはどうですか。

山本：　おいしそうですね。上田さん、どうですか。

上田：　ええ。私もピザは大好きです。

山本：　じゃあ、そうしましょう。ほかに何がいいですか。

上田：　フライドチキンはどうですか。

石田：　いいですね。じゃあ、飲み物は？

山本：　のどが かわきましたから、ビールにしませんか。

石田：　いいですね。じゃあ、ぼくもそうします。上田さんはどう

　　　　しますか。

上田：　私は水でいいです。

ウェイターが来ました。

　ウェイター：　いらっしゃいませ。ごちゅうもんは。

　　　　石田：　このピザとフライドチキンとビールをおねがいします。

　ウェイター：　ピザを一まいとフライドチキンをお一つですね。

　　　　　　　ビールは何本にしましょうか。

　　　　石田：　一本おねがいします。

　ウェイター：　一本ですね。かしこまりました。

　　　　上田：　あ、それから、私はお水を下さい。

　ウェイター：　はい、かしこまりました。

DIALOGUE PHRASE NOTES

- そろそろ十二時です means *it's about 12 o'clock.*
- ほかに means *in addition.*
- のどがかわきました means *I am thirsty.*
- ごちゅうもんは? means *What would you like to order?"*
- かしこまりました   (*Yes, I shall do as you say*) was introduced in the Japanese Culture section for Chapter 8. This phrase is used in restaurants as well as in shops.

ダイアローグの後_{あと}で

A. Circle はい if the statement is true, or いいえ if it is false.

1. はい　いいえ　上田さんは何か食_たべたがっています。

2. はい　いいえ　石田_{いし}さんは山本さんとレストランに行_いきました。

3. はい　いいえ　石田_{いし}さんと山本さんはレストランでビールを飲みました。

4. はい　いいえ　山本さんはピザとフライドチキンをちゅうもんしました。_の

5. はい　いいえ　上田さんは何も飲_のみませんでした。

B. Complete the following passage by filling in the appropriate particle for each blank.

石田_{いし}さん＿＿＿上田さん＿＿＿山本さんは、土曜日＿＿＿しぶや＿＿＿

あそび＿＿＿行_いきました。おなかがすきましたから、イタリアりょうりの

レストラン＿＿＿行_いって、ピザ＿＿＿フライドチキン＿＿＿食_たべました。

石田_{いし}さん＿＿＿山本さん＿＿＿ビール＿＿＿飲_のみました。

日本の文化
ぶん か

日本の食生活 Eating habits in Japan
しょくせいかつ

For many Japanese, not a day goes by without eating some rice. A traditional Japanese breakfast consists of a bowl of rice, miso soup, a raw egg with some soy sauce, seaweed, pickles, and a small piece of fish. Western-style breakfasts consisting of buttered toast, an egg, green salad, and coffee or tea are also very popular. Many restaurants and cafes offer special breakfast sets for

commuters. These are called モーニングサービス or モーニングセット, and the breakfast may be either Japanese- or Western-style.

At lunchtime, some people bring a box lunch (おべんとう), go to the company or university cafeteria, or eat at restaurants and cafes that offer a choice of special lunch sets of the day (日替りランチ). Popular lunches
ひ がわ
include noodles, Italian pasta, curried rice, fried rice, or bowls of rice topped with stewed beef, pork cutlet, and eggs, or tempura. Local eateries, convenience stores, supermarkets, and department stores also sell a variety of おべんとう. Most primary schools provide lunch for the children, while students at secondary schools usually bring their own.

For most Japanese, dinner is the largest meal of the day, and is eaten around 6 or 7 p.m. A wide range of dishes (tempura, sashimi, grilled fish, sukiyaki

[stewed pork]) as well as other foreign dishes are cooked at home. Many local food shops offer a variety of prepared dishes for working mothers and businesspeople. Small local restaurants usually offer free delivery, so sushi, noodles, and Chinese dishes, can be ordered by phone as well.

The most popular international dishes are Chinese, Italian, and French. Some Korean and Indian dishes, such as grilled beef and curry, are also popular. American franchise stores like McDonald's have Western fast food. Hamburgers, pizza, and fried chicken are popular, particularly among young people. Mexican cuisine is still not well known in Japan.

Before a meal, the Japanese say いただきます (literally, *I humbly receive this*). After the meal, they say ごちそうさまでした (literally, *It was a feast*). Both are expressions of gratitude to those who made the meal possible (farmers, fishermen, cooks), as well as for natural phenomena, like rain.

日本のレストラン

Restaurants in Japan range from the very inexpensive to outrageously expensive places. Many restaurants display realistic-looking models of food in the front window to give an idea of the dishes they serve and their prices. Moderately priced restaurants tend to have free seating, that is, you don't have to wait to be seated. As soon as you are seated, a waiter or waitress often brings a steaming hot towel called おしぼり to wipe your hands and face. Since the service charge is included in the bill, it is customary not to tip.

Dining out or going for drinks is very common among Japanese business people and students. Instead of hosting parties at home, Japanese people prefer to hold parties in restaurants, pubs, and hotels. The organizer often sets the menu and collects cash from the guests ahead of time. At the beginning of a party, it is customary to have a toast, or かんぱい. Pouring a drink into your own glass or drinking directly from a bottle is not polite. Instead, you should fill other people's glasses and let them fill yours.

If you are treated to a restaurant meal, thank the person after the meal (ごちそうさまでした), and again the next time you meet. You might say 昨日／先日はどうもごちそうさまでした . (Thank you for the feast yesterday/the other day.) And remember that the reciprocation of invitations and other favors plays a vital role in relationships among the Japanese.

文法
ぶんぽう

I. Indicating choices using 〜にします ; making requests using 〜をおねがいします

When ordering something in a restaurant, you may say 〜にします or 〜をおねがいします as well as 〜を下さい, as you learned in Chapter 8. します in the 〜にします construction does not mean *do* but something like *decide on* 〜. It may also be used in other contexts, as in トヨタにします (*decide on a Toyota when you buy a car*).

ウェイター：お飲みものは、何に しますか。
の
What would you like to drink? (literally, *As for drinks, what will you decide on?*)

きゃく (*customer*)：オレンジジュースに します。
I will have orange juice. (literally, *I decide on juice.*)

オレンジジュースを おねがいします。
I will have orange juice. (literally, *I request orange juice.*)

オレンジジュースを 下さい。
Please give me orange juice.

With 〜をおねがいします and 〜を下さい (but not with 〜にします), you can use a number of quantity expressions depending on what it is you are asking. Use 〜つ (Japanese origin number) to order dishes and drinks and 〜本 for bottles. The quantity expression directly follows the particle を. When two or more items are listed, the sentence takes the form of "X を Quantity Expression と Y を Quantity Expression . . ." おねがいします.

コーヒーを一つ下さい。
Please bring one coffee.

ビールを二本おねがいします。
Please bring two bottles of beer.

こうちゃを一つとコーヒーを一つおねがいします。
Please bring one tea and one coffee.

鈴木：何、飲みますか。
すず　　　　の
What would you like to drink?

リン：そうですね。鈴木さんは？
すず
Let's see. How about you, Mr. Suzuki?

鈴木：ぼくはコーラにします。
すず
I will have some cola.

リン：　そうですか。じゃあ、私もコーラにします。
Well then, I will have cola, too.

鈴木：　(to the waiter) すみません。コーラを二つおねがいします。
すず
Excuse me. We will have two colas.

話してみましょう
はな

Activity 1

Place an order using 〜を　おねがいします. Use すみません to get the server's attention.

Example:　そば／1

　　　　　　すみません。そばを一つおねがいします。

1. コーラ／1　　　　5. ラーメン／5
2. サンドイッチ／2　　6. A ランチ／1
3. こうちゃ／1　　　　7. おさしみ／4
4. ハンバーガー／3　　8. うどん／2

Activity 2

Work with a partner. You are going to a restaurant with your partner. Think about a dish that you would like to order. Discuss with your partner and decide on the restaurant.

Example:　A: 今、何が食べたいですか.
た

　　　　　B: そうですね。スパゲティが食べたいですね。
た

　　　　　A: そうですか。じゃあ、イタリアりょうりのレストランにしませんか。

　　　　　B: あ、いいですね。

Activity 3

Work with a new partner. You are a customer and your partner is the waiter or waitress. Circle one item that you would like to have from each category in the table below. The waiter/waitress will ask for your order by saying ごちゅうもんは？ (Your order?). Place your order.

Example:　　　ウェイター：　ごちゅうもんは？

おきゃくさん (*customer*)：　こうちゃとサンドイッチとケーキを
　　　　　　　　　　　　　　　　おねがいします。

　　　　　　　ウェイター：　こうちゃとサンドイッチとケーキですね。
　　　　　　　　　　　　　　かしこまりました。

飲み物 （の　もの）	ミルク　オレンジジュース　おちゃ　水　ワイン　ビール コーヒー　こうちゃ
食べ物 （た　もの）	スープ　サンドイッチ　ハンバーガー　サラダ　スパゲティ ピザ　（お）すし　（お）さしみ　てんぷら　チャーハン カレーライス　ステーキ
デザート	ケーキ　アイスクリーム　クッキー

Activity 4

Work in groups of three. One person is the waiter/waitress at a restaurant. The other two are customers. Look at the menu to decide what you are going to order. The waiter/waitress will ask ごちゅうもんは？, then write down your orders and confirm them by saying X と Y ですね。かしこまりました. Change roles and repeat the role play until everyone has had a turn taking orders.

Example:　　ウェイター：　ごちゅうもんは？

　　　　　　　A：　飲み物はどうしますか。
　　　　　　　　　　（の　　もの）
　　　　　　　B：　ぼくはビールにします。

　　　　　　　A：　私はオレンジジュースにします。じゃあ、
　　　　　　　　　　ビールを一本とオレンジジュースを一つ
　　　　　　　　　　おねがいします。

　　　　　　ウェイター：　ビールを一本とジュース一つですね。
　　　　　　　　　　　　　かしこまりました。

メニュー

オードブル

オードブル取り合わせ	¥800
スモークサーモン	¥1,000
シュリンプ・カクテル	¥900

スパゲティ

スパゲティ・ナポリタン	¥900
スパゲティ・ミートソース	¥1,000

スープ

コンソメスープ	¥400
オニオングラタンスープ	¥600

サラダ

グリーンサラダ	¥500
ミックスサラダ	¥500
チキンサラダ	¥700

魚料理

エビフライ	¥1,200
エビグラタン	¥1,200
カニコロッケ	¥1,000

米飯料理

カレーライス	¥800
オムライス	¥900
エビピラフ	¥800

肉料理

サーロインステーキ	¥3,500
ビーフシチュー	¥3,000
ハンバーグステーキ	¥1,000
ポークソテー	¥1,200
チキンコロッケ	¥1,000

サンドイッチ

ハムサンド	¥600
タマゴサンド	¥500
やさいサンド	¥500
ミックスサンド	¥600

飲み物

ビール	¥400
オレンジジュース	¥500

II. Eliciting and making proposals using ～ましょうか and ～ましょう

In Chapter 6, the negative question form of a verb ～ませんか is used for extending an invitation or making a suggestion. ～ましょうか (*shall we*) and ～ましょう (*let's ～*) are used to elicit or make proposals.

Eliciting proposal	Making proposals
どこへ行きましょうか。 *Where shall we go?*	きょうとへ行きませんか。 *Why don't we go to Kyoto?* きょうとへ行きましょう。 *Let's go to Kyoto.*
何を食べましょうか。 *What shall we eat?*	和食にしませんか。 *Why don't we have Japanese food?* 和食にしましょう。 *Let's have Japanese food.*
どこで会いましょうか。 *Where shall we meet?*	えきで会いませんか。 *Why don't we meet at the station?* えきで会いましょう。 *Let's meet at the station.*

リー：　上田さん、今週の金曜日にコンサートに行きませんか。
　　　　Ms. Ueda, why don't we go to a concert together this Friday?

上田：　ええ、ぜひ。何時にどこで会いましょうか。
　　　　Yes I would love to. Well, what time and where shall we meet?

リー：　そうですね。三時十五分ごろに学生会館のまえはどうですか。
　　　　Let's see, how about around three fifteen in front of the student union?

上田：　いいですね。じゃあ、三時十五分に学生会館のまえで。
　　　　That would be fine. Okay then, in front of the union at three fifteen.

話してみましょう
（はな）

Activity 1

Work with a partner. Extend an invitation by rephrasing the following sentences with the 〜ませんか form. Your partner will accept your invitation saying えぇ、〜ましょう. Then switch roles.

Example:　A: 〜さん、明日こうえんに行って、テニスをしませんか。
（あした）（い）
　　　　　　B: ええ、しましょう。

1. 木曜日に一緒にえいがを見る
2. アイスクリームを食べに行く
（た）（み）
3. 明日一緒にべんきょうする
（あした）（しょ）
4. うちに来て、コーヒーを飲む
（あした）（しょ）（の）
5. あのカフェに入る
（はい）
6. 今日ばんごはんを一緒に食べる
（しょ）（た）
7. 一緒に帰る
（しょ）（かえ）

Activity 2

Invite a new partner to do the following activities. Then decide on the time and place together.

Example:　A: 一緒に買い物に行きませんか。
（しょ）（か）（もの）（い）
　　　　　　B: ええ、いいですね。いつ行きましょうか。
（い）
　　　　　　A: 明日はどうですか。
（あした）
　　　　　　B: いいですよ。どこに行きましょうか。
（い）
　　　　　　A: 〜に行きませんか。
（い）
　　　　　　B: ええ、いいですよ。　じゃあ、〜に行きましょう。
（い）

	いつ	どこ
一緒に買い物に行く （しょ）（か）（もの）（い）		
コンサートに行く （い）		
一緒にしゅくだいをする （しょ）		
一緒にばんごはんを作る （しょ）（つく）		
おちゃを飲む （の）		

Activity 3

Work in small groups. You want to go on a trip for vacation. Think about a fun place to go, then invite a few people to come along, and negotiate the details of when to meet, where to go, what to do, etc. 今度の休みに means the next vacation.

Example:　鈴木：　木村さん、スミスさん、今度の休みにハワイに
　　　　　　　　　あそびに行きませんか。

　　　　　木村：　ハワイですか。いいですね。

　　　　　スミス：　そうですね。私も、ぜひ行きたいです。

　　　　　鈴木：　じゃあ、そうしましょう。

　　　　　木村：　いつ行きましょうか。

　　　　　　　　　どんなホテルにしましょうか。

　　　　　　　　　何をしましょうか。

> ## III. Using question word + か + (particle) + affirmative and question word + (particle) + も + negative

Question words can be combined with other words to form new expressions in Japanese. This chapter introduces both indefinite and negative expressions using question words.

A. Using question word + か + (particle) ～ affirmative statement or question.

Indefinite expressions are formed by adding か to a question word.

なに ＋ か ＝ なにか　　something
どこ ＋ か ＝ どこか　　somewhere
だれ ＋ か ＝ だれか　　someone
いつ ＋ か ＝ いつか　　sometime

Question word ＋ か is used with affirmative sentences and in questions.

何か　食べ<u>ます</u>。　　*(I) eat something.*

あそこに　だれか　<u>いますか</u>。　　*Is there someone over there?*

Question word ＋ か can also be used with ～ませんか, as in the following examples. Although the verbs here are in the negative form, their meanings are not negative.

何か　食べませんか。　*Why don't we eat something?*

どこか　行きませんか。　*Why don't we go somewhere?*

The particles は, も, or に (of time) are not used with indefinite expressions. The particles が and を are usually omitted with indefinite expressions, and the particles へ／に (of direction) are optional. Other particles are added after か.

だれか	来ました。	*someone came*
何か	食べます。	*eat something*
いつか	帰ります。	*come/go back sometime*
どこか (へ／に)	行きました。	*went somewhere*
どこかで	会いました。	*met somewhere*
だれかと	話します。	*talk with someone*

山本：	何か飲みませんか。	*Why don't we drink something?*
中川：	ええ、いいですよ。	*Sure. (literally, Yes, that would be fine.)*
山本：	何にしましょうか。	*What will you have?*
中川：	私はジュースにします。	*I'll have some juice.*

山田：　どこかに今日の新聞はありませんか。
Is today's paper somewhere?

中山：　そこにありますよ
It's right there.

NOTES

- Questions that employ question word + か + (particle) are はい／
  いいえ questions, even though they appear to be information
  questions:

  友田：　何か飲みますか。
  Are you going to drink something?

  中本：　いいえ、どうぞ おかまいなく。
  No, please don't bother.

  友田：　何を飲みますか。
  What are you going to drink?

  中本：　コーヒーを飲みます。
  I will drink coffee.

- To decline an offer of food or drinks, use the following phrases.

  いいえ、どうぞおかまいなく。　*No, please don't bother.*

  いいえ、けっこうです。　　　　*No, thank you.*

- To form indefinite expressions such as *something delicious*, add
  adjective + noun after question + か

  何かおいしいものを作ります。
  I will make something good.

  だれか好きな人がいるんですか。
  Is there someone you like?

  どこかしずかなところへ行きましょう。
  Let's go somewhere quiet.

- Notice that in Japanese, unlike the equivalent English expressions,
  you must include a noun (もの、人、ところ) after the modifying
  adjective.

B. Using question word + (particle) + も～ negative statement.

Question word + (particle) + も～ followed by a negative statement means "not ～
any" or "no ～." The expression must be used with a negative statement.

何も	食べませんでした。	*I did not eat anything.*
だれも	いません。	*There isn't anyone/There is no one.*
どこも	よくありません。	*There isn't any good place.*
		(literally, *None of the places is good.*)

The particles は, も, が, and を are not used with question word + (particle) + も.
Other particles are added before も.

だれも	来ませんでした。	*No one came.*
何も	買いません。	*I am not going to buy anything.*
いつも	来ません。	*(He) never comes.*
どこ (へ／に) も	行きませんでした。	*I didn't go anywhere.*
だれとも	話しませんでした。	*I didn't talk to anyone.*

山本： 昨日、どこかへ出かけましたか。
Did you go somewhere yesterday?

中川： いいえ、どこへも行きませんでした。
No, I didn't go anywhere.

石田： 何か飲みますか。
Would you like to drink something?

ペギー： いいえ、今はいいです。何もいりません。
No, thanks. I don't need anything.

NOTES

- いつも in an affirmative sentence means always, as introduced in Chapter 3.

    いつも　来ます。   *(He) always comes.*

    いつも　来ません。   *(He) never comes.*

- どこでも (どこ ＋ で ＋ も) is an exception to this pattern. It means everywhere and is always used with a positive statement.

話してみましょう

Activity 1

しつもんに日本語でこたえて下さい。

Examples: 今日何か食べましたか。

ええ、食べました。 or いいえ、食べませんでした。

今日何を食べましたか。

サンドイッチを食べました。

1. いつか日本に行きたいですか。
2. よくどこで食事をしますか。
3. いつうちに帰りますか。
4. 今日だれかに会いますか。
5. 週末どこかへ出かけますか。
6. よくだれと話しますか。

Activity 2

Create questions that correspond to each of the following answers.

Example: ええ、コーヒーをおねがいします。

何か飲みませんか。

1. ええ、食べました。 レストランに行って、おいしいフランスりょうりを食べました。
2. 十一時に寝ました。
3. ざっしを買いましょう。
4. いいえ、うちにいました。
5. ええ。田中さんに会って、話しました。
6. 六時ごろ起きます。
7. ええ、図書館に行って、日本語の本を読みました。

Activity 3

Fill in the chart below, then extend invitations to a partner for food, drinks, places to go, and things to do.

Example: A: 何か飲みませんか。

B: いいですね。／ええ、いいですよ。

A: 何を飲みましょうか。

B: こうちゃはどうですか。／こうちゃにしませんか。

	Items / Places / Things
飲み物	
食べ物	
行くところ (place to go)	
すること (thing to do)	

Activity 4

Answer the following questions using いいえ、question word + (particle) + も ～ negative.

Example: (in a dark place) そこに　だれか　いますか。

<u>　いいえ、だれも　いません。　</u>

1. (At a party, your friend is going to a bar counter and says) ～さん、何か いりますか。
2. うちのねこをどこかで見ましたか。
3. そのことについて (about that matter)、だれかと話しましたか。
4. 昨日だれかにメールを書きましたか。
5. しゅくだいについて (about homework)、何か聞きましたか。

Activity 5

You are conducting a survey on breakfast habits. Ask your classmates if they have eaten or drunk anything today. If they have, find out what they had. Then determine how many people in all didn't have anything in the morning and what the most popular breakfast was for the class.

Example: A: スミスさん、今日のあさ、何か食べましたか。
            B: いいえ、何も食べませんでした。
            A: 何か飲みましたか。
            B: ええ、カフェに行って、コーヒーを飲みました。

なまえ	食べ物	飲み物
スミス	-------	コーヒー

IV. Giving reasons using から; expressing opposition or hesitation using けど

In Chapter 7, you learned that the conjunction ので expresses a reason and が expresses a contrast or opposition. This chapter introduces an additional set of conjunctions that are commonly used in conversational Japanese.

A. The conjunction から (*because*)

The conjunction から indicates a reason, and it is attached to the end of the clause that expresses the reason. If a sentence contains both a reason and a result, the clause containing the reason precedes the clause indicating the result. から tends to reflect the speaker's personal opinion or judgment more than ので. Reasons expressed with から may sound a little stronger and those using ので. ので, thus, may sound softer and more polite, especially in formal speech.

Clause with から (reason)	Clause (result)
日本のおちゃが好きですから、	よく買_かいます。

I like Japanese tea, so I often buy some.

〜から can be used with both polite and plain forms. The plain form that precedes から is similar to the forms preceding 〜ので and 〜んです except that だ is used instead of な for the copula verb and な-adjectives.

Verbs	よく<u>食べます</u>／<u>食べる</u>から、げんきです。	*He is healthy because he eats a lot.*
	あまり<u>寝ません</u>／<u>寝ない</u>から、ねむい (*sleepy*) です。	*He is sleepy because he doesn't sleep much.*
い - adjectives	これ、<u>あまいです</u>／<u>あまい</u>から、食べませんか。	*Why don't you eat this because it's sweet?*
	これ、<u>あたたかくありません</u>／<u>あたたかくない</u>から、いりません。	*I don't want it because it isn't warm.*
な - adjectives	ねこが<u>好きです</u>／<u>好きだ</u>から、ほしいです。(ねこが好き<u>な</u>ので、ほしいです。)	*I want it because I like cats.*
	いぬは<u>好きじゃありません</u>／<u>好きじゃない</u>から、いりません。	*I don't want it because I don't like dogs.*
Copula verbs	じゅぎょう<u>です</u>／じゅぎょう<u>だ</u>から、行_いきます。(じゅぎょう<u>な</u>ので、行_いきます。)	*I am going because my class is starting.*
	<u>水じゃありません</u>から／<u>水じゃない</u>から、いりません。	*I don't want it because it is not water.*

NOTES

- ～から can be used without a main clause expressing results.

    A: デザートはいりませんか。
    You don't want any dessert?

    B: ええ、カロリーが高いですから。
    That's right, because they're high in calories.

- Plain form + からです is also commonly used for reasons.

    石田さんと田中さんは、今、学校にいます。スミスさんは
    今日はやく帰りました。

    石田：　スミスさん、今日ははやく帰りましたね。
    Mr. Smith went home early today, didn't he?

    田中：　明日のあさ、日本に行くからですよ。
    It's because he is going to Japan tomorrow morning.

    石田：　ああ、そうなんですか。
    Oh, I see.

B. The conjunction けど (*but, although*)

Like が, the conjunction けど is used to connect two sentences or clauses that oppose each other, and is attached to the end of the first sentence. けど tends to sound more colloquial than が and is often used in casual conversation.

Clause with けど (reason)	Clause (result)
ちょっとにがいです／にがいけど、	日本のおちゃが好きです。

I like Japanese tea although it is slightly bitter.

～けど can be used with both polite and plain forms. The plain form that precedes けど is the same as that used with から.

Verbs	その人にはよく<u>会います</u>／<u>会う</u>けど、なまえはわかりません。	*Although I meet him often, I don't know his name.*
	あまり<u>寝ません</u>／<u>寝ない</u>けど、げんきです。	*He is energetic although he doesn't sleep much.*
い-adjectives	このステーキは<u>やわらかいです</u>／<u>やわらかい</u>けど、ちょっとあぶらがおおいですね。	*This steak is tender but it's a bit fatty.*
	あまり<u>ほしくありません</u>／<u>ほしくない</u>けど、<u>買い</u>ました。	*I bought it though I did not really want it.*
な-adjectives	図書館は<u>きれいだ</u>けど、あまりあかるくありません。	*The library is not very bright but it is pretty.*
	キムチは<u>好きじゃありません</u>／<u>好きじゃない</u>けど、かんこくは<u>好き</u>です。	*I don't like Korean pickles but I like Korea.*
Copula verbs	<u>休みです</u>／<u>休みだ</u>けど、学校へ行きます。	*I am going to school even though it's a holiday.*
	水<u>じゃありません</u>／水<u>じゃない</u>けど、飲みました。	*I drank it even though it wasn't water.*

NOTES

- 〜けど can be also used without a main clause expressing results.
  - A: よくテレビを見ますか。
    Do you watch TV often?
  - B: ええ、いそがしいですけど。
    Yes, though I am busy.
- Like が、〜けど can be used to open a conversation, or to introduce a topic of conversation as well. It does not introduce a strong negative relation, and it is similar to the use of *but* in English as in: *Excuse me, but could you turn on the TV?*

  あのう、すみませんけど、今何時ですか。
  Excuse me, but what time is it?

  明日食事に行くんですけど、田中さんも来ませんか。
  We are going to eat out tomorrow, so why don't you join us?

話してみましょう
はな

Activity 1

Combine the following pairs of sentences using 〜から. Make sure to start with a sentence containing a reason and followed by から.

Example: 明日テストがあります。今日べんきょうします。
あした
明日テストがあるから、今日べんきょうします。
あした
明日テストがありますから、今日べんきょうします。
あした

1. このワインは古いです。すっぱいです。

2. 水がいります。このスープはしょっぱいです。

3. 七時に起きます。八時にじゅぎょうがあります。

4. 水にします。今日はくるまで帰ります。
お   かえ

5. 週末はどこにも行きませんでした。まだ (yet) 友達がいません。
い   だち

6. トマトがたくさんあります。イタリアりょうりを作ります。

7. あぶらがおおいりょうりは好きじゃありません。さかなをちゅうもん
つく
します。

Activity 2

Invite your partner to do one of the activities in the chart below. Your partner will refuse using the corresponding reason and だめなんです。(I can't). Create a conversation using the table and the dialogue model in the example, then switch roles.

Example: A: 明日あそびに来ませんか。
あした
B: すみません、明日は友達がうちに来るから、だめなんです。
あした だち   き
A: そうですか。それは、ざんねんですね。
B: すみません。今度またよんで下さい。
ど

Invitation	Reason for refusal
明日あそびに来る。 あした　　　　く	友達がうちに来ます。 だち
金曜日にえいがを見に行く。 み　い	びょういんへ行きます。 い
今晩一緒にしゅくだいをする。 ばん　しょ	アルバイトがあります。
一緒にテニスをする。 しょ	今日はとてもいそがしいです。
今からひるごはんを食べる。 た	今からじゅぎょうです。
ビールを飲みに行く。 の　い	おさけはあまり好きじゃありません。

Activity 3

Draw lines between the expressions in Column A and Column B that you feel are in opposition to each other. Then create a sentence for each set using けど.

Example:　にくはきらいだけど、やさいは好きですよ。
　　　　　　にくはきらいですけど、やさいは好きですよ。

Column A	Column B
1 さかなはきらいです。	カロリーが高いから、食べません。
2 高いです。	てんぷらはあぶらがおおいです。
3 あまりからいものは食べません。	おすしはよく食べます。
4 和食はカロリーがひくいです。	カレーは大好きです。
5 コーヒーはにがいです。	よくフランスりょうりのレストランに行きます。
6 バター (butter) クッキーをよく作ります。	ブラック (black) で飲みます。

Activity 4

Work with a partner. Using the same situation in Activity 2, invite your partner for an activity. Your partner will refuse the invitation but provide an alternative using けど and the example. Make a conversation and take turns.

Example:　A:　明日あそびに来ませんか。
　　　　　　B:　すみません。
　　　　　　　　明日はいそがしいんですけど、明後日はどうでしょうか。
　　　　　　A:　じゃあ、明後日にしましょうか。
　　　　　　B:　いいですか。ありがとうございます。

Invitation	Solution
明日あそびに来る。	
金曜日にえいがを見に行く。	
今晩一緒にしゅくだいをする。	
一緒にテニスをする。	
今からひるごはんを食べる。	
ビールを飲みに行く。	

V. Making inferences based on direct observation using verb and adjective stems + そうだ

Verb/adjective stem + そうだ expresses an impression or an inference based on what the speaker has seen or felt. The degree of certainty in such statements is fairly low. In some cases, information is visual, but it can be auditory as well. Its meaning is similar to the expressions *to look (like)* or *to appear*. そうだ cannot be used with adjectives of shape, color, and other exressions that show the result direct visual observation, not inferences. That is, anyone can tell if something is pretty, red, or round by just looking at it, so you cannot say きれいそうです, あかそうです, or まるそうです (looks round).

わあ、このステーキおいしそうですね！
Wow, this steak looks delicious!

この水、つめたそうですね。
This water looks cold.

あの人、もうすぐ寝そうです。
It looks like that person might fall asleep at any time.

あかちゃんが起きそうです。
The baby appears to be waking up.

	Plain affirmative form	Affirmative そう (look like 〜)	Plain negative form	Negative そう (doesn't look like 〜)
Verbs	いる (to be)	いそう	いない	いなさそう いそうにない
な - Adjectives	しずかな (quite)	しずかそう	しずかじゃない	しずかじゃなさそう しずかそうじゃない
い - Adjectives	からい (spicy)	からそう	からくない	からくなさそう からそうじゃない
	いい (good)	よさそう	よくない	よくなさそうだ よさそうじゃない

大田：　カレーがありますけど、食べますか。
　　　　There is curry. Would you like to have some?

リー：　わあ、おいしそうですね。いいんですか。
　　　　Wow, it looks delicious. Are you sure?

大田：　もちろん、はい、どうぞ。
　　　　Of course, here you are.

リー：　いただきます！
　　　　Thank you (literally, I humbly receive)

NOTES

- To negate a phrase with そう, you can either negate そう itself or negate the verb or adjective before そう. Because そう is a な-adjective, its negative form is そうじゃない, except that そうにない should be used for verbs. To negate the verb or adjective, change the negative ending ない to なさ before そう. For example, "*It does not look fun,*" using the adjective たのしい (*fun*), could be stated as either たのしそうじゃない or たのしくなさそう. The verb 来(く)る becomes 来(き)そうにない／来(こ)なさそう (*He/She does not appear to come*).
- The affirmative form of the adjective いい becomes よさ before そう.
- Since そう is a な- adjective, it can be used to describe nouns.

あまそうなアイスクリーム	*ice cream that looks sweet*
たのしそうなアルバイト	*a part-time job that looks fun*
むずかしそうなテスト	*a test that looks difficult*

話(はな)してみましょう

⬡ **Activity 1**

Look at the following pictures and state what appears to be taking place.

Example: このアイスクリーム、おいしそうですね。
　　　　　　おいしそうなアイスクリームですね。

1

2

3

4

5

6

7

8

9

10

11

Activity 2

Work with a partner. Choose an adjective from the box below and act it out. Have your partner guess the adjective and comment on your condition using 〜そうですね. Then create a dialogue to explain why you feel the way you do.

たのしい　うれしい　かなしい　つまらない　ひま　いそがしい さびしい　たいへん

Example:　B is singing and smiling while cooking.

A:　たのしそうですね。

B:　ええ、今日は私の誕生日だから、今晩パーティが
　　あるんですよ。

A:　そうですか。それはいいですね。

Activity 3

Work with a partner. Based on the above pictures, create as many short conversations as you can using から or けど .

Example:　A:　おいしそうなアイスクリームですね。

B:　ほんとに (really) おいしいですよ。すこし食べませんか。

A:　ありがとうございます。食べたいけど、今ダイエット中
　　なんです。

B:　そうですか。

聞く練習
き　　れんしゅう

上手な聞き方
じょうず　き　かた

Using context

It is not necessary to understand every single word of a conversation to be able to comprehend what is going on. If you can get the gist or pick up key words, you will probably be able to guess the words you miss. Context provides many clues that help you to figure out the words you don't completely understand.

練習
れんしゅう

You are on the phone with Mr. Li, who is telling you about his vacation in Florida, but the connection isn't very good. Each time you hear static, indicating that the line has cut out, write the word or part of the word you miss by guessing from the context.

言葉のリスト
ことば

オーランド	Orlando
マイアミ	Miami
ディズニーワールド	Disneyworld

　1._____

　2._____

　3._____

レストランの会話　　Restaurant conversations
かいわ

Listen to each conversation and fill in the blanks to complete the sentences below.

1. このレストランは ＿＿＿＿＿ りょうりのレストランです。

　 この人は ＿＿＿＿＿＿＿ を食べます。
　　　　　　　　　　　　　　た

2. このレストランは ＿＿＿＿＿ りょうりのレストランです。

　 おとこの人は今日 ＿＿＿＿＿＿＿ を食べます。
　　　　　　　　　　　　　　　　　　た

　 おんなの人は ＿＿＿＿＿＿＿ をちゅうもんしました。

3. このレストランは ＿＿＿＿＿ りょうりのレストランです。

　 おんなの人は ＿＿＿＿＿＿＿ をちゅうもんしました。

　 さしみていしょくは ＿＿＿＿＿＿＿ 円です。

　 おとこの人は ＿＿＿＿＿＿＿ をちゅうもんしました。

聞き上手話し上手
き　　じょうずはな　　じょうず

上手な話し方
じょうず　　はな　　かた

Introducing a new topic

After greeting someone or getting their attention (あのう、(すみません))、the next step is to introduce a topic of conversation. An unfinished sentence ending with a conjunctive particle such as けど and が as well as んです is often used to introduce a topic. For example, the following phrases may be used as introductory remarks to extend an offer or invitation.

おいしいケーキがあるんですけど、食べませんか。
I have a delicious cake, so would you like to have some?

土曜日は山田さんの誕生日なんですが、何かしませんか。
Saturday is Mr. Yamada's birthday, so why don't we do something?

This function of けど and が is different from their original meaning (*but*) because what follows these words does not contrast with the preceding statement. Phrases such as 〜のことなんですけど／が and 〜についてなんですけど／が are also commonly used to introduce conversational topics. For example:

日本語のプロジェクトのことなんですけど、一緒にしませんか。
About the Japanese project, would you like to do it with me?

クラスのパーティについてなんですが、来週の金曜日はどうですか。
As for the class party, how does next Friday sound?

In some cases けど and が are used to end an utterance without finishing the sentence:

山田：　あのう、スミスさん。
　　　　Well, Mr. Smith.

スミス：　はい。
　　　　Yes?

山田：　明日のミーティングなんですけど、
　　　あした
　　　　About tomorrow's meeting.

スミス：　ええ。
　　　　Yeah?

山田：　すみませんが、キャンセルしたいんです。
　　　　I'm sorry but I want to cancel it.

スミス：　え、どうして？
　　　　Why?

山田：　明後日、大変なテストがあるんです。
　　　あさって　　たいへん
　　　　I have a difficult exam the day after tomorrow.

Following these steps and allowing your listener to respond is considered polite speech in Japanese.

練習
れんしゅう

A. Work with a partner. Think of a fun event. Then initiate a conversation with some small talk and invite your partner to the event by introducing your topic as shown in the examples above.

B. Work with a new partner, who will pretend to be your Japanese instructor. Think of some requests that you can make. Role-play a situation where you approach the instructor, introduce a topic, and make a request. Then switch roles.

漢字
かんじ

Creating inflectional endings with okurigana

Okurigana are the **hiragana** that follow verbs and adjectives written in **kanji**. For example, the きい in 大きい and the く in 行く are **okurigana**. One of the main functions of **okurigana** is to indicate inflectional endings of verbs and adjectives, as shown below.

う - verbs:	行く、 行かない、 行きます、 行って
	買う、 買わない、 買います、 買って
る - verbs:	見る、 見ない、 見ます、 見て
	寝る、 寝ない、 寝ます、 寝て
い - adjectives:	古い、 古くない、 古かったです
	安い、 安くない、 安かったです
な - adjectives:	大変な、 大変じゃない、 大変でした

Cases in which **okurigana** are used for more than just the final verb and adjective endings need to be learned individually.

食べる、 食べない、 食べます、 食べて
大きい、 大きくない、 大きかったです
新しい、 新しくない、 新しかったです

(All い -adjectives ending in しい follow this pattern.)

好きな、 好きじゃない、 好きでした

All of the **kanji** presented in this chapter are used in verbs with **okurigana**.

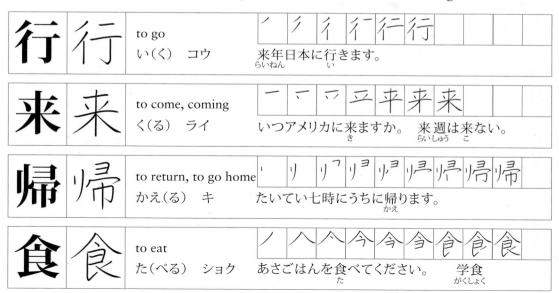

行 行	to go い(く) コウ	ノ ク イ 行 行 行 来年日本に行きます。 らいねん い
来 来	to come, coming く(る) ライ	一 一 一 一 平 来 来 いつアメリカに来ますか。 来週は来ない。 き らいしゅう こ
帰 帰	to return, to go home かえ(る) キ	' リ リ' リ' リ' リ' リ' 帰 帰 たいてい七時にうちに帰ります。 かえ
食 食	to eat た(べる) ショク	ノ 八 へ 今 今 今 食 食 食 あさごはんを食べてください。 学食 た がくしょく

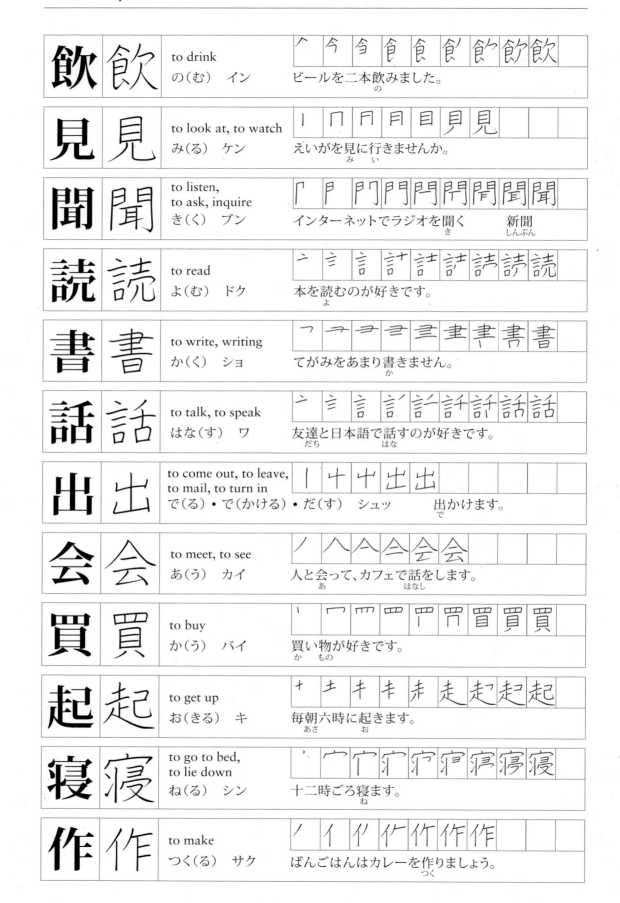

飲	飲	to drink / の（む）　イン	⺈ 今 今 食 食 飠 飲 飲 飲
見	見	to look at, to watch / み（る）　ケン	丨 冂 冂 月 目 貝 見
聞	聞	to listen, to ask, inquire / き（く）　ブン	門 門 門 門 門 門 門 聞 聞 聞
読	読	to read / よ（む）　ドク	二 主 言 言 計 訪 読 読
書	書	to write, writing / か（く）　ショ	⺆ ⺕ ヨ ⺕ 聿 聿 書 書
話	話	to talk, to speak / はな（す）　ワ	二 言 言 計 計 計 話 話 話
出	出	to come out, to leave, to mail, to turn in / で（る）・で（かける）・だ（す）　シュツ	丨 屮 屮 出 出
会	会	to meet, to see / あ（う）　カイ	ノ 人 人 今 会 会
買	買	to buy / か（う）　バイ	丶 冂 罒 罒 罒 買 買 買
起	起	to get up / お（きる）　キ	十 土 キ キ 走 走 起 起 起
寝	寝	to go to bed, to lie down / ね（る）　シン	丶 宀 宀 宀 宵 宵 寢 寢 寝
作	作	to make / つく（る）　サク	ノ 亻 亻 竹 作 作 作

飲: ビールを二本飲みました。
の

見: えいがを見に行きませんか。
み　い

聞: インターネットでラジオを聞く　　新聞
き　　　　　　しんぶん

読: 本を読むのが好きです。
よ

書: てがみをあまり書きません。
か

話: 友達と日本語で話すのが好きです。
だち　　　　　はな

出: 出かけます。
で

会: 人と会って、カフェで話をします。
あ　　　　　　はなし

買: 買い物が好きです。
か　もの

起: 毎朝六時に起きます。
あさ　　　お

寝: 十二時ごろ寝ます。
ね

作: ばんごはんはカレーを作りましょう。
つく

入	入	to enter はい（る）・い（れる）　ニュウ	ノ	入						
			はこに入れます。　店に入ります。 　　　　い　　　　　　　　はい							

読めるようになった漢字
かん　じ

行く　銀行　旅行　来る　来週　来年　帰る　食べる　食べ物　食事
　　　ぎんこう　りょこう　　　　　　　　　　　　　　　　　　もの　　しょくじ

和食　洋食　定食　食品　飲む　飲み物　見る　聞く　新聞　読む
わ しょく　ようしょく　ていしょく　しょくひん　　　　もの　　　　　　　　しんぶん

書く　図書館　教科書　辞書　話す　電話　出る　出かける　会う
　　　としょかん　きょうかしょ　じ しょ　　　　でんわ

学生会館　会話　買う　買い物　起きる　寝る　作る　入る
　かいかん　かいわ　　　　　　もの

押し入れ　中華
お　　い　ちゅうか

練習
れんしゅう

1. 昨日、日本食のレストランで、ビールをすこし飲んで、ばんごはんを
　食べました。

2. カフェでフランス人の友達と日本語で話しました。
　　　　　　　　　　　だち

3. 先週インド人の友達が来たので、カレーを作って、インドの
　　　　　　　　だち
　おんがくを聞きました。

4. 新宿に出かけて、買いものをしました。そして、友達と会って、
　しんじゅく　　　　　　　　　　　　　　　　　　　　だち
　えいがを見に行きました。

5. （私の一日）私は毎日六時半に起きて、新聞を読みます。八時に
　大学に行って、たいてい五時ごろ帰ります。よるはテレビを見て、
　メールを書いて、十時ごろおふろに入ります。たいてい十一時に
　寝ます。

読む練習
れんしゅう

上手な読み方
じょうず　かた

Understanding Japanese e-mail formats

The format of Japanese e-mail programs for the PC is very similar to their counterparts in English, except that all of the English words are written in Japanese. However, Roman letters in parentheses such as (F) and (E) remain part of the menu commands, which will give you some clue as to what a menu is about. For example, (F) often represents File option and (E) usually stands for Editing options. So you can guess the contents of some of the fields using your knowledge of English e-mail.

練習
れんしゅう

Look at the e-mail screen above and try to guess the meaning of the following words.

挿入 (そうにゅう)
書式 (しょしき)
メッセージ
ツール
送信者 (そうしんしゃ)
宛先 (あてさき)
件名 (けんめい)

E - メールが来ました

```
ファイル(F)    編集(E)    書式(O)    送受信(S)    ヘルプ(H)

    〒         ✉          ✉          ↺          📄          🖨

送信者：  大木　高子　　takako@westside.ac.jp
宛先：    Sara Jones sjones@hotmail.com
Cc：
件名：    パーティのこと
```

サラさん、

こんにちは。高子です。

来週の木曜日に山本さんの誕生日パーティがあるんですが、よかったら
来ませんか。６時から、ぎんざのマルスというフランス料理の
レストランでします。会費は一人５０００円です。

カードを買いましたから、あとで何か書いてくれませんか。

じゃあ、おへんじまっています。

読んだ後で Comprehension

A. しつもんに日本語でこたえて下さい。

1. このメールはだれが書きましたか。
2. このメールはだれに書きましたか。
3. どうしてメールを書きましたか。
4. だれのパーティがありますか。
5. パーティはいつどこでありますか。
6. 一人 (per person) いくらかかりますか。

B. Imagine that you are the recipient of this e-mail and write a response.

総合練習
そうごうれんしゅう

Your instructor will give you a card with a day of the week written on it to indicate which day you have off from class. On the card, write in Japanese an activity you'd like to do with someone. Your instructor will then divide the class into two groups. Everyone in the first group must find someone in the second group with a matching card and extend an invitation to do the activity. Together, negotiate the details, such as where to go, what time to meet, and where. Remember to use the expressions and strategies you have learned in this chapter to introduce a topic and extend an invitation.

Example: You are free on: 水曜日

Activity: えいがを見る

ロールプレイ

1. You are with a friend at a Japanese department store and want to have lunch. You go up to the eighth floor, where there are a variety of restaurants (めいてんがい). Discuss your options (和食、 洋食、 中華りょうり わ しょく   ようしょく   ちゅう か etc.) and decide where to eat.

2. You have gone out to eat with your friend. Place your orders and find out how long they will take. If any one of the dishes require more than 15 minutes to prepare, order something else.

Chapter 10

第十課
(だい か)

私の家族
(か ぞく)
My family

単語
たん

Nouns

あし	足	leg, foot
あたま	頭	head, あたまがいい smart, intelligent
あに	兄	older brother (the speaker's)
あね	姉	older sister (the speaker's)
いもうと	妹	younger sister (the speaker's)
いもうとさん	妹さん	younger sister (someone else's)
おかあさん	お母さん	mother (someone else's)
おくさん	奥さん	wife (someone else's)
おこさん	お子さん	child (someone else's)
おじいさん	お祖父さん	grandfather (someone else's)
おとうさん	お父さん	father (someone else's)
おとうと	弟	younger brother (the speaker's)
おとうとさん	弟さん	younger brother (someone else's)
おとこ	男	male, おとこの人 man
おにいさん	お兄さん	older brother (someone else's)
おねえさん	お姉さん	older sister (someone else's)
おばあさん	お祖母さん	grandmother (someone else's)
おんな	女	female, おんなの人 woman
かいしゃいん	会社員	businessperson
かお	顔	face
かぞく	家族	family, speaker's family
かみ	髪	hair
きょうだい	兄弟	sibling(s)
くち	口	mouth
けっこん	結婚	marriage, 〜とけっこんする to marry 〜, けっこんしている to be married

こ	子	child, おとこのこ boy, おんなのこ girl
ごかぞく	ご家族	family (someone else's)
ごきょうだい	ご兄弟	siblings (someone else's)
ごしゅじん	ご主人	husband (someone else's)
こども	子供	child
しゅじん	主人	husband (the speaker's)
せ	背	back (part of the body), height (of a person)
そふ	祖父	grandfather (the speaker's)
そぼ	祖母	grandmother (the speaker's)
ちち	父	father (the speaker's)
つま	妻	wife (the speaker's)
て	手	hand
とし	年	age としうえ elder, older としした younger
はな	鼻	nose
はは	母	mother (the speaker's)
ひとりっこ	一人っ子	only child
ブロンド		blond
まんなか	真ん中	center, middle, middle child
みみ	耳	ear
め	目	eye
めがね	眼鏡	glasses

う -verbs

かぶる		to put on (a hat or cap)
すむ	住む	to reside, 〜にすんでいる to live in 〜
はく		to put on (skirt, pants, socks, shoes)
ふとる	太る	to gain weight, ふとっている to be fat
わかる	分かる	to understand, 〜がわかる

る -verbs

| かける | | to put on (glasses) |

きる	着る	to put on (sweater, shirt, jacket)
つとめる	勤める	to become employed 〜につとめている to be employed at, work for
やせる		to lose weight, やせている to be thin

Irregular verbs

| する | | to put on (accessories) |

Auxiliary verbs

| 〜ている | | resultant state |

い -adjectives

あかるい	明るい	cheerful (Chapter 4, bright)
かっこいい		good-looking, cool, neat
かわいい	可愛い	cute, adorable
しかくい	四角い	square
ながい	長い	long
ほそながい	細長い	long/elongated
まるい	丸い	round
みじかい	短い	short (length)

な -adjectives

| じょうず（な） | 上手（な） | good at, skillful |
| しんせつ（な） | 親切（な） | kind |

Question words

| いくつ | | How old 〜? おいくつ (polite form) |

Prefixes

| しょう〜 | 小〜 | elementary, 小学生 elementary school student,
小学校 elementary school |
| ちゅう〜 | 中〜 | middle, 中学生 middle school student,
中学校 middle school, junior high school |

Suffixes

〜さい	〜歳／才	〜 years old
〜にん	〜人	〜 people
〜ばん（め）	〜番（目）	〜 th (ordinal suffix)
〜かた	〜方	person (polite form of 人)
		いいかた (nice person)

Expressions

いいえ、そんなことはありません。	No, that's not the case.
いいえ、まだまだです。	No, I still have a long way to go.

単語の練習
たん　　　れんしゅう

A. 家族　Kinship terms
か ぞく

Japanese has two sets of kinship terms. One is used to refer to one's own family and the other is used to refer to someone else's.

	Your own family member (humble form)	Someone else's family member (polite form)
family	家族（かぞく）	ご家族（かぞく）
father	父（ちち）	お父さん（とう）
mother	母（はは）	お母さん（かあ）
parents	両親（りょうしん）	ご両親（りょうしん）
older brother	兄（あに）	お兄さん（にい）
older sister	姉（あね）	お姉さん（ねえ）
younger brother	弟（おとうと）	弟 さん（おとうと）
younger sister	妹（いもうと）	妹 さん（いもうと）
brothers and sisters	兄弟（きょうだい）	ご兄弟（きょうだい）
grandfather	祖父（そ ふ）	お祖父さん（じ い）
grandmother	祖母（そ ぼ）	お祖母さん（ば あ）
husband	主人（しゅじん）	ご主人（しゅじん）
wife	つま	おくさん
child/children	子供（こ ども）	お子さん（こ）

Note that 子供, 兄弟, 家族 and 両親 can be used in general statements.

日本の子供はよくあそびます。   *Japanese children play a lot.*

ハワイには日本人の家族がたくさんいます。   *There are many Japanese families in Hawaii.*

Activity 1

Look at the family trees. Note that each family member is represented by a letter. Now, form groups of three. One of you will write the letters A through T in random order on a piece of paper and read a letter on the list. The other two will give the kinship term that corresponds to the letter. Remember to say 私の〜 or 山田さんの〜. Whoever calls out the correct term first gets a point. The person with the most points wins. Take turns reading the letters.

Example: The dealer says *H.* Player 1 says 私の弟 first. Player 1 gets a point.

私の家族   山田さんのご家族

Supplementary Vocabulary: 親族 (Kinship terms)

	Your own family member (humble form)		Someone else's family member (polite form)	
cousin	いとこ	従兄弟	いとこさん	従兄弟さん
nephew	おい	甥	おいごさん	甥子さん
uncle	おじ	叔父／伯父	おじさん	叔父さん／伯父さん
aunt	おば	叔母／伯母	おばさん	叔母さん／伯母さん
relatives	しんせき	親戚	ごしんせき	ご親戚
niece	めい	姪	めいごさん	姪子さん
grandchild	まご	孫	おまごさん	お孫さん

B. 人　People

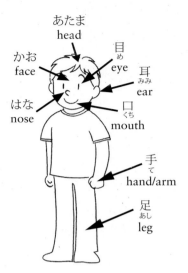

あたま
head

目
め
eye

かお
face

耳
みみ
ear

はな
nose

口
くち
mouth

手
て
hand/arm

足
あし
leg

Activity 2

Work with in class. Everyone claps their hands twice and immediately after that, your instructor will say a body part in Japanese. Touch the part he/she says.

Activity 3

"Simon Says." Work with a partner. Using the vocabulary in this chapter, take turns calling out and identifying parts of the body in Japanese.

Supplementary Vocabulary:　からだ　The Body

あご	顎	chin
うで	腕	arm
おなか		belly
からだ	体	body
くちびる	唇	lip(s)
くび	首	neck
こし	腰	waist
せなか	背中	back
どう	胴	torso, trunk, body
つめ	爪	nail
のど	咽	throat
は	歯	tooth
ひげ	髭	mustache, beard
ほっぺた		cheek
まつげ	睫	eyelash
まゆげ	眉毛	eyebrow
ゆび	指	finger

C. からだのとくちょう   Physical features

せが高い	tall (height)
せがひくい	short (height)
手がながい	have long reach
足がみじかい	have short legs
かおがまるい	have a round face
かおがほそながい	have a narrow face
かおが四角い	have a square face
目があおい	have blue eyes
口が小さい	have a small mouth
はなが高い	have a big nose
かっこいい	good-looking
かみがくろい	have black hair
ブロンド	blond hair
ふとっている	fat, chubby
やせている	thin

おぼえていますか。

きれい（な）　ちゃいろい　あかい　しろい　みどり

Activity 4

Write your guess for the opposite of each attribute listed below.

1. せがひくい　　　　_____
2. ふとっている　　　_____
3. かみがくろい　　　_____
4. かおが小さい　　　_____
5. 足がみじかい　　　_____
6. 手がながい　　　　_____
7. 口が小さい　　　　_____
8. はなが高い　　　　_____
9. 耳が大きい　　　　_____
10. あたまが小さい　_____

Activity 5

Take a moment to think about your own physical features. Then state as many as you can in sixty seconds.

D. Verbs used with clothing and accessories

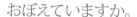

シャツを<u>きる</u>   put on a blouse
スカートを<u>はく</u>   put on a skirt
くつを<u>はく</u>   put on shoes
ぼうしを<u>かぶる</u>   put on a hat
めがねを<u>かける</u>   put on glasses
イヤリングを<u>する</u>   put on earrings
うでどけいを<u>する</u>   put on a wristwatch

おぼえていますか。

コート   ジャケット   シャツ   ジーンズ   スーツ
ストッキング   セーター   Tシャツ   ドレス   ネクタイ
ネックレス   パンツ／ズボン   ふく   ゆびわ   ベルト

Activity 6

Classify the above articles of clothing and accessories that are used with the following verbs:

Verbs	Articles of clothing and accessories
きる	
はく	
する	

E. せいかくとのうりょく   Personality and ability

親切 (な)   kind
しんせつ
あかるい   cheerful
かわいい   cute, adorable
あたまがいい   smart, intelligent
日本語が分かる   understand Japanese
スポーツが上手 (な)   good at sports
じょうず

おぼえていますか。

やさしい   おもしろい   たのしい   いい   つまらない   むずかしい
さびしい   げんきな   りっぱな   しずかな   にぎやかな

Activity 7

しつもんに日本語でこたえて下さい。

1. お父さんはどんな人ですか。
2. お母さんはどんな人ですか。
3. どんな人が好きですか。
4. 一番いい友達はどんな人ですか。

Supplementary Vocabulary:　せいかく　Personality

うちき（な）	内気（な）	shy, introverted
きがつよい	気が強い	strong-minded
きがながい	気が長い	patient
きがはやい	気が早い	impatient, hasty, rash
きがみじかい	気が短い	short-tempered
きがよわい	気が弱い	weak-minded
くらい	暗い	somber, nerdy
たんき（な）	短気（な）	short-tempered
のんびりしている		easygoing, carefree

F. しごととちい　Work and social status

〜と　けっこんする	to get married
〜に　すむ	to reside
〜に　つとめる	to get a job at
会社員	business person
小学生	elementary school student
中学生	middle school student

おぼえていますか。

しごと　学生　大学生　大学院生　高校　高校生

Activity 8

しつもんに日本語でこたえて下さい。

1. けっこんしたいですか。いつけっこんしたいですか。
2. 今、どこにすんでいますか。
3. どんなところにすみたいですか。
4. 日本の会社につとめたいですか。
5. どんなところにつとめたいですか。
6. ご家族に小学生がいますか。中学生がいますか。高校生がいますか。
7. お父さんは／お母さんはどこかにつとめていますか。

Supplementary Vocabulary: Occupations

いしゃ	医者	medical doctor
エンジニア		engineer
かんごし	看護士	nurse, medical assistant
きょうし	教師	teacher
こうむいん	公務員	government official
サラリーマン		white-collar worker (from the Japanese term "salary man")
じえいぎょう	自営業	self-employed
だいがくきょうじゅ	大学教授	college professor
はいしゃ	歯医者	dentist
べんごし	弁護士	lawyer
マネージャー		manager

G.　としと人数　Age and number of people

	～人 (～ people)	～さい (～ years old)
何	なんにん	（お）いくつ／なんさい
0		れいさい
一	※　ひとり	※　いっさい
二	※　ふたり	にさい
三	さんにん	さんさい
四	※　よにん	よんさい
五	ごにん	ごさい
六	ろくにん	ろくさい
七	※　しちにん	※　ななさい
八	はちにん	※　はっさい
九	きゅうにん	きゅうさい
十	じゅうにん	※　じゅっさい ※　じっさい
百	ひゃくにん	ひゃくさい
千	せんにん	
一万	いちまんにん	

Note: 四人家族 means *a family of four including yourself.* 兄弟が二人います
however, means that you have two brothers and sisters excluding yourself.

⬡ **Activity 9**

Sing a version of this popular counting rhyme in Japanese!

ひ　とり ふ　たり　さん にん いる よ　　よ にん ご にん　ろく にん いる よ

し ち　に ん は ち　に ん　きゅう　に ん　い る　よ　じゅう にん のこ　ども　　た

ちー　　　ヘーイ!
（右手の掌を振り上げ　回れ右）

⬡ **Activity 10**

Form groups of varying sizes according to the directions your instructor calls out. Try to join each group as quickly as possible so that you won't be left behind.

Example:　三人のグループを作って下さい。
　　　　　　　にん

⬡ **Activity 11**

Write down three numbers on a piece of paper. Your instructor will call out an age. Cross out a number if it corresponds to what you hear. Whoever crosses out all the numbers first wins.

⬡ **Activity 12**

しつもんに日本語でこたえて下さい。

1. この大学には学生が何人ぐらいいますか。
　　　　　　　　　　　　　　にん

2. この大学には先生が何人ぐらいいますか。
　　　　　　　　　　　　　　にん

3. 日本語の先生は何人いますか。
　　　　　　　　にん

4. 日本語の学生が何人ぐらいいますか。
　　　　　　　　　にん

5. 今、きょうしつにクラスメートが何人いますか。
　　　　　　　　　　　　　　　　にん

6. ご兄弟がいますか。何人いますか。
　　きょうだい　　　　にん

7. 何人家族ですか。
　　にん か ぞく

Activity 13

Work in groups of five or six. Make up a number representing a classmate's age, write it down on a piece of paper, and tape it to the back of someone else in your group. Take turns asking about your ages. Then line up from the "youngest" to the "oldest."

Activity 14

The following table lists typical age ranges for children and young adults who attend school or day care in Japan. The information about Japan is provided. Fill in the information about your country and compare the two.

Example:　日本では　れいさいから三さいの子供がたくじしょに行きます。

アメリカでは／も、〜さいから〜さいの子供がたくじしょ
に行きます。

	日本	
たくじしょ (nursery)	0 さいから　　3 さい	（　　）さいから　（　　）さい
ほいくえん (day care center)	0 さいから　　6 さい	（　　）さいから　（　　）さい
ようちえん (kindergarten)	3 さいから　　6 さい	（　　）さいから　（　　）さい
小学校 しょう	6 さいから　　12 さい	（　　）さいから　（　　）さい
中学校	12 さいから　　15 さい	（　　）さいから　（　　）さい
高校	15 さいから　　18 さい	（　　）さいから　（　　）さい
大学	18 さいから　　22 さい	（　　）さいから　（　　）さい

Activity 15

しつもんに日本語でこたえて下さい。

1. お父さんはおいくつですか。
2. お母さんはおいくつですか。
3. 〜さんは、今何さいですか。

ダイアローグ

はじめに　　**Warm Up**

A. しつもんに日本語でこたえて下さい。

1. 何人家族ですか。
   <small>にん か ぞく</small>
2. お兄さんがいますか。お姉さんはどうですか。
   <small>にい</small>　　　　　　　　　<small>ねえ</small>
3. 妹さんがいますか。弟さんはどうですか。
   <small>いもうと</small>　　　　　　　　<small>おとうと</small>

私の家族は五人家族です。 *There are five people in my family*
<small>か ぞく</small>　　<small>にん か ぞく</small>

上田さんの友達の川口さんがあそびに来ています。上田さんと
<small>だち</small>
川口さんは、上田さんのへやにいます。

川口：　あ、あのしゃしん、上田さんのご家族ですか。
　　　　　　　　　　　　　　　　　　　　　<small>か ぞく</small>

上田：　ええ、そうです。これが父で、これが母です。
　　　　　　　　　　　　　　<small>ちち</small>　　　　　<small>はは</small>

川口：　かっこいいお父さんですね。それにとてもきれいなお母さん
　　　　　　　　<small>とう</small>　　　　　　　　　　　　　　　<small>かあ</small>
　　　　ですね。

上田：　ああ、でも、父も母も四十九さいなんですよ。
　　　　　　　　　<small>ちち</small>　<small>はは</small>

川口：　そうですか。とてもわかく見えますけど。

上田：　父はくるまの会社につとめていて、母は英語の先生なんです。

川口：　そうなんですか。じゃあ、この帽子をかぶっている男の子は
　　　　弟さんですか。

上田：　ええ、そうです。なまえはデービッドで、今、小学三年生です。

川口：　かわいいですね。じゃあ、この人はお姉さんですか。

上田：　いいえ、それは妹のパムです。パムはまだ十七さいなんですが、
　　　　パムのほうが私よりせが高くて大きいから、よく年上に
　　　　見られるんですよ。

川口：　そうなんですか。

DIALOGUE PHRASE NOTES

- It is rude to refer to people using これ, それ, あれ, but you can do so when you talk about a person in a photograph or drawing because they are not actual human beings.
- わかく見えます means *look young*. わかい means *young*, and it is usually used for teenagers or adults but not for children.
- 年上に見られる means *to be mistaken for an older (sibling)*.

ダイアローグの後で

1. Look at the picture of a family tree on page 138. Using it as an example, draw Ms. Ueda's family tree.
2. Based on the dialogue, complete the following paragraphs using appropriate words and phrases.

上田さんの家族は五人家族です。お父さんとお母さんと＿＿＿＿＿＿
と＿＿＿＿＿＿＿がいます。上田さんの＿＿＿＿＿＿＿は四十九さいで、
くるまの会社につとめています。上田さんの＿＿＿＿＿＿＿＿も
四十九さいです。＿＿＿＿＿＿＿＿は　英語の先生です。上田さんの
＿＿＿＿＿＿＿のなまえは＿＿＿＿＿で、高校生ですが、せがとても高
いです。上田さんの＿＿＿＿＿＿のなまえはデービッドで、小学校の
＿＿＿＿＿＿です。とてもかわいいです。

日本の文化
ぶん か

日本の家族
か ぞく

According to a 2005 government survey, about 60 percent of Japanese families fall under the category of nuclear families, and 27 percent are single-person households. Only 13 percent are three-generation families.

Since the end of World War II, the number of children in a Japanese family has decreased substantially. The average for 2006 was only 1.3 children per household, compared with 2.0 for the same year in the U.S. and France. Some reasons for the decline are economic; others are social, such as later marriages and a lack of support for women to continue to work after having children. According to 2005 statistics from the Japanese

Ministry of Health, Labor and Welfare, the average age for a man to marry was 29.8 years. For a woman, it was 28 years. Nearly 90 percent of women work before getting married, but only 65 percent continue to work after marriage. After a child is born, the percentage plummets to a scant 23 percent. Traditionally, wives are expected to take care of the house and children, even

while holding down a job. Despite recent efforts to update traditional roles, the current support infrastructure, such as day-care facilities and baby-sitting services, is still inadequate to allow many women to work.

Conversely, Japanese husbands are expected to support the family financially, and they tend to work long hours. For example, according to a 2004 ILO survey, over 28 percent of Japanese workers logged more than 50 hours a week, which is much higher than the European average of 1.4 to 15.5 percent or the U.S. average of 20 percent. Although some companies offer parental leave for men in addition to maternity leave, new fathers rarely take advantage of this benefit, as it would lower their income significantly, could inconvenience their co-workers, and might even affect chances for promotion.

Despite these pressures, the divorce rate in Japan is extremely low. Until 1972, it was less than one percent. After climbing to a high of 2.3 percent in 2002, the rate as of 2005 declined to under 2.1 percent.

ウチとソト Insiders and Outsiders

The Japanese rarely praise members of their own family when they are talking to someone outside the family. They are very conscious of the distinction between "in-groups" (ウチ) and "out-groups" (ソト). It is very important to be polite to those who are not in one's in-group, and praising members of your own family—the primary in-group—is considered impolite. Accordingly, you may often hear a Japanese man complaining that his wife is not good at cooking when in fact she is an excellent cook, or you may hear a woman say that her husband is impractical and inept at household matters. Similarly, boasting about yourself is considered socially inappropriate.

Within one's own family, お父さん, お母さん, お兄さん, お姉さん

and similar terms are used to address senior members. First names are used only to address younger members. A daughter or son would address their mother as お母さん, お母ちゃん (ちゃん being the more familiar form), or ママ (Mom); older brothers as お兄さん or お兄ちゃん; and a younger sister named Michiko as みち子ちゃん. Senior members tend to refer to themselves using their kinship terms when talking to a younger member of the family. Instead of using their first names with their children, parents usually call each other お父さん／パパ (Dad, Papa) , and お母さん／ママ.

In addition, Japanese forms of address do not distinguish between biological parents and stepparents. Using the Japanese equivalent of terms such a stepfather and stepmother can imply a distant relationship between the stepchild and the stepparents, so both biological and stepparents are addressed in the same way.

文法
ぶんぽう

I.   Stating the order within a family using 番（目）
め

Expressing the order within a family using 番（目）
め

番（目）converts cardinal numbers into ordinal numbers, and it is used to describe
め
one's standing in his/her family such as:

一番上	oldest (*literally*, the first from the top, the highest)
上から二番目 め	second oldest (*literally*, the second from the top, the second highest)
まん中	right in the middle
下から二番目 め	second youngest (*literally*, the second from the bottom, the second lowest)
一番下	youngest (*literally*, the first from the bottom, the lowest)

The pronunciation of numbers preceding ばん（め）is regular and follows the same
pattern as the pronunciaiton for counter 〜まい.

	〜番（目）(ordinal, 〜 th)		
何	なんばん（め）	六	ろくばん（め）
一	いちばん（め）	七	ななばん（め）
二	にばん（め）	八	はちばん（め）
三	さんばん（め）	九	きゅうばん（め）
四	よんばん（め）	十	じゅうばん（め）
五	ごばん（め）	百	ひゃくばん（め）

家本：　私の家族は五人家族です。
いえもと　　　　　かぞく　　にんかぞく
My family consists of five members.

小山：　そうですか。ゆみ子さんは何番目ですか。
こやま　　　　　　　　　　こ　　　　　なんばんめ
Where do you come in the family (literally, *what order are you*), *Yumiko?*

家本：　一番上です。
いえもと
I am the oldest.

小山：　そうですか。じゃあ、一番下はだれですか。
こやま
I see. Who is the youngest?

家本：　妹のみかです。みかは、今十五さいです。
いえもと　いもうと
My younger sister Mika. She is fifteen years old now.

Note that the term for *only child* is 一人っ子.
ひとり　こ

話してみましょう

Activity 1

Take turns asking your classmates how many people are in their family. Then compare the results. Whose family is the largest or the smallest? Discuss the advantages and disadvantages of coming from large and small families.

Example: A: ～さんのご家族は何人家族ですか。

B: 四人家族です。

or 母と私と妹が二人います。

Activity 2

Work in groups of four or five. Take turns asking your classmates how many siblings they have and their order in the family. Then compare the results. Who is the oldest or the youngest?

Example: A: ～さんはご兄弟がいますか。

B: はい、二人います。

A: ～さんは何番目ですか。

B: 私は一番上です。

Activity 3

Work with a partner. Take turns describing your family members in terms of name and age, and complete the table with your partner's descriptions.

Example: 私の家族は三人家族です。兄が一人います。なまえは
トーマスで、二十五さいです。父のなまえはジョンです。今、
五十二さいです。

ご兄弟	おなまえ	～さい

ご両親	おなまえ	～さい

II. Describing a resultant state using verb て - form ＋ いる

The verb て - form ＋ いる describes a state (of being) that is the result of a past action. For example, めがねをかける means *to put on* (*glasses*), and めがねをかけている means *as the result of putting glasses on, the person is now wearing them.*

めがねをかける   めがねをかけている

Similarly, けっこんする means *to get married* whereas けっこんしている means *to be married.*

Action: けっこんする (*get married*)	Resultant state: けっこんしている (*is married*)

Action: ふとる (gain weight)	Resultant state: ふとっている (is fat)

山本：　田中さんはめがねをかけていますか。
Does Ms. Tanaka wear glasses?

チョイ：　いいえ、めがねはかけていませんが、イヤリングを
　　　　　していますよ。
No, she doesn't, but she wears earrings.

NOTES

* The past form 〜ていました describes a (resultant) state at a specified time in the past.

たくさん食べて、ふとりました。
I ate a lot and gained some weight.

私は小さい時、ふとっていました。
とき
I was fat (chubby) when I was small.

- ～ている can be used to describe a person who wears something habitually.

田中さんはよくジーンズをはいています。
Mr. Tanaka often wears jeans.

山田さんはいつもネクタイをしています。
Mr. Yamada always wears a tie.

- The verbs すむ and つとめる are usually used with ～ている. The particle に is used to indicate a location, company or organization.

私はとうきょうにすんでいます。
I live in Tokyo.

山田さんはアパートにすんでいました。
Mr. Yamada used to live (was living) in an apartment.

ぼくはじょうとう大学につとめています。
I work for Joto University.

話してみましょう

Activity 1

Describe what each person is wearing, using the verb ている form.

Example: さとうさんはスーツをきています。そして、ネクタイを
しています。

さとうさん　　　山本さん　　　こんどうさん　　　木村さん
　　　　　　　　　　　　　　　　　　　　　　　　むら

Activity 2

Work with a partner. Pick a classmate and have your partner guess who it is by asking what the person is wearing, using はい／いいえ questions.

Example: A:　その人は帽子をかぶっていますか。
　　　　　　　　ぼう　し
　　　　　B:　いいえ、かぶっていません。
　　　　　A:　その人はスカートをはいていますか。
　　　　　B:　はい、はいています。

Activity 3

Your instructor will ask the class to walk around the classroom observing what the others are wearing. When he/she tells the class to stop, each student will stand back to back with the person who is closest and describe his/her clothing. How many items can you describe correctly?

Example: ～さんはあかいセーターをきていて、ジーンズを
はいています。

Activity 4

Work with a series of partners. Take turns finding out where your classmates have lived up until now. Note that ～ の時 means *at the time of* ～ or *when I was / am* ～ .

Example: A: ～さんは、今、どこにすんでいますか。

B: ハリソン・ホールにすんでいます。

A: ずっと *(for a long time)* そこにすんでいますか。

B: いいえ、高校の時は 両親の家にすんでいました。

A: そうですか。ご両親はどこにすんでいますか。

B: バーリントンにすんでいます。

III. Describing physical appearance and skills using ～は ～が

The ～は ～が construction is used to describe the characteristics of a variety of things such as people, places, and other physical objects. This chapter introduces how ～は ～が can be used to describe people's physical appearance, skills, and personality.

A. Describing physical appearance

The construction "person は body parts が adjectives" is used to describe a person's physical appearance.

山下さんは	はなが	高いです。	Mr. Yamashita has a large nose.
リーさんは	目が	ちゃいろいです。	Ms. Li has brown eyes.
上田さんは	かみが	ながいです。	Ms. Ueda has long hair.
キムさんは	かおが	四角いです。	Mr. Kim has a square face.

本木：　あの人はせが高くて、足がながくて、かっこいいですね。
That person over there is good-looking. She is very tall, and has long legs.

山口：　ああ、あの人はモデルですからね。
Oh yes, that's because she is a model.

B. Describing skills and ability

～は ～が can be used with other personal traits such as personality and ability. In the following example, いい and 上手 are adjectives and 分かる is an intransitive verb. Unlike a transitive verb, an intransitive verb does not take a direct object or the direct object marker を. Instead, the particle が is used.

チョイさんは	あたまが	いいです。	Mr. Choi is smart.
石田さんは	テニスが	上手です。	Mr. Ishida is good at tennis.
山田さんは	フランス語が	分かります。	Mr. Yamada understands French.

田口：　あの人は日本語が分かりそうですね。
That person over there appears to understand Japanese.

三上：　ええ、でも、あまり上手じゃなさそうです。
Yes, but it does not look like he is good at it.

NOTES

- Like 好き and きらい, the plain present affirmative form of a verb + の can be used with 上手.
  アリソンさんはうたをうたうのが上手です。
  Allison is good at singing songs.

話してみましょう

Activity 1

Using the following chart listing various physical characteristics, describe the persons named.

Example: 私

私はせがひくいですが、手と足はながいです。

かおがまるくて、かみがながいです。そして、目もはなも口も小さいです。

からだ	大きい　小さい					
せ	高い　ひくい					
手	ながい　みじかい　きれい					
足	ながい　みじかい　きれい					
かお	まるい　四角い　ほそながい　たまごがた (egg-shaped)					
かみ	ながい　みじかい　くろい　あかい　ちゃいろい　ブロンド					
目	大きい　小さい　あおい　ちゃいろい　くろい　みどり					
はな	大きい　小さい　高い　ひくい					
口	大きい　小さい					

1. 私
2. 父
3. 母
4. 一番いい友達
5. Other members of your family

Activity 2

Work with a partner. Pick one face in the drawing and describe it to your partner. Have him/her identify the face by the number on the illustration.

Example:　この人はかおがまるいです。
　　　　　この人は目が大きいです。

1　　2　　3　　4　　5　　6

7　　8　　9　　10　　11　　12

Activity 3

Work with a partner. Draw a person's face. Then, describe the face to your partner. Your partner will try to draw the face according to your description. Compare the two faces.

Example:　この人はかおがほそながくて、目が小さいです。

Activity 4

Work with the class. Find out which languages your classmates can speak, who knows the most languages, and any other talents they may have. List the information you obtain in the chart.

Example:　　1. A:　〜さんはどんなことばが分かりますか。

B:　かんこく語が分かります。

A:　そうですか。かっこいいですね。

2. A:　〜さんはどんなことをするのが上手ですか。

B:　かんじを書くのが上手です。

A:　そうですか。いいですね。私はかんじを書くのが上手じゃないんです。

クラスメートの　なまえ	ことば　(language)	上手なこと

IV. Describing people and things using nouns and modifying clauses

A noun may be modified by another noun, an adjective, or a modifying clause. The modifier always comes before the noun. In a noun-modifying clause, the verb must be in the plain form. The negative forms of adjectives and the copula verb must be in the plain form as well.

ブロンドの	かみ	*blond hair*
日本のくるまじゃない	くるま	*a car that is not a Japanese car*
きれいな	家	*a clean house*
きれいじゃない	家	*a house that is not clean*
りょうりが上手な	人	*a person who is good at cooking*
そうじが上手じゃない	人	*a person who is not good at cleaning*
小さい	くつ	*small shoes*
小さくない	くつ	*not so small shoes*
かみがながい	人	*a person who has long hair*
かみがながくない	人	*a person who does not have long hair*
英語が分かる	人	*a person who understands English*
新聞をよく読む	人	*a person who often reads the paper*
けっこんしている	人	*a person who is married*
けっこんしていない	人	*a person who is not married*

ホン： 田中さんのお母さんはどの方ですか。
Which (person) is Mr. Tanaka's mother?

木村： あそこにいる人ですよ。せが高くてかみがながい人です。
(She is) the person over there—the tall person with long hair.

ホン： ああ、 あの方ですか。とてもきれいな方ですね。
Oh, that person? She's very beautiful, isn't she?

木村： 本当にそうですね。
Indeed.

話してみましょう

Activity 1

Look at the drawing and answer the questions using a noun-modifying clause wherever appropriate.

さとうさん　　山本さん　　こんどうさん　　木村さん

Example:　さとうさんはどの人ですか。

　　　　　　スーツをきている人です。

1. さとうさんはどの人ですか。

2. こんどうさんはどの人ですか。

3. 木村さんはどの人ですか。

4. 山本さんはどの人ですか。

5. ジーンズをはいている人は木村さんですか。

6. ネックレスをしている人はどの人ですか。

7. めがねをかけている人はこんどうさんですか。

Activity 2

Fruit Basket. Work with the class. Arrange your chairs in a circle so that everybody except for one person has a place to sit. That person stands in the center of the circle and calls out a physical descriptor. Anyone who fits the description must move to another seat. Whoever is left without a seat then takes the center and calls out another descriptor.

Example:　The person in the center says: めがねをかけている人
　　　　　　People who wear glasses must move to another seat.

Activity 3

Take turns finding out how many in the class fall into the categories listed in the chart. Then check your answers with each other. Note that 私のデータでは means *according to my data*.

Example:　1.　A: ～さんはけっこんしていますか。

　　　　　　　　B: いいえ、していません。

　　　　　　2.　A: けっこんしている人は何人いますか。

　　　　　　　　B: 二人います。／ぜんぜんいません。

　　　　　　　　A: そうですか。私のデータでは一人です。

	はい	いいえ
けっこんしている		
お姉さんがいる		
妹さんがいる		
一人っ子だ		
りょうにすんでいる		
スポーツが上手だ		
スペイン語が分かる		

Activity 4

Work in groups of four. One student thinks of a classmate but does not say his/her name. The other members ask questions about his/her characteristics to find out who he or she is. They can ask up to six questions. Anyone who guesses the answer after the first question receives six points. After the second question, he/she receives five points. If no one is able to get the correct answer after the sixth question, the person who has chosen the name receives six points. The person who earns the most points wins.

Example:　A:　女の人ですか。
　　　　　　　　おんな
　　　　　　B:　はい。
　　　　　　C:　かみがながい人ですか。
　　　　　　B:　いいえ、かみはみじかいです。
　　　　　　D:　じゃあ、ブロンドですか。
　　　　　　B:　いいえ、ちゃいろいかみの人です。

Activity 5

With a partner, take turns asking what kind of person appeals to each of you. Have your partner describe the person in terms of physical appearance, personality, interests, and ability, using noun modifiers. Take turns. Take detailed notes on the information that your partner gives you.

Example:　A:　スミスさんはどんな人が好きですか。
　　　　　　B:　せが高くて、かみがブロンドの人が好きです。
　　　　　　　　そして、やきゅうが上手な人がいいですね。
　　　　　　　　　　　　　　　　じょうず
　　　　　　　　おいしいものを食べるのが好きな人もいいですね。
　　　　　　A:　せいかくは (personality) どんな人がいいですか。
　　　　　　B:　そうですね。あたまがよくて、やさしい人がいいですね。

Activity 6

You are a dating consultant looking for the best match for your partner from the previous activity. Take turns asking about your classmates' favorite types. They will give information about their previous partner's preferences.

Example:　A:　どの人のデータ (data) がありますか。
　　　　　　B:　スミスさんのデータがあります。
　　　　　　A:　スミスさんはどんな人が好きなんですか。
　　　　　　B:　せが高くて、かみがブロンドの人が好きです。
　　　　　　　　そして、あたまがよくて、やさしい人が好きです。

V. Expressing opinions using 〜とおもう

〜とおもう expresses the speaker's opinion about things or events. The subject of おもう, the speaker, is often deleted. The clause before とおもう must end in the plain form.

Copula verb			
ご主人は	会社員 だと	おもいます。	*I think her husband is a businessman.*
ご主人は	日本人じゃないと	おもいます。	*I think her husband is not Japanese./ I don't think her husband is Japanese.*
い - adjectives			
上田さんは	かわいいと	おもいます。	*I think Ms. Ueda is cute.*
このテストは	むずかしくないと	おもいます。	*I think this test isn't difficult./ I don't think this test is difficult.*
な - adjectives			
先生は	とても親切だと	おもいます。	*I think my teacher is very kind.*
弟は さしみが好きじゃないと		おもいます。	*I think my younger brother doesn't like sashimi./ I don't think my younger brother likes sashimi.*
Verbs			
友田さんは	けっこんしていると	おもいます。	*I think Mr. Tomoda is married.*
山田さんは	明日来ないと	おもいます。	*I think Ms. Yamada is not coming tomorrow./I don't think Mr. Yamada is coming tomorrow.*

The speaker can be specified for emphasis to clarify the context.

私はアリソンさんは明日来るとおもいます。
I think Allison is coming tomorrow.

私はこの本はいいとおもいます。
I think this book is good.

When the subject of the main clause is someone other than the speaker, the form おもっている is used instead of おもう.

トムさんは足がながいと　おもっています。
あし
Tom thinks he has long legs.

トムさんは足がながいと　おもいます。
あし
I think Tom has long legs.

木村さんはふとっていないと　おもっています。
むら
Mr. Kimura doesn't think he is fat.

木村さんはふとっていないと　おもいます。
むら
I don't think Mr. Kimura is fat.

ペギーさんは和食は高いと　おもっています。
わしょく
Peggy thinks Japanese food is expensive.

私も和食は高いと　おもいます。
わ しょく
I also think that Japanese food is expensive.

To form an information question, use a question word and end the sentence and か. To ask for a general impression or opinion, use 〜をどうおもいますか, what do you think of 〜.

高田：　このクラスでだれが一番せが高いとおもいますか。
Who do you think is the tallest in this class?

キム：　イアンさんが一番高いとおもいます。
I think Ian is the tallest.

さとう：　どの新聞がいいとおもいますか。
Which newspaper do you think is good?

もり：　朝日新聞がいいとおもいます。
あさ ひ
I think Asahi Newspaper is good.

ゆみ：　田中さんをどうおもいますか。
What do you think of Ms. Tanaka?

トム：　ちょっとしずかだけど、いい人だとおもいます。
I think she's rather quiet but a nice person.

石田：　この本、どうおもいますか。
いし
What do you think of this book?

大川：　むずかしくて、あまりおもしろくないとおもいます。
I think it's difficult and not very interesting.

石田：　ぼくもそうおもうんですよ。
いし
I think so, too!

NOTES

- The plain form とおもう cannot express the speaker's wish or intention without an additional suffix attached to the verb. You will learn how to express intentions in Nakama 2.

日本に行くとおもいます。
I think (someone, in context) is going to Japan.

キムさんは日本に行くとおもいます。
I think Ms. Kim is going to Japan.

- 〜たいとおもいます to express a wish is often used instead of たいです in conversation, because it sounds softer and more polite.

私は日本に行きたいとおもいます。
I would like to go to Japan.

キムさんは日本に行きたいとおもっています。
Ms. Kim would like to go to Japan.

話してみましょう

Activity 1

A friend of Mr. Ishida is thinking about applying to your school. Answer his/her questions using plain form + とおもう.

Example: 〜さんの大学は大きいですか。

いいえ、あまり大きくないとおもいます。

1. 〜さんの大学には日本人がたくさんいますか。
2. 大学があるまちには日本のレストランがありますか。
3. 大学のじゅぎょうは大変_{たいへん}ですか。
4. どんな大学ですか。
5. 大学があるまちはどんなまちですか。

Activity 2

Work with a partner. Look at the following pictures and guess what kind of people they show.

Example:　A:　この男_{おとこ}の子_こはどんな子_こだとおもいますか。

　　　　　　B:　げんきな子_こだとおもいます。

　　　　or　げんきそうな子_こだとおもいます。

1　　　　　　2　　　　　　3

4　　　　5　　　　6　　　　7

Activity 3

Work with a partner. Think about the strengths (ちょうしょ) of each one of your classmates and write down your opinions using ～とおもう.

Example:　A:　スミスさんのちょうしょは何だとおもいますか。

　　　　　　B:　そうですね。スミスさんはかんじがとても上手だ_{じょうず}
とおもいますね。

　　　　　　A:　ええ、私もそうおもいます。

Activity 4

Work with the class. Think of a famous person or cartoon figure, and write out a description, including your opinion of the person or character. After reading your description to the class, have them guess who it is.

Example:　A:　この人は高いところが好きだとおもいます。そして、
スポーツが上手だ_{じょうず}とおもいます。あかいマスク (mask) を
していて、あかくてあおいスーツをきています。

　　　　　　B:　スパイダーマンですか。

　　　　　　A:　はい、そうです。

聞く練習
れんしゅう

上手な聞き方
じょうず　　　かた

Using one's background knowledge about a person

Besides visual cues, background knowledge about a person such as his/her age, sex, and occupation can help you to understand better what is being said or asked.

練習
れんしゅう

Look at the photo below. Then listen to each question and circle the letter of the answer you think is correct. The questions will be repeated.

1. a   b   c   d

2. a   b   c   d

3. a   b   c   d

私たちの家族　Our family
（かぞく）

テープを聞いて、家系図 (family tree) を書いて下さい。そして、「はい」
（かけいず）
か「いいえ」にまるをつけて下さい。(Then circle はい if a statement below
is true or いいえ if it is false.)

1. 中山あやかさんの家族
　　　　　　　　　　（かぞく）

　家系図
　（かけいず）

```
┌─────────────────────────────────────┐
│                                     │
│                                     │
│                                     │
│                                     │
│                                     │
└─────────────────────────────────────┘
```

はい　　　いいえ　　　　中山さんはお兄さんがいます。
　　　　　　　　　　　　　　　　（にい）
はい　　　いいえ　　　　中山さんの弟さんはせが高いです。
　　　　　　　　　　　　　　　（おとうと）
はい　　　いいえ　　　　中山さんのお母さんはびょういんに
　　　　　　　　　　　　　　　　　（かあ）
　　　　　　　　　　　　つとめています。
はい　　　いいえ　　　　中山さんのお姉さんは大学生です。
　　　　　　　　　　　　　　　　（ねえ）

2. 吉田けい子さんの家族
　　（よしだ）（こ）　　　（かぞく）

　家系図
　（かけいず）

```
┌─────────────────────────────────────┐
│                                     │
│                                     │
│                                     │
│                                     │
│                                     │
└─────────────────────────────────────┘
```

はい　　　いいえ　　　　けい子さんは兄弟がいます。
　　　　　　　　　　　（こ）　（きょうだい）
はい　　　いいえ　　　　けい子さんのお祖父さんは七十五さいです。
　　　　　　　　　　　（こ）　　（じい）
はい　　　いいえ　　　　けい子さんのお父さんはふとっています。
　　　　　　　　　　　（こ）　　（とう）

聞き上手 話し上手
じょうず　　　じょうず

上手な話し方
じょうず　　かた

Being modest about yourself and your family

As noted earlier in this chapter, the Japanese generally refrain from praising or bragging about their families. Again, if someone praises a family member, they usually deny the compliment or try to steer the conversation in another direction. For example, when someone says to a Japanese person that his mother is beautiful, he will say something like *No, she isn't.* or *Do you really think so?* This is not an attempt to milk the compliment, and may seem strange to people from cultures where praise is received in a straightforward manner. In Japan, however, it is best to observe this protocol. If you receive a compliment in Japanese, try using the following standard replies:

いいえ、そんなことありません／ないですよ。
No, that isn't the case.

いいえ、まだまだです。
No, I still have a long way to go.

練習
れんしゅう

Work with a partner. Respond to each compliment appropriately. Ask your instructor to check your manner of delivery.

1. ～さんは日本語が上手ですね。
じょうず
2. ～さんのお母さんはとてもきれいな方ですね。
かあ　　　　　　　　　　　　かた
3. ～さんはあたまがいいですね。
4. ～さんは足がながくて、かっこいいですね。
あし
5. ～さんのおじいさんはりっぱな方ですね。
かた
6. ～さんの家は大きくてりっぱですね。
うち

漢字
かんじ

Kanji derived from pictures (3)

(Rice field and an strong arm came to mean *male*.)

(女, "female" with breasts came to mean *mother*.)

(An axe and a strong hand → *man* → *father*)

(A person with a big head → *bigger brother*)

(A pig under a roof. → *house*. Pigs were important livestock.)

男 男	male, man			
	おとこ　ダン	女の人と男の子がいます。 おんな　　おとこ　こ		
女 女	female, woman	∠ 女 女		
	おんな　ジョ	山本さんは帽子をかぶった女の人です。 ぼうし　　　　おんな		
目 目	eye	｜ 冂 冃 月 目		
	め　モク	目がわるいです。　上から二番目です。 め　　　　　　　　　　　め		
口 口	mouth	｜ 冂 口		
	くち・ぐち　コウ	口が小さいです。　川口 くち　　　　　　　ぐち		

耳	耳	ear みみ　ジ	一	丁	干	下	甘	耳			
		私は耳があまりよくありません。									

足	足	foot, leg あし　ソク	丶	口	口	早	足	呈	足		
		ジョンはせが高くて、足がながいです。									

手	手	hand て　シュ	一	二	三	手					
		手がきれいですね。　テニスが上手です。									

父	父	father ちち・とう	丶	八	分	父					
		父のなまえはジョンです。　お父さん									

母	母	mother はは　・　かあ	く	口	口	口	母				
		母のしごとは高校の先生です。　お母さん									

姉	姉	older sister あね・ねえ　シ	く	夕	女	女	女	妒	姉	姉	
		姉は私より三さい上です。　お姉さん									

兄	兄	older brother あに・にい　ケイ　キョウ	丶	口	口	尸	兄				
		兄が一人います。　お兄さん　兄弟									

妹	妹	younger sister いもうと　マイ	く	夕	女	女	好	奸	妹	妹	
		妹はいません。									

弟	弟	younger brother おとうと　ダイ	丶	丷	兰	兰	兰	弟	弟		
		弟は四時にアルバイトに行きます。　兄弟									

家	家	house いえ・（うち）　カ	丶	宀	宀	宁	宇	宋	家	家	家
		父は七時ごろ家に帰ります。　新しい家									

族	族	tribe ゾク	一	亠	方	方	扩	扩	斿	斿	族
		私の家は四人家族です。									

両	両	both リョウ	一	冂	冂	两	両	両			
		両親はニューヨークにすんでいます。									

| 親 親 | parent おや　シン | 両親はアメリカが好きです。　親切な人 りょうしん　　　　　　　　　　しんせつ | 亠 宀 立 辛 亲 亲 剎 親 親 |
| 子 子 | child こ　　シ | 男の子が三人います。　母のなまえは「よし子」です。 おとこ こ さんにん　　　　　　はは　　　　　　　こ | 了 了 子 |

読めるようになった漢字
　　　　　　かん じ

男の人　男の子　女の人　女の子　目　～番目　口　耳　足　手
　　　　　　　　　　　　　　　　　　　め

上手　父　お父さん　お祖父さん　祖父　母　お母さん　お祖母さん
じょうず　　　　　　　　　じ い ふ　　そ ふ　　　　　　　　　　　ば あ

祖母　姉　お姉さん　兄　お兄さん　妹　弟　兄弟　家族　私の家
そ ぼ

両親　親切　子供　お子さん　一人っ子　帽子　いい方　一人　二人
　　　しんせつ　ども　　　　　　ひとり こ　ぼうし　　　かた　ひとり　ふたり

三人　何人　ご主人　会社員　真ん中　四角い　小学生　小学校
にん　にん　しゅじん　かいしゃいん　ま なか　しかく　　しょう　　　　しょう

日本人のなまえ：家本　小山　田口　山口　三上　吉田
　　　　　　　　　いえもと　こやま　たぐち　やまぐち　みかみ　よしだ

練習
れんしゅう

Read the following sentences written in a mixture of **hiragana, katakana,** and **kanji.**

1. 父は先週の月曜日に川につりに行きました。弟はえいがを見に行きました。私と母は家にいました。

2. 中山さんのお父さんはせが高くて、目が大きいですね。

3. 妹は小学生で、弟は中学一年生です。

4. 高田：「ご兄弟は何人いますか。」

   川口：「三人います。」

5. めがねをかけている女の人が山田さんのお姉さんで、スーツをきている人がお兄さんです。

6. 山本：「川口さんは何人家族ですか。」

   川口：「両親と弟の四人家族です。」

7. 田中さんのお子さんは目が大きくて、口が小さくて、とてもかわいいいですよ。

8. 本田さんの親子はよくにていますね。(にている = *resemble*)

9. 　A：「あの男の人は手と足がながくて、スタイルがいいですねえ。」

   　B：「そうですか。あの人は、私の兄なんですよ。」

10. 父はこのごろ耳がとおくなりました。(耳がとおい = *hard of hearing*)

読む練習
れんしゅう

Creating charts and figures

People usually read with a specific purpose in mind, such as to gather specific information or to skim for the main ideas. When reading an assignment, you might jot down only the information that you need. If you organize your notes systematically, you may understand the assignment better and retain the information longer. One way to organize material is to make charts or tables.

練習
れんしゅう

A. Review the dialogue on pages b-146–b-147 and complete the following table.

上田さんの家族	なまえ	しごと	Physical appearance

B. Now read the following passage. It was written by Ms. Ueda, but some of the information is different from what the dialogue contains on pages b-146–b-147. Circle the discrepancies or write them on a separate piece of paper. Don't worry about any unfamiliar words or **kanji** you may encounter.

上田さんの家族

私の家族は五人家族です。父は四十五歳の会社員で、銀行に勤めています。父は目があまりよくないので、たいていめがねをかけています。ゴルフが大好きで、日曜日にはよくゴルフに行きます。母は四十三歳で、大学で英語を教えています。背があまり高くないので、たいていハイヒールの靴を履いています。母はとても優しくて明るい人です。弟のトムは十三歳で、中学生です。背が高くて、目がとても大きいです。スポーツは好きなんですが、勉強がきらいなので、こまります。そして、妹の名前はパムです。パムは背が高くありませんが、とてもかわいいです。頭がよくて、勉強もスポーツも大好きな高校一年生です。

C. Underline all the sentence and clause connectors in the above passage.

D. Describe your ideal family (りそうの家族). Use the following questions as cues.

1. 何人家族がいいですか。

2. 子供は何人がいいですか。

3. どんな子供がいいですか。

4. お父さんとお母さんはどんな人ですか。

5. どんなところにすみたいですか。

6. お父さんは／お母さんはどんなしごとをしますか。

総合練習
そうごうれんしゅう

Work with the class. Your instructor will give you a card similar to the one in the example below. It will have a description of two people, A and B. You are A. You are looking for B. Go around the class and ask your classmates questions using B's description. After you find B, check his/her identity card against yours.

Example:

Features	A Your identity	B The person you are looking for
かみ	ながい	くろい
目	あおい	みどり
すんでいる	とうきょう	ニューヨーク
上手	日本語	英語 えい

A: その人はかみがくろいですか。

B: はい、くろいです。

A: その人は目があおいですか。

B: いいえ、あおくありません。

A: そうですか。それじゃあ、また。

(Go to a different person.)

ロールプレイ

1. You are introducing a member of your family to your instructor. Your instructor will praise the person. Respond appropriately.
2. You are looking for a new roommate. Tell your partner what type of person you are looking for and ask for help.

Chapter 11

第十一課(だいじゅういっか)

きせつと天気(てんき)
Seasons and Weather

Objectives	Describing the weather
Vocabulary	Weather, climate, temperature, compass directions
Dialogue	寒(さむ)いですね。 *It's cold.*
Japanese Culture	Japan's climate
Grammar	I. Expressing ongoing and repeated actions using the て- form of verbs + いる
	II. Plain past forms and casual speech
	III. Describing characteristics of places, objects, and time using 〜は 〜が
	IV. Expressing manner of action or outcome of a change using the adverbial forms of adjectives and noun + に
	V. Expressing uncertainty using 〜でしょう, 〜かもしれない, and 〜かな
Listening	Understanding the organization of prepared speech
Communication	Expressing agreement and solidarity using ね and も
Kanji	Component shapes of **kanji** 1—Introduction
	天 気 雨 雪 風 晴 温 度 東 西 南 北 寒 暑 多 少 冷
Reading	Getting used to vertical writing

単語
たん

Nouns

あき	秋	fall, autumn
あめ	雨	rain
かぜ	風	wind
きおん	気温	air temperature
きこう	気候	climate
きせつ	季節	season
きた	北	north
きょねん	去年	last year
くも	雲	cloud
くもり	曇り	cloudy
けさ	今朝	this morning
ことし	今年	this year
さいきん	最近	recent, recently
たいふう	台風	typhoon
つゆ	梅雨	rainy season
てんき	天気	weather
てんきよほう	天気予報	weather forecast
なつ	夏	summer
なんせい	南西	southwest
なんとう	南東	southeast
にし	西	west
にわかあめ	にわか雨	shower (rain)
のち	後	after
はる	春	spring
はれ	晴れ	sunny weather
ひがし	東	east

ふゆ	冬	winter
ほう	方	direction
ほくせい	北西	northwest
ほくとう	北東	northeast
マイナス		minus
みなみ	南	south
ゆうがた	夕方	evening
ゆき	雪	snow
よる	夜	night

う -verbs

あがる	上がる	to rise, to go up
くもる	曇る	to become cloudy
さがる	下がる	to fall, to go down
しる	知る	to come to know　しっている to know しらない　don't know
つづく	続く	to continue
ふく	吹く	to blow
ふる	降る	to fall

る -verbs

| はれる | 晴れる | to become sunny |

い -adjectives

あたたかい	暖かい／温かい	warm　暖かい (air temperature)　温かい (other objects such as water, food, heart, etc.)
あつい	暑い／熱い	hot　暑い (air temperature) 熱い (other objects such as water, food, heart, etc.)
さむい	寒い	cold
すずしい	涼しい	cool
つよい	強い	strong
はやい	早い	early

よわい	弱い	weak
むしあつい	蒸し暑い	humid
わるい	悪い	bad

な -adjectives

きゅう（な）	急（な）	sudden， きゅうに suddenly
いや（な）	嫌（な）	unpleasant, yuck

Suffixes

〜ど	〜度	degree, temperature
〜がつ	〜月	month

Expressions

〜のち〜	after, あめのちはれ　sunny after rain
ほんとう（に）/ ほんと（に）本当（に）	truly, really, indeed
	ほんと（に）　is more conversational than ほんとう（に）

単語の練習
たん　　　れんしゅう

A. 天気予報　Weather forecast
てんきよほう

晴れ
は
sunny

くもり
cloudy

雨
あめ
rain, rainy

雪
ゆき
snow, snowy

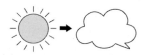

晴れのちくもり
は
sunny then cloudy

くもり時々雨
ときどきあめ
cloudy with occasional rain

Activity 1

Write the readings of the following weather symbols.

1	2	3	4
5	6	7	8
9	10	11	12
13	14	15	16
17	18	19	20
21	22	23	24

Supplementary Vocabulary: Nouns to indicate regions

たいへいようがわ	太平洋側	Pacific ocean side (east side) of Japan
にほんかいがわ	日本海側	Sea of Japan side (west side) of Japan
さんがくぶ	山岳部	mountain area (in any country)
にしかいがん	西海岸	West coast region (USA)
ちゅうせいぶ	中西部	Midwest region (USA)
なんぶ	南部	South region (USA)
なんせいぶ	南西部	Southwest region (USA)
ひがしかいがん	東海岸	East coast region (USA)

Supplementary Vocabulary: Nouns expressing weather

おんど	温度	temperature
かし	華氏	Fahrenheit
きあつ	気圧	air pressure
こうすいりょう	降水量	amount of precipitation
さいこうきおん	最高気温	highest temperature
さいていきおん	最低気温	lowest temperature
しつど	湿度	humidity
せっし	摂氏	Celsius
てんきず	天気図	weather map

B. 天気　Weather
てんき

暑い　あつ	hot	晴れる　は	to clear up
寒い　さむ	cold	くもる	to become cloudy
すずしい	cool	風がふく　かぜ	wind blows
あたたかい	warm	雨がふる　あめ	to rain
むし暑い　あつ	humid	雪がふる　ゆき	to snow
天気がいい　てんき	good weather	にわか雨がふる　あめ	sudden showers
天気がわるい　てんき	bad weather	台風が来る　たいふう	a typhoon comes
くもが多い　おお	cloudy	梅雨になる　つゆ	the rainy season comes
風がつよい　かぜ	strong winds	大雨がふる　おおあめ	heavy rain falls
風がよわい　かぜ	mild winds	大雪がつづく　おおゆき	heavy snow continues

おぼえていますか。

多い　おお	少ない　すく	少し　すこ	冷たい　つめ

NOTES

- Both 寒い and 冷たい mean *cold*, but 寒い refers to cold temperatures, as in 今日は寒い (*It is cold today*). On the other hand, 冷たい refers to objects that are cold, e.g., 水が冷たい, 風が冷たい.

- 梅雨 refers to the rainy season particular to Japan. It usually starts in early June and ends in mid-July.

Supplementary Vocabulary: 天気の言葉

あらし	嵐	storm
あられ		hail
いなびかり	稲光り	lightening
かみなり	雷	thunder
きり	霧	fog
こうずい	洪水	flood
こさめ	小雨	light rain
たつまき	竜巻	tornado
つなみ	津波	tidal wave, tsunami
どしゃぶり	どしゃ降り	downpour
ハリケーン		hurricane
ひでり	日照り	drought
ふぶき	吹雪	snowstorm
みぞれ		sleet
ゆうだち	夕立ち	evening shower

Activity 2

Imagine that the following chart shows tomorrow's weather in some of the major cities in the world. そして、下のしつもんに日本語でこたえて下さい。

Example: 明日、カイロの天気はいいですか。
　　　　ええ、明日は晴れますよ。

まち	東京	ニューヨーク	モスクワ	シドニー	カイロ
天気		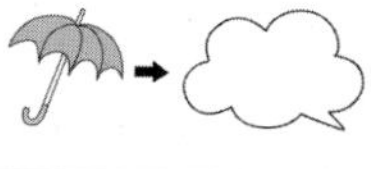		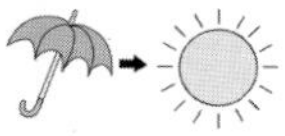	
気温	61.9/48.9° F 16.6/9.4° C	49.8/39.0° F 9.9/3.9° C	34.7/26° F 1.5/-3.3° C	75.2/58.1° F 24/14.5° C	98.2/60.3° F 36.8/15.7° C
風	SSW 5 mph	NE 20 mph	NE 15 mph	SE 10 mph	E 3 mph

1. 明日、モスクワは天気がいいですか。
2. 東京は明日晴れますか。ニューヨークはどうですか。
3. 明日、どこで雨がふりますか。
4. シドニーとカイロとどちらの方が暑いですか。
5. ニューヨークと東京とどちらの方が寒いですか。
6. どこがあたたかいですか。
7. どこがすずしいですか。
8. 明日、東京は風がつよいですか。ニューヨークはどうですか。
9. カイロは風がつよいですか。よわいですか。
10. モスクワではつよい風がふきますか。

Activity 3

Select the item that describes recent weather in your area.

1. 寒い／すずしい／あたたかい／暑い／むし暑い
2. 天気がいい／天気がよくない
3. いやな天気がつづく／いやな天気がつづかない
4. 雨がぜんぜんふらない／雨があまりふらない／雨が時々ふる
5. 雨がよくふる／毎日雨がふる
6. にわか雨が多い／にわか雨が少ない
7. 雪がぜんぜんふらない／雪があまりふらない／雪が時々ふる
8. 雪がよくふる／毎日雪がふる
9. 大雪になる／大雪にはならない
10. よく風がふく／あまり風がふかない
11. 風がつよい／風がよわい

Activity 4

Describe the recent weather in your area using your answers from Activity 2. It is unnecessary to use all of your responses, but make sure that your description is cohesive.

Example: このへんは、さいきん天気がよくて、むし暑いです。雨はぜんぜんふりません。そして、風もあまりありません。

C. きせつ Seasons

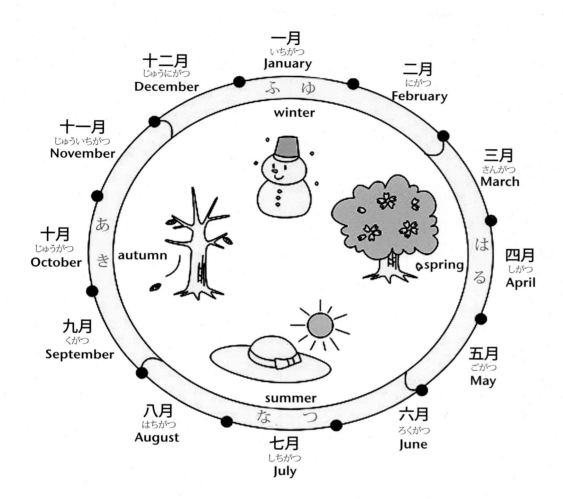

> ⬡ **Activity 5**

Complete the following statements about Japanese seasons.

Example: 日本では、__六月__に梅雨がはじまって、__七月__におわります。
　　　　　　　　　　　つ ゆ

1. 日本では＿＿＿＿＿＿＿＿＿にはるがはじまって、＿＿＿＿＿＿＿＿＿におわります。

2. 日本では＿＿＿＿＿＿＿＿＿になつがはじまって、＿＿＿＿＿＿＿＿＿におわります。

3. 日本では＿＿＿＿＿＿＿＿＿にあきがはじまって、＿＿＿＿＿＿＿＿＿におわります。

4. 日本では＿＿＿＿＿＿＿＿＿にふゆがはじまって、＿＿＿＿＿＿＿＿＿におわります。

5. このへんは＿＿＿＿＿＿＿＿＿にはるがはじまって、＿＿＿＿＿＿＿におわります。

6. このへんは＿＿＿＿＿＿＿＿＿になつがはじまって、＿＿＿＿＿＿＿におわります。

7. このへんは＿＿＿＿＿＿＿＿＿にあきがはじまって、＿＿＿＿＿＿＿におわります。

8. このへんは＿＿＿＿＿＿＿＿＿にふゆがはじまって、＿＿＿＿＿＿＿におわります。

> **Activity 6**

For each season, write five things that describe where you live.

Example: このへんは　ふゆに雪がたくさんふります。
_{ゆき}

はる	
なつ	
あき	
ふゆ	

D. 気温　Air temperature
_{き おん}

気温が下がる　　air temperature falls
_{き おん　さ}

気温が上がる　　air temperature rises
_{き おん　　あ}

何度	なんど
−１度	マイナスいちど
０度	れいど
１度	いちど
２度	にど
３度	さんど
４度	よんど
５度	ごど
６度	ろくど
７度	ななど、しちど
８度	はちど
９度	きゅうど、くど
１０度	じゅうど

Japan uses the Celsius scale for temperature, and the metric system for other measurements. The following table shows equivalent temperatures for Celsius and Fahrenheit.

せっし (Celsius)	かし (Fahrenheit)
０℃	３２℉
１０℃	５０℉
２０℃	６８℉
３０℃	８６℉
４０℃	１０４℉

Activity 7

しつもんに日本語でこたえて下さい。

1. 今の気温は何度ぐらいですか。
　　（き　おん）　　　（ど）

2. 今朝の気温は何度ぐらいでしたか。
　　（けさ）（き　おん）　（ど）

3. あさから何度ぐらい気温が上がりましたか。
　　　　　　（ど）　　　（き　おん）（あ）

4. 今晩、何度ぐらいまで気温が下がるとおもいますか。
　　（ばん）　（ど）　　　（き　おん）（さ）

5. 寒い日は何度ぐらいまで気温が下がりますか。
　（さむ）（ど）　　　　　（き　おん）（さ）

6. 暑い日は何度ぐらいまで気温が上がりますか。
　（あつ）（ど）　　　　　（き　おん）（あ）

7. せっし (Celsius) 0 度はかし (Fahrenheit) 何度ですか。
　　　　　　　　　　（ど）　　　　　　　　　　　（ど）

8. かし (Fahrenheit) 0 度はせっし (Celsius) 何度ですか。
　　　　　　　　　　（ど）　　　　　　　　　　（ど）

Activity 8

Using your answers from Activity 5, give a short description of your town in its four seasons.

E.　方角　Compass directions
　　（ほうがく）

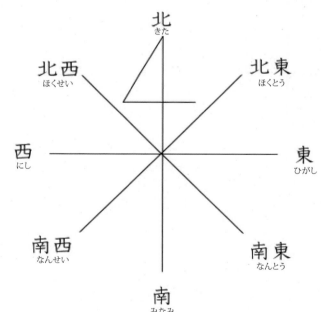

〜の方　　toward 〜
　（ほう）

北の方　　to the north
（きた）（ほう）

Activity 9

Write the appropriate direction word in each blank.

Example:　オーストラリアは日本の＿＿南＿＿にあります。
　　　　　　　　　　　　　　（みなみ）

1. カナダはアメリカの＿＿＿＿＿にあります。

2. 日本はかんこくの＿＿＿＿＿にあります。

3. メキシコはアメリカの＿＿＿＿＿にあります。

4. フランスはスペインの＿＿＿＿＿にあって、ドイツの＿＿＿＿にあります。

5. 中国はかんこくの＿＿＿＿＿にあります。
　　　（ごく）

Activity 10

えを見て、しつもんに日本語でこたえて下さい。

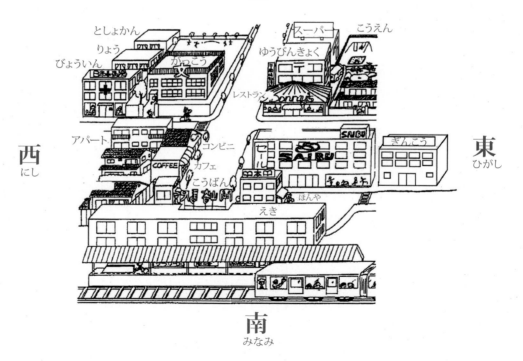

1. このまちの北の方には何がありますか。南の方には何がありますか。
　　　　　　（きた）（ほう）　　　　　　　　　（みなみ）（ほう）

2. 学校はどこにありますか。

3. 学校の東の方に何がありますか。西の方に何がありますか。
　　　　（ひがし）（ほう）　　　　　（にし）（ほう）

4. こうえんはどこにありますか。

5. 図書館はどこにありますか。
　　　（と）（かん）

6. えきの北には何がありますか。
　　　　　（きた）

ダイアローグ

はじめに

しつもんに日本語でこたえて下さい。

1. 今日のお天気はどうですか。

2. ふゆの寒い日の気温は何度ぐらいですか。

3. ふゆのあたたかい日の気温は何度ぐらいですか。

寒いですね。　*It's cold.*

鈴木道子さんは石田さんにきょうしつで会いました。

鈴木：　あ、石田さん。おはよう。

石田：　あ。鈴木さん。寒いね。

鈴木：　ええ、今日は風がつよいから。

石田：　たしかに、今晩は雪かな。

鈴木：　そうね。くもってるから、ふるかもしれないね。

石田：　でも、まだ十一月だよ。

鈴木：　そうね。今年はいつもよりはやく寒くなりそうね。ざんねんだけど。

石田：　いやだなあ。

先生がきょうしつにいらっしゃいました。
(*The professor has come to the classroom.*)

鈴木：　あ、先生。おはようございます。

先生：　あ、鈴木さん、石田くん。おはよう。寒いね。

石田：　ええ、それにくもっていますね。

先生：　そうだね。雪がふりそうな天気だね。

鈴木さんはまどのそとを見ました。雪がふっています。

鈴木：　あ、先生、雪がふっていますよ。

先生：　本当だね。みんな風邪ひかないように気をつけるんだよ。

DIALOGUE PHRASE NOTES

- たしかに means *certainly*.
- いつもより means ~ *than usual*.
- いやだなあ means *unpleasant*.
- みんな風邪ひかないように気をつける means *Everybody, take care so that you don't catch cold.* 風邪 means *cold*. Note that the **kanji** is different from 風, *wind*.

ダイアローグの後で

1. The following manga frames are scrambled—they are not in the order described in the dialogue. Read the dialogue and unscramble the frames by writing their correct order in the box located in the upper right corner of each frame.

2. しつもんに日本語でこたえて下さい。

   1. 今、何月ですか。時間はいつごろですか。

   2. 今どんな天気ですか。
       _{てんき}

   3. 天気予報によると今日の天気はどうですか。
       てんきよほう　　　　　　　　　　てんき

   4. 石田さんはふゆが好きだとおもいますか。
      いし

3. Work with a partner. The following conversation is a simplified version of the dialogue. You meet each other in the classroom in the morning. Decide on a season and the weather, and complete the following conversation using appropriate phrases.

    A: あ、_____さん。おはよう。

    B: あ、_____さん。今日は_____ね。

    A: ええ、_____ね。

    B: _____かもしれないね。

    A: そうだね。

日本の文化
ぶんか

気候　Climate
きこう

Japan lies in the temperate zone and has four distinct seasons. The climate is predominantly temperate, but it varies from subarctic to subtropical because

the country extends so far from north to south. Southeast winds blow across Japan from the Pacific in summer, bringing humidity to the Pacific side of the country (たいへいようがわ). The northwest winds blow across from continental Asia in winter, bringing sunny and dry weather to the Pacific Ocean side but heavy snow to the Japan Sea side (日本海側).
にほんかいがわ

　　Between June and July, there is a period of predominantly rainy weather, called tsuyu (梅雨), in all parts of
つゆ
Japan except 北海道. Typhoons (台風) occur most frequently from August
ほっかいどう　　　　　　　たいふう
through October.

　　Japan's climate is further divided into six principal zones because of its geographical features. On the northernmost island, 北海道,
ほっかいどう
spring and summer are short, and it is cool with little rain throughout the year. Although precipitation is not heavy, winters are severe with deep snow banks from November through April.

The Japan Sea side of the northern main island, such as 北陸 region and the east coast of
ほくりく
東北, experiences heavy snowfall in the winter,
とうほく
but it is cooler than the Pacific Ocean side in

the summer. The Pacific Ocean side, such as 関東, 東海, and きんき, is
generally sunny, cold, and dry in winter, but the summer is hot and humid.

Temperatures in the central highland region, 中部, range widely between
summer and winter, and between day and night, although precipitation is
generally light.

Southwestern regions such as 四国, 中国 and 九州 tend to have mild
weather throughout the year, especially in せとないかい (Seto-Inland Ocean)
area, the area surrounded by these three regions.

The southern islands, おきなわ and いしがきじま, have a subtropical
climate and are known for high temperatures and precipitation throughout the
year. The rainfall is heavy during 梅雨, and 台風 are very common.

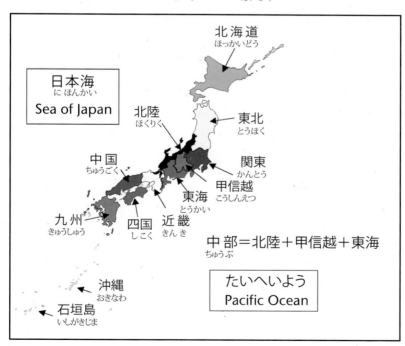

文法
ぶんぽう

> ## I.   Expressing ongoing and repeated actions using the て - form of verbs + いる

In Chapter 10, you learned the verb て- form + いる, which expresses resultant state. This interpretation is common for verbs used to express wearing clothes or accessories.

田中さんはめがねをかけている。	*Mr. Tanaka has glasses on.*
田中さんはネクタイをしている。	*Mr. Tanaka has a tie on.*

Also, if the verb indicates an instantaneous change of state or transfer (e.g., 行く, けっこんする), then the verb て-form + いる will express a resultant state.

田中さんはけっこんしている。	*Mr. Tanaka is married.*
田中さんは高校につとめている。	*Mr. Tanaka works for a high school.*
田中さんは学校に行っている。	*Mr. Tanaka has gone to school and is there.*
田中さんはここに来ている。	*Mr. Tanaka has come here and is here now.*
田中さんはその人をしっている。	*Mr. Tanaka knows that person.*
今日は晴れている。	*It is sunny today.*
くもっている。	*It is cloudy.*

In the above example, the て-form of the verb しる (*to come to know*), しっている (*to know*), expresses the result of one's discovery of information.

In addition to this usage, the verb て-form + いる can express ongoing action and repeated action. This chapter introduces these two usages of the verb て-form + いる.

A. Ongoing action

The verb て-form + いる can express ongoing action when used with certain action verbs. The verbs indicate activities that take place for a period of time. For example, the act of eating, drinking, raining, etc., can take place for a long time.

石田さんはおすしを<u>食べている</u>。	*Mr. Ishida is eating sushi.*
石田さんはおちゃを<u>飲んでいる</u>。	*Mr. Ishida is drinking tea.*
石田さんは本を<u>読んでいる</u>。	*Mr. Ishida is reading.*
雨が<u>ふっている</u>。	*It is raining.*
風が<u>ふいている</u>。	*The wind is blowing.*

The verb て-form + いる is often contracted to the verb て-form + る in conversation (in both formal and casual styles).

ドレスを<u>きています</u>。　　　ドレスを<u>きてます</u>。
けっこん<u>しています</u>。　　　けっこん<u>してます</u>。
しゅくだいを<u>しています</u>。　しゅくだいを<u>してます</u>。
さとみさんを<u>しっている</u>。　さとみさん、<u>しってる</u>。
ごはんを<u>食べている</u>。　　　ごはん、<u>食べてる</u>。

かおり：何、しているの。　　　　*What are you doing?*

まさお：しゅくだい、してるんだ。　*I am doing homework.*

リン：どうしたんですか。
　　　What's wrong?

鈴木：雨がふっているんですが、かさがないんです。
すず　*It's raining but I don't have an umbrella.*

リン：そうですか。じゃあ、私のくるまで行きませんか。
　　　I see. Well, why don't we take my car?

鈴木：いいんですか。
すず　*Is that okay?*

リン：ええ、どうぞ。
　　　Yeah, sure.

B. Repeated action

Many verbs, including action verbs or change-of-state verbs, can be used to express habitual action with the verb て-form + いる.

鈴木さんはよくあかいジャケットをきている。
すず
Ms. Suzuki often wears a red jacket.

田中さんは時々バスでびょういんへ行っています。
　　　ときどき
Mr. Tanaka sometimes goes to hospital by bus.

毎週土曜日にテニスをしています。
I play tennis every Saturday.

健一：　ブラウンさんはよくサングラスをかけているけど、どうして？
けん　　*Ms. Brown often wears sunglasses, but why?*

道子：　サラは目がよわいからよ。
みち　　*Because Sarah has weak eyes.*

健一：　そうなんだ。
けん　　*Oh, I see.*

話してみましょう

Activity 1

Make sentences from the following expressions using the verb て -form + いる.
Then say whether the sentence indicates an ongoing action or a resultant state.

Example: ごはんを食べる

ごはんを食べています。   Ongoing action

1. 雪がふる
   ゆき
2. くもる
3. 気温が下がる
   き おん さ
4. 本を読む

5. 家に帰る
6. つよい風がふく
   かぜ
7. 手紙を書く
   て がみ
8. 気温が三十度まで上がる。
   き おん   ど   あ

Activity 2

Work with a partner. Your partner will write a name for each person in the
picture. Ask your partner who is who by describing what the people are doing.

Example: A: コーヒーを飲んでいる人はだれですか。

B: スミスさんです。

Activity 3

Work with a partner. Think of five actions, then act them out and have your partner guess what you are doing by asking questions using 〜ている.

Example:　You act as though you are drinking coffee.

　　　　　A: おちゃを飲んでいるんですか。

　　　　　B: いいえ。

　　　　　A: コーヒーを飲んでいるんですか。

　　　　　B: はい。

Activity 4

Work as a class. Ask your classmates what kinds of things they practiced or learned recently for fun or personal improvement.

Example:　A: さいきん、どんなことをよくしていますか。

　　　　　B: テニスをよくしています。

なまえ	さいきんよくしていること

II.   Plain past forms and casual speech

The plain forms are used in a variety of structures and contexts in Japanese. For example, they are used in the structure ので (*because*) in Chapter 7, ～んです in Chapter 8, から and けど in Chapter 9, and とおもう and noun modification in Chapter 10. So far the plain present forms have been used with these structures, but the plain past forms can be used with all of them. This chapter introduces the plain past forms of verbs and adjectives. It also introduces another usage of the plain form, namely casual and self-directed speech.

Plain past forms

1. Plain past affirmative form

The plain past affirmative form of the verbs is formed by taking the て-form of a verb and replacing it with た (or だ).

Verb types	Dictionary form	て -form	Plain past affirmative form
う -verb	つづく (to continue)	つづいて	つづいた (continued)
	読む (to read)	読んで	読んだ (read)
る -verb	晴れる (to become sunny)	晴れて	晴れた (became sunny)
	食べる (to eat)	食べて	食べた (ate)
Irregular verb	する (to do)	して	した (did)
	来る (to come)	来て	来た (came)

The plain past affirmative form of い-adjectives is formed by deleting です from the polite past affirmative form.

Dictionary form	Polite past affirmative form	Plain past affirmative form
暑い (hot)	暑かったです	暑かった (was hot)
いい (good)	よかったです	よかった (was good)

The plain past affirmative form of な-adjective and the copula verb is formed by adding った to the plain present affirmative form.

	Dictionary form	Polite past affirmative form	Plain past affirmative form
な -adjective	好き (like)	好きだ	好きだった (liked)
	元気 (healthy)	元気だ	元気だった (was healthy)
Noun + copula	台風 (typhoon)	台風だ	台風だった (was typhoon)
	くも (cloud)	くもだ	くもだった (was a cloud)

2. Plain past negative form

The plain past negative form of the verbs and adjectives of all types is formed by replacing the plain present negative ending ない with なかった.

	Dictionary form	Plain present negative form	Plain past negative form
う -verb	行く (to go)	行か<u>ない</u>	行か<u>なかった</u> (didn't go)
	飲む (to drink)	飲ま<u>ない</u>	飲ま<u>なかった</u> (didn't drink)
	ある (to exist)	<u>ない</u>	<u>なかった</u> (didn't exist)
る -verb	起きる (to get up)	起き<u>ない</u>	起き<u>なかった</u> (didn't get up)
	食べる (to eat)	食べ<u>ない</u>	食べ<u>なかった</u> (didn't eat)
Irregular verb	する (to do)	し<u>ない</u>	し<u>なかった</u> (didn't do)
	来る (to come)	来<u>ない</u>	来<u>なかった</u> (didn't come)
い -adjective	わるい (bad)	わるく<u>ない</u>	わるく<u>なかった</u> (wasn't bad)
	いい (good)	<u>よくない</u>	<u>よくなかった</u> (wasn't good)
な -adjective	元気 (healthy)	元気じゃ<u>ない</u>	元気じゃ<u>なかった</u> (wasn't healthy)
	きれい (pretty)	きれいじゃ<u>ない</u>	きれいじゃ<u>なかった</u> (wasn't pretty)
Noun + Copula	雪 (snow)	雪じゃ<u>ない</u>	雪じゃ<u>なかった</u> (wasn't snow)
	南 (south)	南じゃ<u>ない</u>	南じゃ<u>なかった</u> (wasn't south)

梅雨が<u>ながかったので</u>、今年のなつはむし暑いとおもいます。
Because the rainy season was long, I think this summer will be humid.

いい天気が<u>つづかなかったので</u>、ざんねんでした。
I was disappointed because the nice weather did not last long.

風が<u>冷たかったから</u>、ジャケットをきました。
I put on a jacket because the wind was cold.

元気が<u>よくなかったから</u>、家にいました。
I stayed home because the weather was not good.

お母さんは<u>親切だったけど</u>、お父さんはあまり話しませんでした。
The mother was kind but the father did not talk much.

そのアパートは<u>きれいじゃなかったけど</u>、安かったです。
The apartment was not very clean but cheap.

<u>元気そうだったけど</u>、本当は病気でした。
He looked healthy, but he was actually sick.

去年の三月は<u>あたたかかったとおもいます</u>。
I think last March was warm.

図書館はまちの北の方に<u>あった</u>とおもいます。
<small>と かん</small>　<small>きた ほう</small>
I think the library is on the north side of the town.

今年の梅雨はあまり<u>ながくなかった</u>んです。
<small>こ とし</small>　<small>つ ゆ</small>
This year's rainy season was not very long.

あれは台風<u>じゃなかった</u>んです。
<small>たいふう</small>
That was not a typhoon.

昨日<u>ふった</u>大雪ででんしゃがストップしました。
<small>きのう</small>　<small>おおゆき</small>
The train stopped because of the heavy snow that fell yesterday.

日本へ<u>帰った</u>友達にメールを書きました。
<small>だち</small>
I wrote a letter to a friend who went back to Japan.

Plain forms in casual conversation

Plain forms are used in conversations among close friends and family members, because the plain forms indicate closeness, intimacy, and carefree attitudes. On the other hand, です／ます indicates that the speaker is more aware of the listener's presence and intends to maintain a proper social distance.

　The use of plain and polite forms is not always determined by the degree of formality. For example, in relatively casual situations such as a home party and going out after work, a person may use です／ます toward someone who holds a higher social status or someone who is much older, in order to show respect. In this situation, です／ます signals that the speaker is aware of the social difference and does not consider his/her interlocutor a true equal. Conversely, the social superior may use the plain form toward the junior interlocutor in order to show close carefree attitudes. Also, it is very common for two people of the same age group who meet for the first time to start conversation in です／ます forms but switch to plain forms as the conversation progresses. In other words, the choice between です／ます and the plain form depends on the speaker's perception about his/her social relationship with his/ her interlocutor. For this reason, it is common for a teacher to use the plain form to show familiarity to his/her students while the students use です／ます toward the teachers to show respect in the same conversational context.

> 子供：お母さん、かさ、いるよ。　*Mom, I need an umbrella.*
> <small>ども</small>
> お母さん：え、どうして？　　　　*Why?*
> 子供：雨、ふってるよ。　　　　*It's raining.*
> <small>ども</small>　<small>あめ</small>
> お母さん：ええっ！　　　　　　*Oh, really?*

In answering a yes-no question, use うん (the casual form of はい or ええ) or ううん (the casual form of いいえ).

Mr. Li and Ms. Ueda are friends:

リー：ねえ、上田さん、今日いそがしい？
　　Hey, Ms. Ueda, are you busy today?

上田：<u>ううん</u>、ひまだけど。
No, not really.

学生：先生、少し寒くありませんか。　*Professor, isn't it a bit cold here?*

先生：<u>うん</u>、ほんとに寒いね。　*Yeah, it's really cold.*

学生：ヒーター、入れましょうか。　*Shall I turn on the heater?*

先生：うん、そうして。　*Yes, please.*

NOTES

- The thematic particle は、the subject particle が, and the direct object particle を are not used in conversations often.

  今日、すずしいね。　*It's cool today.*

  あ、雪、ふってる。　*Gee, it's snowing.*

  雨、ふった。　*It rained.*

- In casual conversation, the question marker か is often omitted in questions. It usually has a rising intonation toward the end.

  リー：寒い？　*Are you cold?*

  上田：うん、ちょっと寒い。　*Yes, a little bit.*

  リー：これ、きる？　*Do you want to put this on?*

  上田：ありがとう。　*Thank you.*

- The copular verbs だ and だ in な- adjective are also deleted in questions. Deleting だ before particles like ね and よ makes the speech sound feminine.

  リー：大丈夫？　*Are you OK?*

  上田：うん、大丈夫（だ）よ。　*Yes, I am.*

  リー：あの人、学生？　*Is he a student?*

  上田：うん、学生（だ）よ。　*Yes, he is.*

- The plain form of んです is んだ or の. In questions の is usually used. In statements, both の and んだ can be used.

  上田：昨日どうしたの？　*What happened yesterday?*

  リー：あ、病気で寝てたんだ。　*I got sick and stayed in bed.*

- 〜てください is 〜て:

  リー：わるいけど、あれとって。　*Sorry, but can you take that?*

  上田：ああ、いいよ。　*Sure.*

話してみましょう

Activity 1

The following conversations take place between two acquaintances. Change the style so that the conversation takes place between close friends.

Example: A: 昨日はすずしかったですね。
　　　　　　 B: ええ。

　　　　　　 A: 昨日はすずしかったね。
　　　　　　 B: ええ／うん。

1. A: 先週の火曜日は休みでしたか。

　　B: いいえ、じゅぎょうはありましたよ。

2. A: 昨日は本当にあつかったですね。
　　B: ええ、気温が三十五度まで上がりましたからね。

3. A: 今朝、雨がふっていましたか。
　　B: いいえ、ふりませんでしたよ。昨日のばん、雪がふっていましたけど。

4. A: 去年のはるは寒い日がつづきましたけど、今年はあたたかい日が
　　　 多くていいですね。

　　B: そうですね。去年の三月と四月は気温がぜんぜん上がりません
　　　 でしたから、寒かったですね。

5. A: 昨日の台風は大きかったですね。

　　B: ええ、雨はあまり多くありませんでしたけど、風がとても
　　　 つよかったですね。

Activity 2

Work with a partner. One person restates the following questions using the plain form, and the other person responds to them using 〜とおもいます。

Example: 日本のなつをどうおもいますか。

A: 日本のなつ（を）どうおもう。

B: そう（だ）ね。アメリカよりむし暑いとおもう。

1. 今朝の気温は何度ぐらいでしたか。

2. 今日は気温が何度ぐらいまで上がりますか。

3. 昨日のばんは気温が何度ぐらいまで下がりましたか。

4. 昨日と今日とどちらの方があたたかいですか。

5. 昨日と一昨日とどちらの方があたたかかったですか。

Activity 3

Work with partner. Ask and answer questions using the sentences provided.

Example: 今までいろいろなえいがを見ましたが、〜が一番おもしろかったです。
（いろいろな = *various*）

A: 今まで見たえいがの中で何が一番おもしろかったですか。

B: 〜です。

1. 今までいろいろなところに行きましたが、〜が一番たのしかったです。

2. 今までいろいろなりょうりを食べましたが、〜が一番おいしかったです。

3. 今までいろいろな本を読みましたが、〜が一番おもしろかったです。

4. 今までいろいろな先生に会いましたが、〜先生が一番よかったです。

5. 今までいろいろなアルバイトをしましたが、〜が一番大変でした。

	パートナーのこたえ
一番たのしかったところ	
一番おいしかったりょうり	
一番おもしろかった本	
一番よかった先生	
一番大変だったアルバイト	

III. Describing characteristics of places, objects, and time using 〜は〜が

In addition to describing physical appearance, as you learned in Chapter 10, 〜は 〜が is used to describe other characteristics or to comment on things and concepts. The particle は indicates what the rest of the sentence is going to be about. You can interpret 〜は as *as for 〜*.

十二月は雨が少ない。	*We have little rain in December.*
あきは食べものがおいしい。	*Food tastes good in fall.*
ふゆは水が冷たい。	*Water is cold in winter.*
ハワイは気候がいい。	*Hawaii has a nice climate.*
東京はものが高い。	*Things are expensive in Tokyo.*
日本は山が多い。	*Japan is mountainous.*
まどは南の方がいい。	*The south (side) is good for a window.*
和食は天ぷらがおいしい。	*When it comes to Japanese food, tempura is good.*
山は富士山が一番だ。	*Mt. Fuji is No.1 of all mountains.*
ここは水がきれいだ。	*The water is clean here.*

リー：今日は風がつよいね。	*The wind is strong today.*
上田：ほんと。	*Indeed.*

山中：このへんはどのきせつがいいですか。
Which season is the best around here?

高山：はるが一番きれいですね。

Spring is the nicest.

話してみましょう

▶ **Activity 1**

しつもんに日本語でこたえて下さい。

Example:　アメリカはどのまちが一番好きですか。
　　　　　　ニューヨークが一番好きです。

1.　〜さんの大学は何がゆうめいですか。
2.　〜さんは何が上手ですか。
3.　〜さんのまちはどのきせつが一番いいですか。
4.　アメリカはどの大学が一番大きいですか。
5.　先生はどんな人がいいですか。
6.　日本語は何が大変ですか。むずかしいですか。

Activity 2

The following charts indicate average temperature or precipitation in various cities. Describe the climate in each city, using 〜は〜が . Find similarities among different cities.

Example: 東京は八月が暑いです。　　シンガポールは雨が多いです。
　　　　　とうきょう　　　あつ　　　　　　　　　　　　　あめ　おお

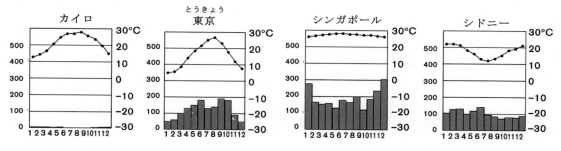

Activity 3

Work with a partner. Choose a town you like. One person will ask the following questions about his /her partner's favorite town and take notes. Then write a short description about the partner's favorite town using the 〜は〜 が forms. Speak casually.

Example:　A:　〜さん、どのまちが好き？

　　　　　B:　メルボルンが好きだね。

　　　　　A:　そう。メルボルンのどんなところが好きなの？

　　　　　B:　メルボルンはこうえんが多くてきれいだから。
　　　　　　　　　　　　　　　　　　おお

　　　　　A:　いいねえ。じゃあ、気候はどう？
　　　　　　　　　　　　　　　き こう

　　　　　B:　そう（だ）ね。なつは暑いけど、ふゆはあまり寒くないよ。
　　　　　　　　　　　　　　　　　あつ　　　　　　　　　　さむ

〜さんが好きなまちはメルボルンです。メルボルンはこうえんがたくさん
あって、きれいです。なつは暑いですが、ふゆは寒くありません。
　　　　　　　　　　　　　　あつ　　　　　　　　　さむ

1. 〜さんはどのまちが好きですか。

2. どうしてそのまちが好きなんですか。

3. そのまちの気候はどうですか。
　　　　　　き こう

4. そのまちはどのきせつがいいですか。どうしてですか。

5. そのまちは何がゆうめいですか。どこがおもしろいですか。

Activity 4

Work in groups of three or four. One person will select a city in the box without telling the rest of the group. The others will take turns asking questions about various characteristics of the city to find out which it is.

ニューヨーク	シカゴ	アンカレッジ
ホノルル	デンバー	ロサンゼルス
アテネ	ローマ	シドニー
東京 <small>とうきょう</small>	きょうと	ロンドン

Example: A: そのまちは古いたてものが多いですか。
<small>おお</small>

B: いいえ。

C: くるまや人が多いですか。
<small>おお</small>

B: ええ、多いです。
<small>おお</small>

D: そのまちは日本にありますか。

B: ええ。

C: 東京ですか。
<small>とうきょう</small>

B: はい、そうです。

IV. Expressing manner of action or outcome of a change using the adverbial forms of adjectives and noun + に

The く- form of い- adjectives and the に- form of な- adjectives modify verbs. They are called adverbial forms.

Adjective type	Dictionary form	Adverbial form
い -adjective	おもしろ<u>い</u>	おもしろ<u>く</u>
な -adjective	きれい	きれい<u>に</u>

The adverbial forms modify a verb indicating how an action takes place.

	元気に _{げんき}	あるいて下さい。	*Please walk cheerfully.*
かんじを	上手に	書いた。	*I wrote kanji skillfully (beautifully).*
雪が _{ゆき}	<u>しずかに</u>	ふっている。	*It is snowing quietly (softly).*
雨が _{あめ}	<u>きゅうに</u>	ふった。	*It rained suddenly.*
	<u>あかるく</u>	わらう。	*to smile brightly (cheerfully)*
今日は	<u>はやく</u>	起きた。	*I woke up early (or quickly).*
風が _{かぜ}	<u>やさしく</u>	ふいていた。	*The wind was blowing gently yesterday.*

They are also used to express change of state or outcome. The adverbial form + する means "to make something/someone into 〜," and the adverbial form + なる means "to become 〜."

子供を _{ども}	<u>先生に</u>	する	*(Parents) make a child into a teacher.*
子供が _{ども}	<u>先生に</u>	なる	*A child becomes a teacher.*
	<u>しずかに</u>	する	*to make (something/someone) quiet*
	<u>しずかに</u>	なる	*to become quiet*
じゅぎょうを	<u>おもしろく</u>	する	*(A teacher) makes the class interesting.*
じゅぎょうが	<u>おもしろく</u>	なる	*A class becomes interesting.*

お母さん：	へや、きれいにしてね。	*Clean this room.*
子供： _{ども}	は〜い。	*Okay./Yes.*

川田：　くるまを新しくしたんですよ。
_だ
　　　I got a new car.

山下：　ええっ、新しいくるまを買ったんですか。
　　　What? You bought a brand-new car?

川田：　いいえ。くるまは古いんですけど、さいきん買ったんです。
_だ
　　　No, the car is old, but I got it recently.

話してみましょう

> **Activity 1**

しつもんに日本語でこたえて下さい。

Example:　なつはあさ何時ごろあかるくなりますか。
　　　　　五時ごろあかるくなります。

1. なつは何時ごろくらくなりますか。
2. ふゆは何時ごろあかるくなりますか。
3. ふゆは何時ごろくらくなりますか。
4. このへんはいつごろ寒くなりますか。
5. このへんはいつごろあたたかくなりますか。
6. ふゆの気温温は何度ぐらいになりますか。
7. なつの気温は何度ぐらいになりますか。

> **Activity 2**

Describe the following pictures using the adverbial forms of adjectives.

Example:　　風がつよくふいています。

Example　　　　　1　　　　　2

3　　　　　4　　　　　5

6

Activity 3

Work with a partner. Your partner first draws a face without showing it to you, then gives you instructions on how to draw this face. Compare the two faces when you are done. Use casual speech.

Example: A: かおを大きく書いて。まるく書いて。

　　　　　　 B draws a big round face.

　　　　　 A: そして、目を小さく書いて。はなはみじかく書いて。

　　　　　　 B draws small eyes and a short nose.

Activity 4

A home remodeling expert is trying to make suggestions to make a room more comfortable. Help the expert make suggestions by completing the sentences using the adverbial form of adjective + する or noun + にする.

Example: かべ (*wall*) がきれいじゃないから、きれいにしましょう。

1. 押し入れがせまいから、_____。
2. このへやは小さいから、_____。
3. まどが少ないから、_____。
4. ドアが古いから、_____。
5. トイレがくらいから、_____。

Activity 5

Discuss the results of the remodeling performed in Activity 4.

Example: かべをきれいにしたので、へやがあかるくなりました。

V. Expressing uncertainty using 〜でしょう , 〜かもしれない , and 〜かな

〜でしょう, 〜かもしれない, and 〜かな express the speaker's conjecture, but they vary in degree of certainty and the intended interlocutor. All of these expressions are preceded by the plain form of verbs and adjectives. However, with な- adjectives and the copula verb, だ is deleted.

Verb くもる (*to become cloudy*)

	Probably	Maybe	I wonder
Present affirmative	くもるでしょう	くもる かもしれない	くもるかな
Present negative	くもらないでしょう	くもらない かもしれない	くもらないかな
Past affirmative	くもったでしょう	くもった かもしれない	くもったかな
Past negative	くもらなかった でしょう	くもらなかった かもしれない	くもらなかったかな

い - adjective 寒い (*cold*)

	Probably	Maybe	I wonder
Present affirmative	寒いでしょう	寒いかもしれない	寒いかな
Present negative	寒くないでしょう	寒くない かもしれない	寒くないかな
Past affirmative	寒かったでしょう	寒かった かもしれない	寒かったかな
Past negative	寒くなかった でしょう	寒くなかった かもしれない	寒くなかったかな

な- adjective いや (*unpleasant*)

	Probably	Maybe	I wonder
Present affirmative	いやでしょう	いや かもしれない	いやかな
Present negative	いやじゃない でしょう	いやじゃない かもしれない	いやじゃないかな
Past affirmative	いやだった でしょう	いやだった かもしれない	いやだったかな
Past negative	いやじゃなかった でしょう	いやじゃなかった かもしれない	いやじゃなかったかな

Noun + copula verb

	Probably	**Maybe**	**I wonder**
Present affirmative	風でしょう	風かもしれない	風かな
Present negative	風じゃない でしょう	風じゃない かもしれない	風じゃないかな
Past affirmative	風だった でしょう	風だった かもしれない	風だったかな
Past negative	風じゃなかった でしょう	風じゃなかった かもしれない	風じゃなかったかな

〜でしょう／だろう   probably, I suppose

〜でしょう indicates probability or conjecture. It can be used for future and past events or actions. The probability expressed by でしょう ranges from probably to must be/must have been. 〜でしょう is often used in weather forecasts.

いい天気でしょう。	*It will probably be good weather.*
にぎやかでしょう。	*It will probably be lively.*
東京はくもり時々雨でしょう。	*It will be cloudy with occasional rain in Tokyo.*
よこはまは雨でしょう。	*It will be rainy in Yokohama.*

In addition, 〜でしょう can be used with a rising intonation to ask for confirmation. This usage of 〜でしょう is rather casual and should not be used toward someone in a superior status.

そとはむし暑いでしょう。	*It is humid outside, don't you think?*
あの人は上田さんでしょう。	*That's Ms. Ueda over there, isn't it?*

The question form of 〜でしょう, 〜でしょうか is used for questions that are more polite than those ending in 〜ですか.

あのう、えきはどこでしょうか。	*Excuse me, but where is the station? (more polite)*
あのう、えきはどこですか。	*Excuse me, but where is the station?*
今、何時でしょうか。	*Do you have the time? (more polite)*
今、何時ですか。	*What time is it now?*

田中：明日の天気はどうでしょうか。	*How will tomorrow's weather be?*
川口：さあ、よく分かりませんが。	*Well, I'm not sure.*
鈴木：田中さんは来ますか。	*Is Mr. Tanaka coming?*
川口：雨だから、たぶん来ないでしょう。	*It's raining, so he probably won't come.*

NOTES

- でしょう is sometimes used with たぶん (*perhaps*).

  たぶん雨<ruby>雨<rt>あめ</rt></ruby>でしょう。 *It will probably rain*

- The plain form of でしょう is だろう. When ～だろう is used in a question such as あの人は日本人だろうか, it can be interpreted as a self-directed question: *I wonder if that person is Japanese*. The polite speech version, あの人は日本人でしょうか, would be consistently interpreted as being a polite question.

～かもしれない   might

～かもしれない also indicates probability or conjecture and can be used for future and past events or actions. The probability expressed by かもしれない is about 50% or lower.

石田<ruby>石田<rt>いし</rt></ruby>：　にわか<ruby>雨<rt>あめ</rt></ruby>がふりそうですね。
It looks like we will have a shower.

チョイ：　そうですね。くもが<ruby>多<rt>おお</rt></ruby>いから、ふるかもしれませんね。
I agree. It's very cloudy, so it might rain.

イアン：　あの人は山田先生でしょうか。
Is that person (perhaps) Professor Yamada?

本田：　さあ、どうでしょうね。Tシャツ、きてるから、学生かもしれませんよ。
Well, I am not sure. He is wearing a T-shirt, so he may be a student.

～かな   I wonder ～ (Casual speech)

～かな is used when the speaker asks himself/herself about something. Since it expresses the speaker's monologue question, *I wonder* ～, it cannot be used as someone else's monologue questions such as *he/she wonders* ～. Also, it indicates present tense and cannot be used in cases such as *I wondered* ～ or *he/she wondered* ～.

<ruby>台風<rt>たいふう</rt></ruby>かな。　　　　　　　　*I wonder if it is a typhoon.*

そとは<ruby>寒<rt>さむ</rt></ruby>いかな。　　　　　　*I wonder if it is cold outside.*

今<ruby>晩<rt>ばん</rt></ruby>は<ruby>気温<rt>きおん</rt></ruby>が<ruby>下<rt>さ</rt></ruby>がるかな。　*I wonder if the temperature will fall tomorrow.*

～かな is not used as a straightforward question to others like ～でしょうか but can be used to solicit the listener's answer indirectly. However, it should not be used toward someone of superior status, because it is used in fairly informal speech.

アリス：　今日も雨かな。
あめ

I wonder if it will rain today, too.

健一：　ううん。昨日のばん、ふったから、今日は大丈夫だよ。
けん　　　　　　　きのう　　　　　　　　　　　　　　　　だいじょうぶ

No. It won't because we had rain last night.

道子：　これは石田さんのかな。リーさんのかな。
みち　　　　　いし

I wonder if this is Mr. Ishida's or Mr. Li's.

ふみえ：　さあ、よく分からないけど。イニシャルがT.I. だから、石田さん
のかもしれないね。　　　　　　　　　　　　　　　　　　　いし

Well, I don't know, but it might be Mr. Ishida's because the initials are T.I.

古田：　上田さんは来るかな。　*I wonder if Ms. Ueda is coming.*

山下：　さあ、どうかな。　　　　*Well, I wonder that, too.*

NOTES

- In feminine speech 〜かしら is used instead of かな.

  大雪になるかしら。　　*I wonder if the snow will get heavy* (feminine).
  おおゆき

話してみましょう

Activity 1

Convert the following questions into monologue questions using 〜かな .

Example:　今年のなつは暑いですか。
　　　　　ことし　　　　あつ

　　　　　今年のなつは暑いかな。
　　　　　ことし　　　　あつ

1. 去年の八月は暑い日が多かったですか。
   きょねん　　　　あつ　　おお

2. 今年のふゆは寒いでしょうか。
   ことし　　　　さむ

3. 去年は雨がたくさんふりましたか。
   きょねん　　あめ

4. 去年のふゆは雪が少なかったでしょうか。
   きょねん　　　　ゆき

5. 一昨年のふゆはあまり寒くありませんでしたか。
   おととし　　　　　　　さむ

6. 今年のなつは暑くなりますか。
   ことし　　　　あつ

Activity 2

Work with a partner. The following chart shows today's weather forecast for various cities. One person asks a question using the words in 1–8 and 〜でしょう. The other person answers the questions, using 〜でしょう or 〜かもしれません.

Example: 東京／いい天気
とうきょう　　てんき

A: 東京はいい天気でしょうか。
とうきょう　　てんき

B: いいえ、天気はあまりよくないでしょう。
てんき

東京／雨
とうきょう　あめ

A: 今日東京は雨がふるでしょうか。
とうきょう　あめ

B: そうですね。東京は雨がふるかもしれませんね。
とうきょう　あめ

	東京 とうきょう	アラスカ	ニューヨーク	シドニー	ロサンゼルス
天気 てんき	くもり	雪 ゆき	くもりのち雨 あめ	晴れ は	くもり時々晴れ ときどき は
気温 きおん	59° F 15° C	-4° F -20° C	41° F 5° C	91.4° F 33° C	77° F 25° C
雨 あめ	50%	0%	80%	0%	30%
雪 ゆき	0%	100%	15%	0%	0%

1. 東京／あたたかい
とうきょう

2. アラスカ／雪
ゆき

3. ニューヨーク／寒い
さむ

4. ニューヨーク／雨
あめ

5. シドニー／晴れる
は

6. ロサンゼルス／あたたかい

7. ロサンゼルス／雨
あめ

8. シドニー／むし暑い
あつ

Activity 3

Using the state of Illinois (イリノイしゅう , しゅう = *state*) as a reference point, ask your classmates where other states are in respect to Illinois. Your classmates will answer using direction words and 〜でしょう , 〜かもしれない , or 〜と おもう depending on their level of certainty. Tally the results.

Example: A: イリノイしゅうの北に何しゅうがありますか。

  B: ウィスコンシンしゅうがあるでしょう／

  かもしれません／とおもいます。

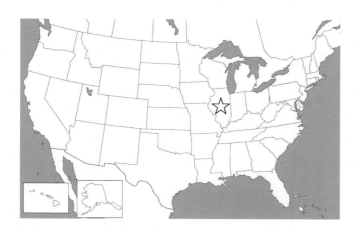

Activity 4

Work with a partner. Look at the following weather map and say what seems to be happening weather-wise in various places. Use casual speech.

Example: 今日、テキサスはいい天気になるでしょう。

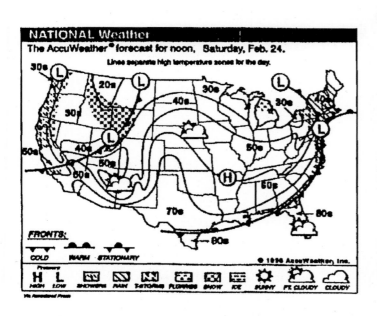

U.S. temperatures

	Today			Tomorrow		
	HI	Lo	Otlk	HI	Lo	Otlk
Atlanta	78	55	clr	68	56	cdy
Baltimore	61	44	cdy	64	48	cdy
Boston	49	41	cdy	56	41	rn
Buffalo	51	33	cdy	45	41	clr
Charlotte, N.C.	73	50	cdy	75	56	cdy
Cincinnati	70	45	cdy	48	40	cdy
Columbus, Ohio	68	45	cdy	46	40	cdy
Dallas-Ft Worth	84	56	clr	75	43	cdy
Dayton	68	45	cdy	45	40	cdy
Denver	52	25	clr	58	22	cdy
Detroit	52	31	cdy	44	38	cdy
Grand Rapids	52	30	rn	41	37	cdy
Greensboro, N.C.	68	48	cdy	73	53	cdy
Hartford Spgfld	54	39	cdy	55	41	rn
Honolulu	79	69	cdy	80	70	cdy
Houston	88	65	cdy	75	58	cdy
Indianapolis	70	46	rn	51	39	cdy
Los Angeles	64	47	clr	66	50	cdy
Louisville	72	52	cdy	57	44	cdy
Memphis	81	59	cdy	61	47	cdy
Miami Beach	83	64	cdy	85	65	cdy
Nashville	77	54	cdy	58	47	cdy
New Orleans	74	63	cdy	74	63	cdy
New York City	60	43	cdy	59	47	rn

聞く練習
_{れんしゅう}

上手な 聞き方
_{かた}

Understanding the organization of prepared speech

Unlike face-to-face conversations, news reports and weather forecasts are based on prepared text and hence do not have much redundant information. It is thus very important to understand the information the first time. Luckily, prepared speech usually has a set pattern. Being aware of the organization of speech helps you to identify when to pay attention and to what. For example, news reports usually start with what happens, to whom, where, and when. The details come later.

聞く 前に
_{まえ}

Write an outline of the organization of a weather report. Include the types of information provided and their order.

天気予報を聞く　　Listening to weather forecasts
_{てん き よ ほう}

聞いてみましょう

Listen to the following weather forecasts. Then complete the chart, in English, by writing in the weather as well as high and low temperatures for each city listed.

言葉のリスト
_{こと ば}

最高気温　　highest temperature　　　　さいてい気温　　lowest temperature
_{さいこう き おん}　　　　　　　　　　　　　　　　　　　　_{き おん}

	天気予報 _{てん き よ ほう} （Example）	天気予報 1 _{てん き よ ほう}	天気予報 2 _{てん き よ ほう}	天気予報報 3 _{てん き よ ほう}
まち	きょうと	東京 _{とうきょう}	よこはま	きょうと
天気 _{てん き}	雪 _{ゆき}			
気温 _{き おん}	1度／ー1度 _ど　　_ど			

聞いた後で
_{あと}

しつもんに日本語でこたえて下さい。

1. 天気予報 1のきせつはいつですか。
_{てん き よ ほう}
2. そのきせつの東京と〜さんのまちとどちらの方が寒いですか。
_{とうきょう}　　　　　　　　　　　　　　　_{さむ}
3. 天気予報 2のきせつはいつですか。
_{てん き よ ほう}
4. そのきせつのよこはまと〜さんのまちとどちらの方があたたかいですか。
5. 天気予報 3のきせつはいつですか。
_{てん き よ ほう}
6. 〜さんのまちでは、そのきせつに雨がたくさんふりますか。
_{あめ}

聞き上手　話し上手

Expressing agreement and solidarity using ね and も

Conversation is like two people playing catch. Both people need to throw the ball in a way that is easy for the other person to catch. To facilitate conversation, it is important to give feedback and show a willingness to participate in the conversation.

Expressing agreement or emphasizing similarity is one way to show your support to the listener. This will help to create a sense of sharing or solidarity. In Japanese, two particles, ね and も, are often used to show agreement. For example, the particle ね in Ms. Suzuki's speech below indicates that she is requesting a confirmation of her impression about the weather. The particle ね in Mr. Yamamoto's speech indicates that he agrees with Ms. Suzuki's assertion that it is humid today.

鈴木：　今日はむし暑いですね。　　　　*It's humid today, isn't it?*

山本：　ええ、本当に暑いですね。　　*It certainly is.*

Similarly, the particle も in the following example emphasizes agreement between Ms. Suzuki and Mr. Yamamoto and indicates what they have in common.

鈴木：　私はいぬが好きです。　　　　　　　*I like dogs.*

山本：　そうですか。ぼくもいぬが好きなんですよ。　*Really? So do I.*

Even if you disagree with a person, it is good to start off by agreeing about something before stating a disagreement. Starting a conversation with a disagreement often sounds rude or cold.

鈴木：　今年は雪が多いですね。　　　　*It has snowed a lot this year.*

山本：　本当によくふりますね。でも、去年より少ないかもしれませんね。
　　　　It's really snowed a lot, hasn't it? But, it may be less than last year.

練習
（れんしゅう）

1. Listen to people expressing their opinions. For each person, first express your agreement using ね and も. Then express your disagreement, but (1) show your support by using ね and も, and (2) articulate the point on which you disagree.
2. Work with a partner. Your partner will express opinions about class, school, weather, a particular hobby, parents. Agree with him/her using ね and も.
3. Work with a partner. Your partner will again express opinions about class, school, weather, a hobby or parents, but this time, show your support for his/her opinion using ね and も, and then express your disagreement.
4. The following conversation is unnatural. Make it more natural by using ね and も.

A:　今日は。おでかけですか。

B:　今日は。ええ、今日は暑いから、およぎに行くんです。

A:　そうですか。今日は本当に暑いです。私はおよぎに行きたいです。明日は暑いでしょうか。

B:　さあ、よく分かりませんが、むし暑いから、よるは雨がふるかもしれません。

A:　そうですか。じゃあ、少しすずしくなるでしょうか。

B:　そうおもいます。

漢字
かん じ

Component shapes of kanji 1 – Introduction

Many **kanji** consist of more than one component. Certain components appear in many different **kanji**. Some of them are **kanji** by themselves while others are not. Since the number of these component shapes is much smaller than the number of **kanji**, approximately 300 in total, they serve as organizers and aid in memorizing.

The term *radical* (部首) is traditionally used to refer to components of
ぶ しゅ
characters. The concept of radicals was developed to classify and index a large number of **kanji**. In modern Japanese, a little over 200 radicals are used to index kanji. A radical is assigned to every **kanji**. Although radicals are very useful in studying **kanji**, they are sometimes deceptive. For example, the radical of 家 is 宀 , but the radical of 字 is 子 .

In this book, we use the term *component shape* to refer to any shape that repeatedly appears as part of **kanji** (e.g., 寸 , 口 , 又 , 月 , 宀 , etc.). Some component shapes are **kanji** by themselves, while some others only appear in other **kanji**. There are about 300 such shapes, which include all of the shapes used as radicals. Some of the component shapes indicate the meaning (or meaning category) of **kanji**. For example, if a **kanji** contains 日 , it is likely that the meaning of the **kanji** is related to day or sun. Some other component shapes may indicate an on-reading of **kanji**.

Component shapes appear in various places within **kanji**, but some shapes have a strong tendency to appear in fixed locations such as the left, the right, the top, or the bottom of the character. The following is a list of major types of component shapes based on where they are found within the character.

Type *	Example		Use Example			
へん (left side)	イ	meaning: person	休	体	住	
つくり (right side)	冓	on-reading: /kou/	講	構	購	
かんむり (top)	宀	meaning: roof	家	寒い		
きゃく (bottom)	儿	meaning: leg	兄	見	先	元
たれ (top to left)	疒	meaning: sickness	病	痛	疲	
かまえ (enclosure)	門	meaning: gate	間	聞	閉	
くにがまえ (enclosure)	囗	meaning: border	回	国		
にょう (left to bottom)	辶	meaning: walk, round	週	道	進	近

* These names are used to label radicals.

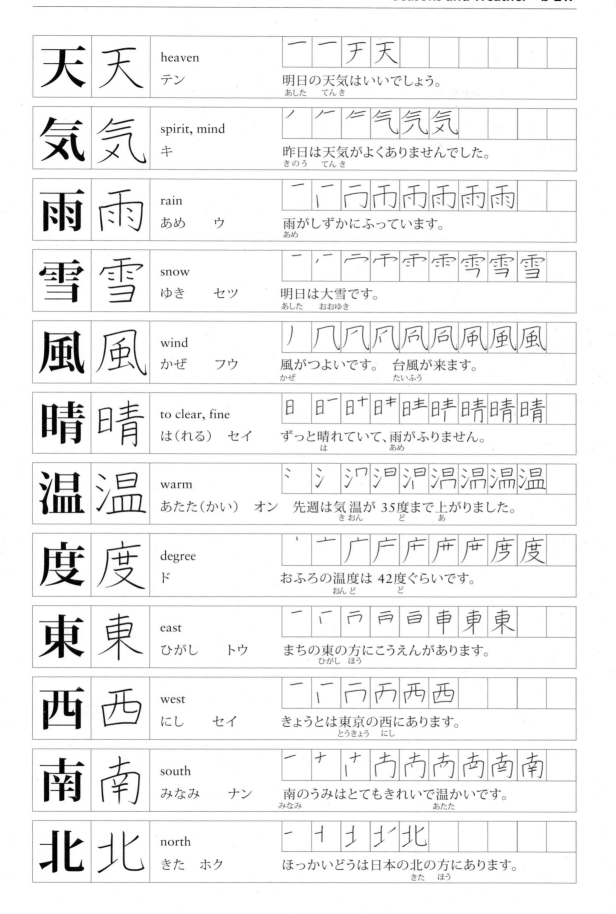

| 天 | 天 | heaven | 一 二 チ 天 |
| | | テン | 明日の天気はいいでしょう。
あした　てんき |

| 気 | 気 | spirit, mind | ノ 二 午 気 気 気 |
| | | キ | 昨日は天気がよくありませんでした。
きのう　てんき |

| 雨 | 雨 | rain | 一 二 冂 市 雨 雨 雨 雨 |
| | | あめ　ウ | 雨がしずかにふっています。
あめ |

| 雪 | 雪 | snow | 一 二 テ 千 雪 雪 雪 雪 雪 |
| | | ゆき　セツ | 明日は大雪です。
あした　おおゆき |

| 風 | 風 | wind | ノ 几 凡 凡 同 同 風 風 風 |
| | | かぜ　フウ | 風がつよいです。　台風が来ます。
かぜ　　　　　たいふう |

| 晴 | 晴 | to clear, fine | 日 日一 日十 日キ 晴 晴 晴 晴 晴 |
| | | は（れる）　セイ | ずっと晴れていて、雨がふりません。
は　　　　　　　　　あめ |

| 温 | 温 | warm | ゝ シ シ冂 シ目 シ目 温 温 温 温 |
| | | あたた（かい）　オン | 先週は気温が 35 度まで上がりました。
きおん　ど　あ |

| 度 | 度 | degree | ` 亠 广 庐 庐 庐 度 度 |
| | | ド | おふろの温度は 42 度ぐらいです。
おんど　　ど |

| 東 | 東 | east | 一 二 冂 百 車 東 東 |
| | | ひがし　トウ | まちの東の方にこうえんがあります。
ひがし　ほう |

| 西 | 西 | west | 一 二 冂 丙 西 西 |
| | | にし　セイ | きょうとは東京の西にあります。
とうきょう　にし |

| 南 | 南 | south | 一 ナ ナ 内 内 南 南 南 |
| | | みなみ　ナン | 南のうみはとてもきれいで温かいです。
みなみ　　　　　　　　　あたた |

| 北 | 北 | north | 一 十 北 北 北 |
| | | きた　ホク | ほっかいどうは日本の北の方にあります。
きた　ほう |

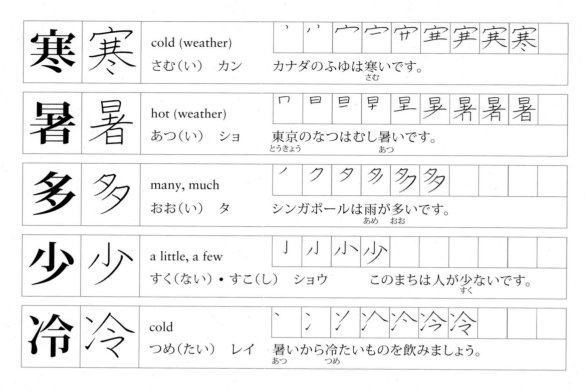

寒	寒	cold (weather) さむ（い）　カン カナダのふゆは寒いです。 さむ	` 、 宀 宀 宀 宯 宯 実 寒
暑	暑	hot (weather) あつ（い）　ショ 東京のなつはむし暑いです。 とうきょう　　あつ	冂 日 旦 早 星 昇 暑 暑 暑
多	多	many, much おお（い）　タ シンガポールは雨が多いです。 あめ おお	ノ ク タ タ 多 多
少	少	a little, a few すく（ない）・すこ（し）　ショウ このまちは人が少ないです。 すく	丿 小 小 少
冷	冷	cold つめ（たい）　レイ 暑いから冷たいものを飲みましょう。 あつ つめ	` 、 ソ 冫 冷 冷 冷 冷

読めるようになった漢字

天気　天気予報　天ぷら　気温　気候　雨　梅雨　にわか雨　雪　風
　　　　　　よほう　　　　　きおん　きこう　　　つゆ
台風　晴れる　温かい　温度　何度　東　西　南　南東　南西　北
たいふう
北東　北西　寒い　暑い　多い　少ない　冷たい　上がる　下がる
　　　　　　　　　　　　　　　　　　　　つめ
去年　今朝　今年　方　夕方　本当に　少し
きょねん　けさ　ことし　ほう　ゆうがた　ほんとう

日本人のなまえ：川田
　　　　　　　　かわだ

練習
れんしゅう

1. 東京の天気は雨のち晴れです。ごごには気温が二十五度まで上がる
   とうきょう
   でしょう。
2. 今晩は北の風がつよいですが、明日は南東の風になって、よわくな
   ばん　　　　　　　　　　　　あした
   るでしょう。
3. 西の方が暗いですから、晴れないでしょう。
   　　　くら
4. なつは暑くて、ふゆは寒いです。雪もたくさんふります。
5. ひるごはんの時は人が多いですが、そのあとは少なくなります。
6. 大阪は東京の西にあります。せんだいは東京の北です。
   おおさか　とうきょう　　　　　　　　　　　　　とうきょう
7. 今日はあたたかかったけど、明日は雨がふるそうだから、気温が下
   　　　　　　　　　　　　あした
   がって、寒くなるかもしれないね。

読む練習
れんしゅう

上手な読み方
かた

Getting used to vertical writing

Japanese text can be written either horizontally or vertically. In vertical writing, text is read from top to bottom, right to left. Japanese newspaper articles are written vertically, including the weather forecast. Popular magazines and literary works are also usually written vertically. Texts requiring scientific symbols, equations, formulas, and foreign words, such as science textbooks, language texts, and computer magazines, tend to be written horizontally.

練習
れんしゅう

1. Mark the beginning and end of each of the following short paragraphs.

メルボルンに給水制限？

メルボルンでは十三年ぶりに給水制限がしかれる可能性が大きいと見られている。一五〇年ぶりの低雨量を記録したメルボルン供給ダムの水量は、七二％と去年の同時期の九五％を大幅に下回り、関係者もこの状態を深刻に受け止めている様子。メルボルン水道局のベイリー氏は、市民に対し節水に協力してくれるよう積極的に呼びかけている。ちなみに、年間平均降雨量六三九ミリに対し、去年の降雨量はわずか三五九ミリだった。

2. Rewrite the following text vertically in two or more lines.

東京は今日は晴れ時々くもりで、ごぜんちゅうは少し寒いですが、
とうきょう　　　　　　　　ときどき
ごごには十度ぐらいになるでしょう。よるになって、雨がふる
でしょう。この雨はあしたのごごまでつづくでしょう。

読む前_{まえ}に

1. The numbers in the following map represent various regions in Japan. Read the description of each region below and write the number that matches the description. Note that しま means *island*.

山陰
さんいん　　本州_{ほんしゅう}にあります。大阪_{おおさか}の西で、四国_{しこく}の北です。

　　　　　かんこくにちかいです。

北海道
ほっかいどう　日本で一番北にあるしまです。

関東
かんとう　　本州_{ほんしゅう}にあります。東京_{とうきょう}の近くです。

近畿
きんき　　　本州_{ほんしゅう}にあります。東京_{とうきょう}の南です。大阪_{おおさか}やきょうとが
　　　　　あります。四国_{しこく}にちかいです。

九州
きゅうしゅう　四国_{しこく}の南西にあるしまです。

北陸
ほくりく　　本州_{ほんしゅう}にあります。東京_{とうきょう}の北西の方です。

本州
ほんしゅう　　日本で一番大きいしまです。

東北
とうほく　　本州_{ほんしゅう}にあります。東京_{とうきょう}の北の方です。

東海
とうかい　　本州_{ほんしゅう}にあります。東京_{とうきょう}の少し南の方です。

四国
しこく　　　日本にある四つのしまの中で一番小さいしまです。

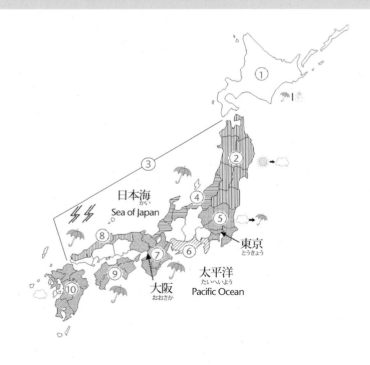

新聞の天気予報　A weather forecast in a newspaper

前線を伴った低気圧が日本海から東北東に進み、全国的に天気はくずれる。本州の日本海側や四国、九州は朝から雨、関東、東北、北陸は午後から雨になる。山陰地方の海岸では所々で雷雨を伴い風も強まる。北海道は雪か雨、沖縄も晴れ後曇りで、昼過ぎから雨。

読んだ後で

A. After reading the above weather forecast, choose the weather map that corresponds to the forecast.

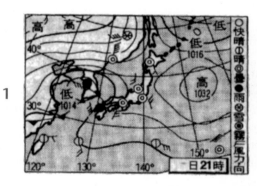

1

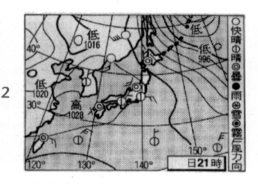

2

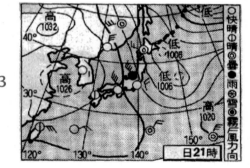

3

B. しつもんに日本語でこたえて下さい。

1. 四国にすんでいる人は今日かさをもって、出かけた方がいいですか。

2. 九州にすんでいる人は今日どんなふくをきて、出かけた方がいいですか。

3. 北海道にすんでいる人は今日はかさをもって、出かけた方がいいですか。

C. An out-of-town friend is planning to visit you for a week and has asked what the weather is like now. Compose an e-mail message to your friend giving details about the forecast for each of the next seven days. Information should include high and low temperatures, the chance of precipitation, and so forth.

総合練習
そうごうれんしゅう

明日のお天気
あ し た

You are a TV meteorologist forecasting tomorrow's weather. Work with a partner to create a map of your country and region. As you make your forecast, add the appropriate weather symbols and temperatures to your map. Give your weather report to the class.

ロールプレイ

Work with a series of partners to act out the following role play activities.

1. You are talking to your roommate. You are planning to go out tonight, but the weather is getting worse. Ask your roommate what he/she knows about tonight's weather.
2. You meet your neighbor on your way to school. Yesterday was a cold, rainy day, but the weather today is nice. Greet him/her and make small talk.
3. A typhoon is approaching your city. It is getting windy and starting to rain hard. Discuss these weather conditions with a partner.
4. Walk around the classroom. As soon as your instructor names a season, pair up with a classmate, greet him/her as if you have bumped into one another on the street, and chat about the weather.

Chapter 12

第
<ruby>十<rt>だい</rt></ruby>
二
<ruby>課<rt>か</rt></ruby>

年中行事
ねんちゅうぎょうじ
Annual Events

Objectives	Describing seasonal holidays and yearly events
Vocabulary	Dates, years, other time expressions, attractions and leisure activities, and memorable events
Japanese Culture	National holidays and annual events
Dialogue	子供の時の上田さん *Ms. Ueda as a child* <small>ども　とき</small>
Grammar	I. Talking about time using noun/adjective + 時, duration + 前 / 後 <small>とき　　　　　　　　　　まえ　ご</small>
	II. Talking about past experiences using 〜たことがある; listing representative activities using 〜たり〜たりする
	III. Expressing frequency using time-span に frequency / duration / amount
	IV. Expressing hearsay using the plain form + そうだ
	V. Using noun modifying clauses in the past and present
Listening	Taking turns in conversation
Communication	Phrases for filling in pauses
Kanji	Which one should I use, kanji or kana? 春 夏 秋 冬 朝 昼 晩 午 前 後 去 昨 供 元 思 明 回
Reading	Understanding the format of a postcard

単語
たん

Nouns

うみ	海	ocean, sea
おととし	一昨年	the year before last
おもいで	思い出	memories
がいこく	外国	foreign countries
がっき	学期	semester, quarter　いちがっき　one semester
		はるがっき　spring semester/quarter
かぶき	歌舞伎	kabuki (Japanese traditional performing art)
きもの	着物	traditional Japanese clothes, kimono
キャンプ		camping
きょうかい	教会	church
クリスマス		Christmas
けんか		fight, quarrel　けんかをする　to fight
こんげつ	今月	this month
しょうがつ	正月	the New Year (often used with the polite prefix お，おしょうがつ)
じんじゃ	神社	Shinto shrine
すいぞくかん	水族館	aquarium
せんげつ	先月	last month
ちゅうがく	中学	junior high school (shortened form of 中学校)
デート		dating, デートする go out on a date
てら	寺	Buddhist temple (often used as おてら)
どうぶつえん	動物園	zoo
とき	時	when, at the time of ～ (子供の時 when I was a child) どもゃ
はくぶつかん	博物館	museum
バレンタインデー		St. Valentine's Day
ハロウィン		Halloween
はんとし	半年	a half year
ひこうき	飛行機	airplane
びじゅつかん	美術館	art museum

プレゼント		present, gift
まつり	祭り	festival (often used as おまつり)
ミュージカル		musical
やまのぼり	山登り	mountain climbing
ゆうえんち	遊園地	amusement park
らいげつ	来月	next month

う -verbs

なく	泣く	to cry
のる	乗る	to get on, to ride (ひこうきに　のる　get on a plane)
もらう		to receive, to get

Irregular verbs

しつれんする	失恋する	to be disappointed in love

Adverbs

はじめて	初めて	for the first time

Particles

なあ		A particle of exclamation to express desires or feelings without addressing anyone in particular. Used in casual speech.

Suffixes

～かい	～回	～ times
～かげつ	～か月	counter for months
～ご	～後	from ～, after ～ (三 年ご three years from now)
～しゅうかん	～週間	for ～ weeks
～ど	～度	～ times
～にち	～日	day
～ねん	～年	specific year (1996年), counter for year (十年)
～まえ	～前	～ ago　(一年まえ one year ago)

Expressions

えーと		Well, Let's see . . .
あけましておめでとうございます。	明けましておめでとうございます。	Happy New Year

単語の練習
たん　　れんしゅう

A. 日にち　Days of the month

日	月	火	水	木	金	土
		一日 ついたち *	二日 ふつか	三日 みっか	四日 よっか	五日 いつか
六日 むいか	七日 なのか	八日 ようか	九日 ここのか	十日 とおか	十一日 じゅういち にち	十二日 じゅうに にち
十三日 じゅうさん にち	十四日 じゅう よっか	十五日 じゅうご にち	十六日 じゅうろく にち	十七日 じゅうしち にち	十八日 じゅうはち にち	十九日 じゅうく にち
二十日 はつか	二十一日 にじゅう いちにち	二十二日 にじゅうに にち	二十三日 にじゅう さんにち	二十四日 にじゅう よっか	二十五日 にじゅうご にち	二十六日 にじゅう ろくにち
二十七日 にじゅう しちにち	二十八日 にじゅう はちにち	二十九日 にじゅうく にち	三十日 さんじゅう にち	三十一日 さんじゅう いちにち		

NOTE

● いちにち means *one day*; ついたち means the *first of the month*. Both are written as 一日 in **kanji** but the context makes the reading clear. The other expression of dates can be used for the duration of time. For example, ふつか may mean the *second day of the month* or *two days*, depending on context.

おぼえていますか。

何月　一月　二月　三月　四月　五月　六月　七月　八月　九月
十月　十一月　十二月

Activity 1

Work with the class. Ask your classmates about their birthdays, and put them in the following charts.

Example: A: スミスさんのお誕生日はいつですか。

   B: 一月一日です。

月	日にちと名前
一月	一日　スミスさん
二月	
三月	
四月	
五月	
六月	
七月	
八月	
九月	
十月	
十一月	
十二月	

B. とくべつな日   Special days

お正月	New Year's Day
クリスマス	Christmas
バレンタイン・デー	St. Valentine's Day
ハロウィン	Halloween

Supplementary Vocabulary: アメリカの休日　US holidays
きゅうじつ

マーティン・ルーサー・キング・デー	Martin Luther King, Jr. Day
プレジデンツ・デー	President's Day
イースター	Easter
どくりつきねんび　　独立記念日	Independence Day
メモリアルデー	Memorial Day
レーバーデー	Labor Day
コロンブス・デー	Columbus Day
ハヌカ	Hanukkah

▶ Activity 2

Work with a partner. Ask your partner about the dates of holidays this year.

Example:　A: 今年のハヌカ (Hanukkah) はいつですか。

　　　　　　B: 十二月十一日です。

C. ほかの時間のいい方　Other time expressions

	日	週	月	年
〜 before last 〜	1 day before yesterday	N/A	N/A	一昨年 おととし year before last
Last	2 Yesterday	5	先月 せんげつ last month	8
This	3 Today	6	今月 こんげつ this month	9
Next	4 Tomorrow	7	来月 らいげつ next month	来年 next year

▶ Activity 3

Fill in the blanks in the above table with appropriate time expressions that you have learned in previous chapters.

Activity 4

しつもんに日本語でこたえて下さい。

1. 今月は何月ですか。
   こんげつ
2. 来月は何月ですか。
3. 先月は何月でしたか。
   せんげつ
4. 今年は何年ですか。
5. 来年は何年ですか。
6. 一昨年は何年でしたか。
   お と と し
7. 去年は何年でしたか。
   きょ

D. 時間のながさ　Duration of time

～度／回 かい (times)	～週間 しゅうかん (for ～ week)	～か月 げつ (for ～ month)	～年 (year)
いちど／いっかい	いっしゅうかん	いっかげつ	いちねん
にど／にかい	にしゅうかん	にかげつ	にねん
さんど／さんかい	さんしゅうかん	さんかげつ	さんねん
よんかい	よんしゅうかん	よんかげつ	よねん
ごかい	ごしゅうかん	ごかげつ	ごねん
ろっかい	ろくしゅうかん	はんとし ／ろっかげつ	ろくねん
ななかい	ななしゅうかん	ななかげつ	しちねん
はちかい ／はっかい	はっしゅうかん	はちかげつ ／はっかげつ	はちねん
きゅうかい	きゅうしゅうかん	きゅうかげつ	きゅうねん ／くねん
じゅっかい	じゅっしゅうかん	じゅっかげつ	じゅうねん

NOTES

- 〜度 refers to frequency and temperature up to 3. Beyond that, it usually refers to temperature only.

- 〜年 indicates both the specific point of time, as in 2008年 (*the year 2008*), and the duration of time as in 八年 (*for 8 years*).

- When 〜かい is written as the **kanji** 階 (かい), it refers to *floor levels*, as in Chapter 8, but when it is written as 回 (かい), it refers to *frequency*. There are some differences between them in terms of pronunciation as well. For example, the first mora is pronounced with a low pitch and the following mora have high pitch when the expression refers to a floor level, such as いっかい, にかい, and さんかい, but this is not the case with the frequency, as in いっかい、にかい、さんかい. Also, *3rd floor* is pronounced さんがい or さんかい but *3 times* is さんかい. On the other hand, *8th floor* is usually pronounced はちかい but *8 times* can be はちかい or はっかい.

- Instead of the western (Gregorian) calendar, the Japanese frequently use the current Emperor's era to refer to a certain year. For example, へいせい五年 is 1993. Recent eras are: 明治 (めいじ) (1868 –1912), 大正 (たいしょう) (1912-1926), しょうわ (1926–1989), and へいせい (1989–).

Activity 5

Tell the year the following events occurred. If you do not know the answer, ask your classmates.

1. コロンブス（Columbus）がアメリカに来た。

2. アメリカがイギリスからどくりつした (became independent)。

3. アメリカで夏（なつ）のオリンピックがあった。

4. アメリカで冬（ふゆ）のオリンピックがあった。

5. 第二次世界大戦（だいじせかいたいせん）(WWII) がはじまった。

6. 第二次世界大戦（だいじせかいたいせん）(WWII) がおわった。

7. ベトナムせんそう (Vietnam War) がおわった。

8. イラクせんそう (Iraq War) がはじまった。

Activity 6

しつもんに日本語でこたえて下さい。

1. 夏休みは何か月ありますか。冬休みはどうですか。春休みは？

2. 一学期は何週間ありますか。

3. 今週は何度学校に来ますか。

4. 今年、何度えいがを見ましたか。

5. 今月、何度じゅぎょうが休みになりましたか。

E. めいしょとレジャー   Attractions and leisure activities

Activity 7

Identify the picture that depicts each of the buildings and activities in the list by writing the number corresponding to the picture.

1. はくぶつかん　museum
__. ミュージカル　musical
__. 水族館 (すいぞくかん)　aquarium
__. 山のぼり　mountain climbing
__. 旅行 (りょこう)　travel
__. びじゅつかん　art museum
__. かぶき　kabuki
__. がいこく　foreign country

__. ゆうえんち　amusement park
__. 教会 (きょうかい)　church
__. うみ　sea
__. (お) てら　temple
__. じんじゃ　shrine
__. (お) まつり　festival
__. キャンプ　camping
__. どうぶつえん　zoo

おぼえていますか。

図書館　こうえん　たいいくかん　えいが　コンサート
（と）（かん）
パーティ　　ピクニック　　休みの日

Activity 8

Work with a partner. Ask each other whether you have been to any of the places or attractions or have participated in them this year.

Example:　A:　今年、はくぶつかんに行きましたか。
　　　　　　B:　ええ、行きました。
　　　　　　A:　何度ぐらい行きましたか。
　　　　　　　　　　（ど）
　　　　　　B:　一度／一回行きました。
　　　　　　　　　（ど）（かい）

	今年行った／見に行った／した	～度／回
はくぶつかん		
びじゅつかん		
水族館 すいぞくかん		
どうぶつえん		
ゆうえんち		
教会 きょうかい		
おてら／てら		
じんじゃ		
うみ		
がいこく		
ミュージカル		
おまつり／まつり		
山のぼり		
かぶき		
旅行 りょこう		
キャンプ		

F. 思い出　**Memories**

きものをきる
to put on kimono

飛行機にのる
to get on a plane

プレゼントをもらう
to receive a present

デートする
to go on a date

けんかをする
to have a fight, a quarrel

しつれんする
to be disappointed in love

なく
to cry

おぼえていますか。

おふろに入る　和食を食べる　およぐ　出かける

Activity 9

Work in a group of three or four. One person acts out the activity in the list, and the rest of the group will try to guess what it is.

Activity 10

Complete the following statements using ～さいの時 (*when I was ～ years old*).

1. ＿＿＿＿＿＿＿＿＿＿の時、はじめて (for the first time) 人を好きに
なりました。

2. ＿＿＿＿＿＿＿＿＿＿の時、はじめて外国人と話しました。

3. ＿＿＿＿＿＿＿＿＿＿の時、はじめて飛行機にのりました。

4. ＿＿＿＿＿＿＿＿＿＿の時、はじめてデートをしました。

5. ＿＿＿＿＿＿＿＿＿＿の時、はじめて友達とけんかしました。

6. ＿＿＿＿＿＿＿＿＿＿の時、しつれんしました。

7. ＿＿＿＿＿＿＿＿＿＿の時、高いプレゼントをもらいました。

ダイアローグ

はじめに

A. しつもんに日本語でこたえて下さい。

1. 子供の時、どんな子供でしたか。

2. 小学校の時、よくどんなことをしましたか。

3. 中学の時、よくどんなことをしましたか。

4. 高校の時、よくどんなことをしましたか。

B. Work with a partner. Ask your partner about his/her childhood memories.

Example: A: 〜さんは子供の時、どんな子供だったの？

   B: そう（だ）ね。とても元気だったけど、よくなく子供だったんだ／の。

子供の時の上田さん   *Ms. Ueda as a child*

道子さんはたんすの上のしゃしんを見ています。(*Michiko is looking at a picture on the chest*.)

道子：　あら、これ、アリス？

上田：　ええ、そうよ。

道子：　かわいい。何さい？

上田：　そうね。それは、七さいの誕生日の時にとったしゃしんなの。

道子：　そう、アリスはどんな子供だったの？

上田：　そうね。父や母によると、明るくて元気な子供だったそうよ。

道子：　へえ、そうなんだ。

上田：　ええ、スポーツが好きだったから、いつもそとであそんでた。

道子：　そうなの。

上田：　で、道子はどんな子供だったの？

道子：　そうね。私も小さい時は、よくうみにあそびに行ったり、山に
　　　　ハイキング行ったりしてたから、けっこうかっぱつだったかな。
　　　　けど、中学や高校の時は、いつもべんきょうしてた。

上田：　そうか。日本はじゅけんがあるからね。

道子：　え、ないの、アメリカじゃ。

上田：　SAT や ACT はあるけど、じゅけんはないのよ。だから、
　　　　じゅけんべんきょうもしたこと、ないの。

道子：　そう。いいなあ。

上田：　だから、高校の時は、よくパーティに行ったり、友達と
　　　　えいがを見たりしたんだ。

道子：　いいなあ。私もアメリカの学校に行きたかった。

上田：　でも、大学はアメリカの方がずっと大変だよ。

道子：　あ、そうか。じゃあ、おなじことね。

DIALOGUE PHRASE NOTES

- けっこう means *quite* and かっぱつ means *active*.

- ないの、アメリカじゃ。This is an inverted sentence of アメリカ じゃないの, but it does not mean *it is not America*. In this sentence, じゃない is not the negative form of だ. Instead, it consists of じゃ and ない. じゃ is a contraction for では where で refers to the place of action and は is a topic marker. ない is the negative form of ある. Therefore this sentence means: *Doesn't it exist in the U.S.?*

- じゅけん means "entrance examination."

- 私もアメリカの学校に行きたかった。 Literally, *I wanted to go to a U.S. school*, and in this context, it means *I wish I had gone to a U.S. school*.

- おなじ means *same*, and おなじこと means *the same thing*.

ダイアローグの後で

A. Complete the chart with information about Ms. Ueda's and Michiko's childhoods.

	どんな子供でしたか。	よくどんなことをしましたか。
アリス		
道子		

日本の文化
ぶん か

A. National holidays.

There are fourteen national holidays in Japan. Visit the *Nakama 1* student website to learn more about these holidays.

1月1日	元日 がんじつ	New Year's Day
1月第2月曜日 だい	成人の日 せいじん	Coming-of-Age Day
2月11日	建国記念の日 けんこく き ねん	National Foundation Day
3月21日	春分の日 しゅんぶん	Vernal Equinox Day
4月29日	昭和の日 しょう わ	Emperor Showa's (Hirohito; 1901–1989) birthday / ゴールデン・ウイーク (Golden Week).
5月3日	憲法記念日 けんぽう き ねん	Constitution Day
5月4日	みどりの日	Green Day
5月5日	子供の日 ども	Children's Day
7月第3月曜日 だい	海の日 うみ	Ocean Day
9月第3月曜日 だい	敬老の日 けいろう	Day of the Elderly
9月23日	秋分の日 しゅうぶん	Autumnal Equinox Day
10月第2月曜日 だい	体育の日 たいいく	Health and Sports Day.
11月3日	文化の日 ぶん か	Culture Day
11月23日	勤労感謝の日 きんろうかんしゃ	Labor and Harvest Day
12月23日	天皇誕生日 てんのうたんじょう	Emperor Akihito's Birthday

B. Seasonal events and celebrations.

Besides national holidays, the Japanese celebrate a variety of seasonal events: February 3rd is called 節分 , and it is the first day of spring according to the せつぶん

old lunar calendar. On this day, people throw soybeans inside and outside their

house while saying "おに (devils) はそと、ふく (luck) はうち" to keep out evil sprits and allow only good luck into the house.

On バレンタインデー it is the women who give men chocolate. Men reciprocate a month later with candies, marshmallows, and white chocolate on ホワイトデー (March 14).

March 3 is ひなまつり (Girl's Day), and people display dolls depicting ancient wedding ceremonies to express their wish for daughters to grow up to be gentle, beautiful women.

The Japanese national flower is the cherry blossom, and it blooms throughout Japan during late March to early April, when TV news programs provide daily forecasts on the blossoms. Bus tours travel to the best cherry blossom regions, and schoolchildren, college students, and corporate groups alike picnic under the blossoms. This eating, drinking, singing, and dancing under the cherry trees is called お花見 (*flower watching*).
はな み

July 7 is considered one of the most romantic days and is called 七夕.
たなばた
According to Chinese mythology, it is the one day a year when two star-crossed lovers, separated by the Milky Way, meet. Schoolchildren write their wishes on small pieces of paper and tie them on bamboo trees to celebrate this day.

Around the middle of July, the rainy season ends, and the summer festival season starts. Many of the major festivals are held between July and August throughout Japan, especially during the period surrounding おぼん (August 13–15). It is a Buddhist festival in honor of deceased relatives and ancestors, and many people go back to their hometowns to greet their ancestors and family, similar to Thanksgiving break in the U.S. In addition to Golden Week, おぼん is one of the three major holiday seasons in Japan.

Starting in the middle of December, many people organize the end-of-the year party called 忘年会. The Japanese also celebrate クリスマス as
ぼうねんかい
a romantic day for couples and a party day for children and families. After December 29, most companies close until January 4. Traditionally, to prepare for the new year, people launch a major house or office cleaning and pay off personal debts during this period.

文法
ぶんぽう

> ## I. Talking about time using noun/adjective + 時,
> とき
> ## duration + 前／後
> まえ　ご

When you want to express a period of time in your life rather than a date, a day of the week, or a specific time, you can create a phrase using 時 (when), 前 (before) and 後 (after). Grammatically they are nouns so they can be modified by a noun, adjective, or a clauselike noun modification. This chapter introduces 時 with respect to nouns and adjectives and 前／後 in relation to counterexpressions.

A. Noun/adjectives + 時 (when, at the time of ～)
とき

時 can be modified by a noun in the form of noun の noun (時) or adjective + noun. The particle に for a time expression can be used with ～時.

子供の時	*When I was a child*
小学校の時	*When I was in elementary school*
十一さいの時	*When I was eleven*
ひまな時	*When I have free time*
いやな時	*When I am annoyed*
元気な時	*When I am healthy*
いそがしい時	*When I am busy*
寒い時	*When I am cold*
小さい時	*When I was small*

The negative ending ない is grammatically an い -adjective, so it can be combined with 時 just like other い -adjectives.

病気じゃない時	*When I am not sick*
ひまじゃない時	*When I do not have free time*
いそがしくない時	*When I am not busy*

ウィル： いつアメリカに来たんですか。
When did you come to the United States?

あつ子： 高校の時に来ました。
It was when I was in high school.

キム：　ひまな時_{とき}はよくいぬのさんぽをします。
I often walk my dog when I am free.

スミス：　そうですか。どんないぬですか。
I see. What kind of dog do you have?

B. Duration + 前_{まえ}／後_ご

Duration + 前_{まえ} indicates *ago* or *before*; it is used with the particle of time, に .

三年前_{まえ}に日本に行きました。　　*I went to Japan three years ago.*
一か月前_{まえ}にけっこんしました。　*I got married a month ago.*

Duration + 後_ご indicates *later* or *after*, and it can be used with に .

三日後_{みっかご}に会いましょう。　*I will see you three days from now.*
一年後_ごに日本に行きました。　　*I went to Japan a year later.*

ジョン：　ホンコンへはいつ行ったの？
When did you go to Hong Kong?

ひろし：　二か月ぐらい前_{まえ}。
About two months ago.

ジョン：　どうだった？
How was it?

ひろし：　おもしろかったけど、ちょっと暑くて大変_{たいへん}だった。
It was fun, but it was a bit too hot and that was hard to take.

ジョン：　今度はいつ行くの。
When are you going again?

ひろし：　半年後_ごだと思_{おも}う。
I think it will be six months from now.

ジョン：　そうか。いいなあ。
I see. That is nice.

NOTE

- ぐらい can be used with 前_{まえ} and 後_ご. It is used right after the duration and before 前_{まえ} or 後_ご. When ぐらい used with 後_ご, the pronunciation of the **kanji** 後 becomes あと.

  その人に四日_{よっか}ぐらい前_{まえ}に会った。　*I met the person about four days ago.*
  その人に一年ぐらい後_{あと}に会った。　*I met the person about a year later.*

話してみましょう

Activity 1

Answer the following questions using 〜 時.
_{とき}

Example: どんな時にセーターをきますか。
_{とき}
寒い時にきます。
_{とき}

1. どんな時に家でゆっくりしますか。
_{とき}
2. どんな時になきますか。
_{とき}
3. どんな時に友達にメールを書きますか。
_{とき} _{だち}
4. どんな時は時間がありませんか。
_{とき}
5. どんな時にびょういんへ行きますか。
_{とき}

Activity 2

Work with a partner. Ask what he/she does on the occasions listed below.

Example: A: ひまな時に何をしますか。
_{とき}
B: 家でテレビを見ます。
_{とき}

A: 〜さんはひまな時に何をしますか。
_{とき}

B: たいてい友達と電話で話します。
_{だち} _{でん}

	すること
ひまな時 _{とき}	
暑い時 _{とき}	
寒い時 _{とき}	
うれしい時 _{とき}	
かなしい時 _{とき}	
さびしい時 _{とき}	

Activity 3

Work with a partner. Your partner is a psychic. Ask him/her about your future.

Example: A: 私はこれから何をするでしょうか。

B: 二か月後に、だれかを好きになるでしょう。

そして、半年後にけっこんするでしょう。

Activity 4

Work with a partner. Ask your partner about places where he/she visited in the past six months and for how long.

Example: A: どんなところに行きましたか。

B: シカゴに行きました。

A: そうですか。いいですね。いつ行ったんですか。

B: 三週間前です。

A: そうですか。何日ぐらいシカゴにいましたか。

B: そうですね。二日いました。

どこ	いつ	どのくらい

II. Talking about past experiences using 〜たことがある; listing representative activities using 〜たり〜たりする

The plain past affirmative form 〜た can be used in various structures in Japanese. This chapter introduce two commonly used structures, namely 〜たことがある and 〜たり〜たりする.

A. Talking about past experiences using 〜たことがある

The construction 〜たことがある is used to express an experience one has had in the past. In contrast, 〜ました simply expresses a past action. The absence of any experience is expressed by 〜たことが／はない.

> 私はミュージカルを<u>見たことがあります</u>。
> I *have seen* a musical.

> 私はミュージカルを<u>見たことがありません</u>。
> I *have never seen* a musical.

> 私はミュージカルを<u>見ました</u>。
> I *saw* a musical.

> 私はミュージカルを<u>見ませんでした</u>。
> I *did not see* a musical.

The construction 〜たことがある is usually used to talk about experience in the not-so-recent past and not about something that took place as recently as 昨日 or 一昨日.

> 一昨年中国に行ったことがあります。
> I *had the experience of going* to China two years ago.

> 一昨日中国に行きました。
> I *went* to China the day before yesterday.

> チョイ： 田中さんは英語が上手ですね。
> *Mr. Tanaka is good at English, isn't he?*

> 山本： ああ、田中さんは小さい時、がいこくにすんでいた ことがあるそうですよ。
> *Well, I heard that he lived in a foreign country when he was small.*

> チョイ： ああ、それで、上手なんですね。
> *I see, that's why he is so good.*

B. Listing representative activities using ～たり～たりする

The construction ～たり～たりする is used to list representative activities. It is similar to や in Chapter 7, which is used to list nouns and noun phrases.

食べたり飲んだりしました。
I ate and drank. (Literally, I did things like eating and drinking.)

新聞を読んだり、ざっしを見たりします。
I do things like reading newspapers and browsing through magazines.

新聞やざっしを読みます。
I read newspapers and magazines. (etc.)

> 川口： きょうとに行ったことがありますか。
> *Have you ever to Kyoto?*
>
> ワット： ええ、ありますよ。じつは、先月行ったんです。
> *Yes, I have. In fact, I went there last month?*
>
> 川口： そうなんですか。どうでしたか、きょうとは？
> *Is that so? How was it?*
>
> ワット： とてもたのしかったですよ。おてらやじんじゃを見たり、
> 買いものをしたりしました。
> *It was really fun. I saw temples and shrines and did shopping.*
>
> キム： 子供の時、よく何したの？
> *What kinds of things did you do when you were a child?*
>
> 一也： どうぶつえんに行ったり、ゆうえんちであそんだりしたよ。
> *I did things like going to the zoo and playing at the amusement park.*

話してみましょう

Activity 1

Look at the drawings on the following page and make up questions asking whether someone has ever done these things.

1 2 3 4

5 6 7

8 9 10

11 12 13

Example: Picture #1
はな (*flowers*) をもらったことがありますか。

Activity 2

Bingo. Work with the class. Ask whether your classmates have done the things in the Bingo chart. Write the name of the person when he/she answers with yes. The first one to complete a row or column with different names wins.

さしみを食べる	ゴルフをする	日本で教会へ 行く <small>きょうかい</small>	ゆびわを もらう
おてらを見る	日本のざっしを 読む	山のぼりをする	日本人と 日本語で話す
きものをきる	スペイン語を べんきょうする	しつれんして、 なく	ふとんで寝る
はくぶつかんに 行く	くるまを買う	ハワイのうみで およぐ	先生を好きに なる

Activity 3

Look at Mr. Jones's personal history and make sentences that express what kinds of activities he did at different stages in his life.

Example: ジョーンズさんは小学校の時、よくアニメを見たり、こうえんで
やきゅうをしたりしました。

	よくしたこと
1990 12/3　誕生日 たんじょう	
1996 ～ 2001　小学校	どうぶつえんへ行く。こうえんでやきゅうをする。アニメを見る。
2001 ～ 2004　中学	うみへおよぎに行く。キャンプをする。うたをうたう。ケーキを作る。
2004 ～ 2007　高校	アルバイトを する。しゃしんをとる。えをかく。びじゅつかんに行く。デートする。
今　　　　大学	べんきょうする。アルバイトをする。日本人とチャット (chat) で話す。ドライブに行く。

Activity 4

Work with a partner. Ask what kinds of activities he/she did at different times in his/her life.

Example: A:　小学校の時、よくどんなことをしましたか。
　　　　　　B:　そうですね。友達の家にあそびに行ったり、
　　　　　　　　父とどうぶつえんに行ったりしました。

	よくしたこと / よくすること
小学校	
中学	
高校	
今	

Activity 5

Work in groups of three or four. Think about a place, such as a park, department store, supermarket, and so on. Describe to the rest of the group what people do at that place and make them guess what that place is.

Example: A:　ここでジェットコースターにのったり、メリーゴーランドに
　　　　　　　のったりします。
　　　　　　B:　ゆうえんちですか。
　　　　　　A:　はい、 そうです。

Activity 6

Work with a partner. Ask your partner what kinds of places he/she has been to for a vacation, when, and what he/she did there, using plain forms. Then report the result using polite forms.

Example: A:　〜さんは　どんなところにあそびに行ったことがあるの？
　　　　　　B:　ボストンに行ったことがあるけど。
　　　　　　A:　いいなあ。いつ行ったの？
　　　　　　B:　二年前に行ったんだ／の。
　　　　　　　　まえ
　　　　　　A:　ボストンでは、どんなことしたの？
　　　　　　B:　びじゅつかんに行ったり古い教会を見たりしたよ。
　　　　　　　　　　　　　　　　　　　　きょうかい

　　　　〜さんは二年前にボストンへ行ったことがあります。
　　　　　　　　　　まえ
　　　　ボストンではびじゅつかんに行ったり、古い教会を見たりしました。
　　　　　　　　　　　　　　　　　　　　　　　きょうかい

III. Expressing frequency using time-span に frequency / duration /amount

Use of the time-span に with frequency /duration expresses how often, how long, or how much one does a certain thing within a specified time.

	Time frame	Particle	Frequency / duration	
私は	一日 （いちにち）	に	二時間ぐらい	べんきょうします。

I study for about two hours a day.

The time frame can be specified by any expression that specifies a duration of time such as 〜分 (*minute*) , 〜時間 (*hour*), 〜日 (*day*), 〜週間 (*week*), 〜か月 (*month*), and 年 (*year*) .

五分に	一度	トイレに行く。	*I go to the restroom every five minutes.*
一時間に	三回 （かい）	電話が来る。 （でん）	*I receive a call three times in an hour.*
二日に （ふつか）	一度	プールでおよぐ。	*I swim in a pool every other day.*
一週間に	十時間ぐらい	テレビを見る。	*I watch TV for about ten hours a week.*
一か月に	十五万円ぐらい	いる。	*I need 150,000 yen in a month.*
半年に	一度	旅行に出かける。 （りょ）	*I go on a trip every six months.*
一年に	三か月ぐらい	休みがある。	*I have a vacation for about three months a year.*
十年に	一度	会う。	*I see (him) once in every ten years.*

東山：　教会へはよく行きますか。
（ひがしやま）（きょうかい）
Do you often go to church?

中西：　ええ、一週間に一度行きます。
（なかにし）
Yes, I go there once a week.

イアン：　どのぐらい本を読むんですか。
How many books do you read?

チョイ：　そうですね。一週間に三さつぐらい読みますね。
Let's see, about three books a week.

イアン：　すごいですね。
Wow!

話してみましょう

> **Activity 1**

Rephrase the following sentences using the frequency or quantity and time frame in the right column.

	Frequency / Quantity	Time frame
Example: 水族館に行きます。 　　　すいぞくかん	About twice	1 year

一年に二回／二度ぐらい水族館に行きます。
　　かい　　　　　　　　　　すいぞくかん

	Frequency/Quantity	Time frame
1. およぎに行きます。	once	2 weeks
2. デートをします。	twice	1 week
3. びょういんに行きます。	once	2 months
4. テレビを見ます。	30 minutes	1 day
5. アルバイトをします。	once	2 days
6. おまつりがあります。	4 times	1 year
7. メールを読みます。	3 times	1 day
8. 山のぼりをします。	once	1 month

> **Activity 2**

Work with a partner. Find out how often he/she does the following things. Compare this information with your own lifestyle.

Example:　A: 一週間にどのぐらいうんどうしますか。
　　　　　B: そうですね。一週間に三回／三度ぐらいします。
　　　　　　　　　　　　　　　かい

うんどうをします／一週間	
アルバイトをします／一週間	
べんきょうします／一日	
寝ます／一日	
友達と出かけます／一週間 だち	

Activity 3

Work with your class. First find out which classmates do not live with their parents. Then ask them how often they get together with their parents, on what occasions, and what sorts of things they do together.

Example:　A:　ご両親と一緒にすんでいますか。

　　　　　B:　いいえ、一人ですんでいます。

　　　　　A:　そうですか。じゃあ、ご両親とご兄弟にはよく会いますか。

　　　　　B:　そうですね。一年に三回ぐらい会います。

　　　　　A:　そうですか。どんな時に会うんですか。

　　　　　B:　クリスマスやお正月や夏休みですね。

　　　　　A:　そうですか。じゃあ、ご家族とどんなことをしますか。

　　　　　B.　旅行に行ったり、食事をしたりします。

名前	Frequency	Occasion	Activity

IV. Expressing hearsay using the plain form + そうだ

A construction using the stem of the verb + そうだ was introduced in Chapter 9; it expresses the speaker's conjecture based on a direct observation.

おまつりは　<u>おもしろ</u>　　　そうだ。　　*The festival looks interesting.*

おまつりは　<u>おもしろくなさ</u>　そうだ。　　*The festival does not look interesting.*

This chapter introduces a different type of そうだ, which takes the plain form of verbs and adjectives. It expresses hearsay and it means *I heard* or *I have heard.*

おまつりは　<u>おもしろい</u>　　　そうだ。　　*I've heard that the festival is interesting.*

おまつりは　<u>おもしろくない</u>　そうだ。　　*I've heard the festival is not interesting.*

In addition to the present form, 〜そうだ for hearsay is used with the plain past forms.

おまつりは　<u>おもしろかった</u>　　　そうだ。　　*I've heard that the festival was interesting.*

おまつりは　<u>おもしろくなかった</u>　そうだ。　　*I've heard the festival was not interesting.*

Also, 〜そうだ in this usage is often used with 〜によると (according to 〜).

スミスさんによると、ハロウィンはアメリカのおまつりだそうだ。
According to Mr. Smith, (I heard that) Halloween is an American festival.

田中さんによると、キムさんは来年けっこんするそうです。
According to Mr. Tanaka, (I heard that) Mr. Kim is getting married next year.

木村：　クリスマスにハワイ旅行に行ったそうですね。
むら　　*I heard that you went on trip to Hawaii during Christmas.*

リー：　ええ、二十三日から五日行きました。
いつか　　*Yes. I went there for five days starting the 23rd.*

木村：　いいですね。私はハワイへは行ったことがないんですよ。
むら　　*Nice. I've never been to Hawaii.*

NOTE

- It may be difficult to distinguish the そうだ meaning *it looks like* from the そうだ indicating hearsay with い-adjectives, because they can sound very similar. So it is essential to pay attention to pronunciation.

  <u>おいし</u>そうですね。   *It looks delicious.*

  <u>おいしい</u>そうですね。   *I heard that it is delicious.*

話してみましょう

Activity 1

You heard some things about Ms. Tanaka. Make a sentence that reports what you have heard.

Example: 田中さんは小さい時よく寝る子供でした。

            田中さんは小さい時よく寝る子供だったそうです。

1. 田中さんは大学院の学生です。
2. 田中さんは中学の時よく山のぼりをしました。
3. 田中さんはしゃしんをとるのが好きです。
4. 田中さんはがいこくにすんでいたことがあります。
5. 田中さんは先週かぶきを見に行きました。
6. かぶきは少しむずかしかったけど、おもしろかったです。

Activity 2

Work in a group of four or five. The instructor tells something to a member from each team. They then go back to their respective team and take turns whispering the information only to the next person on the team. The last person of each team will come to the board and write the information.

Example: ～さんから本をもらいました。

            先生は～さんから本をもらったそうです。

Activity 3

Work with a partner. Choose one person from the list (or choose yourself) and pretend you are that person. Your partner interviews you. He/She will take detailed notes. Reverse the roles and repeat.

Example: A: アメリカの大統領 (President) は今どこにすんでいますか。

　　　　　 B: ホワイトハウスにすんでいます。

有名人のリスト

アメリカの大統領	ジョージ・ワシントン
ブラッド・ピット	リンカーン
ジャネット・ジャクソン	ウィリアム王子 (Prince William)
コロンブス	ダイアナひ (Princess Diana)
スーパーマン	マーティン・ルーサー・キング
バットマン	イチロー

Activity 4

Work in a group of three or four. Report to the group about your interview from Activity 3 without revealing the name of the interviewee. The rest of the group will try to guess who the interviewee was.

Example: この人はアメリカ人じゃないそうです。そして、旅行がとても好きだったそうです。

V. Using noun modifying clauses in the past and present

Chapter 10 introduced the noun modifying clause (see p. b-158). The modifying clause is in the plain form, and it immediately precedes the noun to be modified. This chapter expands the use of this structure in two ways. First, the modifying clause can be in the past tense as long as it is in plain form.

たのしかった	ミュージカル	*the musical that was fun*
先月キャンプに来た	人	*the person who came to the campsite last month*
けんかをした	友達	*the friend who had a fight*
昨日来なかった	学生	*the student who did not come yesterday*

Second, the subject of the verb in a modifying clause is marked by が. The topic marker は does not appear in a modifying clause

山田さんが よく話す思い出	*the memory that Mr. Yamada often talks about*
弟が 昨日行ったおてら	*the temple that my younger brother went to yesterday*
母が 好きだったかぶき	*the kabuki that my mother liked*
姉が 好きなおんがく	*the music that my elder sister likes*

The subject marker が is often replaced by the particle の when the modifying clause is very short.

母が／の 好きだったきもの	*the kimono that my mother liked*
母が 子供の時に好きだったきもの	*the kimono that my mother liked when she was a child*
父が／の 行った水族館	*the aquarium that my father went to*
父が キムさんと行ったびじゅつかん	*the art museum that my father went to with Mr. Kim.*

Use the present tense when a modifying clause describes a characteristic of a person or thing, although the sentence is in the past tense.

私は よく食べる子供でした。	*I was a child who ate a lot.*
田中さんは せが高い人でした。	*Mr. Tanaka was the person who was tall.*

話してみましょう

Activity 1

Read each statement and make up a question that asks for the underlined thing, place, or person.

Example:　田中さんは今月 どこかに行きました。

　　　　　田中さんが今月行ったところはどこですか。

1. 川本さんは昨日何か食べました。
2. 川口さんは昨日だれかに電話をかけました。
3. 金田さんは一昨日だれかとデートをしました。
4. 東山さんは昨日どこかで本を買いましたか。
5. 大田さんは昨日何か飲みました。
6. 中西さんのねこはどこかにいます。
7. 月本さんは来月だれかに会います。
8. 古川さんは何か作ります。

Actvity 2

Work with a partner. Ask what kinds of things your partner did, using the given verbs. Then, for each thing ask how it was.

Example:　A:　ねえ、どんなものを食べたことがある？

　　　　　B:　アイスクリームの天ぷらを食べたことがあるよ。

　　　　　A:　どうだった？

　　　　　B:　う～ん、あまりおいしくなかった。

	もの／ところ	どうでしたか。
食べる		
飲む		
行く		
見る		
聞く		

Activity 3

Work with a new partner. Convey the information you collected in Activity 2 to your new partner by using noun modifying clauses.

Example:　〜さんが食べたものはアイスクリームの天ぷらですが、

〜さんが食べたアイスクリームの天ぷらはあまり
おいしくなかったそうです。

Activity 4

Work in a group of three or four. One person defines one of the items in the list, and the others try to figure it out. The person who correctly guesses the most items is the winner.

Example:　A: 先生とべんきょうするへやです。

B: きょうしつですか。

A: はい、そうです。

図書館　先生　学生　子供　お母さん　やきゅう　デパート　おてら
スーパー　じんじゃ　ゆうびんきょく　えんぴつ　ノート
ゆうえんち　小学校　がいこく　クリスマス　ハロウィン　教会
はくぶつかん　山　うみ

Activity 5

Work with the class. Ask each other what kind of children your classmates were.

Example:　A: キムさんはどんな子供でしたか。

B: よくあそんで、よく食べる子供でした。

名前	どんな子供

MORE ABOUT CASUAL SPEECH

Some expressions like かな are used only in casual speech. Another common sentence final particle is なあ. It expresses the speaker's surprise, admiration, or desires without addressing anyone in particular. It is used both in monologues and dialogues. In general, it is considered a male speech pattern, but women often use it in casual conversation, especially in monologues. The fact that なあ can be used in the first monologue below can imply that the speaker is less aware of the presence of the listener. Therefore, women may choose to use 〜ね if addressing someone in conversation.

きれいだなあ。   *It is beautiful!*
きれいだね。   *It's beautiful, isn't it?*
きれいねえ。   *It's beautiful! / it is beautiful, isn't it?*

Do not use なあ with polite forms such as です and ます, as the use of なあ with these forms is characteristic of the speech of middle-aged men, called おじさんことば.

Another expression that you hear often is すごく (*very*). It can be used instead of とても, though とても can be used in both formal and casual speech.

すごくきれい！   *Very pretty*

The adjective すごい can be used in casual speech as well. It can be used to describe an extremely positive or negative situation, and it means *great*, *amazing*, *awful*, or *horrible*, depending on the context.

聞く練習
れんしゅう

上手な聞き方

Taking turns in conversation

One important rule in conversation is taking turns, or allowing only one person to speak at a time. Body language, introductory remarks, and silence are some ways to signal who should speak next. Of course, not everyone waits for a turn to speak. In fact, many times you may hear two or more conversations going on at the same time in one group.

練習
れんしゅう

Listen to the conversations and decide which one breaks the rule of turn-taking. Write a check mark next to the conversation.

Conversation 1_____   Conversation 2 _____

日本の思い出
おも で

言葉のリスト
こと ば

北海道   Hokkaido
ほっかいどう

雪まつり   Snow Festival

よこはま   Yokohama

These students are talking about their experiences in Japan. Listen to their descriptions and complete the following chart in English. You may not understand every detail, but try to get the gist of each speech.

	いつ行きましたか。	どんなことがありましたか。 どんなことをしましたか。
チョンさん		
モリルさん		
クリシュナさん		

聞き上手話し上手

Phrases for filling in pauses

Speaking always involves false starts, paraphrases, and pauses. Even native speakers do not speak in fluent and complete sentence all the time. In English one often says *um, uh, let's see,* or *well* to fill in pauses. In Japanese, expressions like あのう,そうですね and えーと serve as conversational "fillers." This usage of あのう differs from that of あのう、すみません, which is used to get someone's attention. あのう is commonly inserted between phrase and utterance breaks to give some time for the speaker to put his thoughts into words. When あのう is used, the speaker is aware of the listener's presence. えーと is also used to fill in time between phrases, but it is used for the sake of speaker and does not imply the speaker's awareness of the listener's presence. For this reason, using えーと frequently, especially toward your superior, is rather rude because you may give an impression that you do not pay much attention to the listener when you speak. In any case, overuse of these fillers can break the natural flow of conversation, so one should be careful not to do so.

山本：　休みによくどんなことをしますか。

木村：　そうですね。テニスをしたり、およぎに行ったり、それから、
むら　　あのう、えいがを見たりしますね。

練習
れんしゅう

1. Listen to the conversation as you read the following text, which does not include any fillers. Write in the fillers as you listen.

   ゆかり：　クリスマス、どうだった？

   ケイト：　とてもたのしかった。みんなでコロラドにスキーに
   　　　　　行ったんだ。

   ゆかり：　ほんと。いいなあ。

   ケイト：　うん、でね。アスペンに行ったんだけど、とまった
   　　　　　ホテルがすごくりっぱで、へやもひろくて、ほんとに
   　　　　　よかった。

   ゆかり：　そう。よかったね。スキーはどうだったの？

   ケイト：　ああ、スキーは、私、あまり好きじゃないから、
   　　　　　しなかったんだ。だから、毎日おいしいもの
   　　　　　食べたり、パーティしたり、あそんでたのよ。

   ゆかり：　そうか。いいなあ。

2. Work with a partner. Ask your partner a question that requires a long answer such as a description of his/her apartment, friend, or past experience. Practice using conversation fillers.

漢字
かんじ

Which one should I use, kanji or kana?

There are several words in Japanese that can be written in **kanji** but are usually expressed in **hiragana** or **katakana**. For example, ここ, そこ, あそこ, and どこ can be written as 此処, 其処, 彼処, and 何処, respectively. The choices between ひらがな or 漢字 for such words are made by convention. That is, words like the こそあど expressions are commonly written in **kana** but you may see the **kanji** versions in novels, for example. Similarly, おいしい is more likely to be written in **kana** instead of as 美味しい. On the other hand, the word 寒い is usually written in **kanji** though さむい is possible. It is impossible to know which words are more likely to be written in **kanji** and which are not at this point, but keep in mind that writing every available **kanji** is not necessarily appropriate.

In general, the more **kanji** are used, the more formal or difficult a piece of writing will look. Therefore, official documents addressed to the public may not contain many **kanji** in order to make it look familiar to the general public, whereas an academic journal may contain a large number of **kanji**. A good text is said to have about 30% of the characters written in **kanji** and will not contain more than 40%. For this reason, writing as many **kanji** as possible just for the sake of using **kanji** is not considered appropriate.

In some situations, **kanji** cannot be used even when available. For example, こと is a noun, meaning an *intangible thing*, and can be written with the **kanji** 事. However, when it is used as a part of a grammar expression, such as ことがある, it must be written in **hiragana**. Similarly, ある can be expressed with the **kanji** 有る but it must be written in **hiragana** in the phrase ことがある. Also, いる (*exist*) can be written with the **kanji** 居る, but this character is never used in the expression 〜ている. The **kanji** for the verbs 行く and 来る are commonly used when these words appear as as the main verb in a sentence, but are not used for the expressions 〜ていく／てくる, which are introduced in volume 2 of *Nakama*.

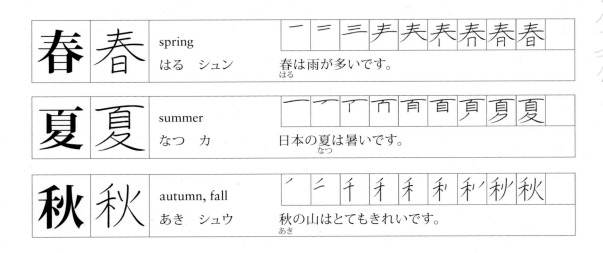

春 春	spring はる　シュン	一 二 三 声 夫 表 春 春 春 春は雨が多いです。 はる
夏 夏	summer なつ　カ	一 一 ㄓ 币 盲 盲 頁 夏 夏 日本の夏は暑いです。 なつ
秋 秋	autumn, fall あき　シュウ	ノ 二 千 手 禾 利 利 秒 秋 秋の山はとてもきれいです。 あき

| 冬 | 冬 | winter
ふゆ　トウ | ノ　ク　タ　冬　冬 |
| 冬は寒いから、時々雪がふります。
　ふゆ　　　　　　　ときどき | | | |

| 朝 | 朝 | morning
あさ　チョウ | 十　十　古　古　卓　朝　朝　朝 |
| 日曜日の朝、おそくまで寝るのが好きです。
　　　　あさ | | | |

| 昼 | 昼 | noon, daytime
ひる　チュウ | フ　コ　尸　尺　尺　尽　尽　昼　昼 |
| 母が昼ごはんを作りました。
　　ひる | | | |

| 晩 | 晩 | evening
バン | 日　日′　日′　日フ　昭　晚　晚　晚　晚 |
| 明日の晩ごはんは天ぷらです。
　　　　ばん | | | |

| 午 | 午 | noon
ゴ | ノ　ヒ　二　午 |
| 午前　　　月曜日の午後、両親と家族が来ます。
ごぜん　　　　　　　　　ごご | | | |

| 前 | 前 | before, front
まえ　ゼン | 、　ソ　兯　苩　前　前　前　前 |
| 午前中にしゅくだいをします。　中学の前　名前
ごぜんちゅう　　　　　　　　　　　まえ　なまえ | | | |

| 後 | 後 | after, later
あと／うし（ろ）
のち　ゴ | ノ　ク　彳　彳　祄　祡　後　後　後 |
| 午後は暑かったです。一か月ぐらい後　つくえの後ろ
ごご　　　　　　　　　　　　　あと　　　　　うし | | | |

| 去 | 去 | to leave, past
さ（る）　キョ | 一　十　土　去　去 |
| 去年、南アメリカに行きました。
きょ | | | |

| 昨 | 昨 | last ~ (yesterday, year)
サク | 1　П　日　日　日′　旷　昨　昨 |
| 一昨年日本に行きました。　　昨日
おととし　　　　　　　　　　　きのう | | | |

| 供 | 供 | attendant,
companion
とも／ども　キョウ | ノ　イ　仁　仁　世　供　供 |
| 子供が二人います。
　ども | | | |

| 元 | 元 | origin, former
もと　ゲン | 一　二　テ　元 |
| 父は元気です。　元気なお母さん
　　げんき　　　げんき | | | |

| 思 | 思 | to think
おも（う）　シ | 1　口　冂　田　田　田　思　思　思 |
| 昨日の朝は風がつよかったと思います。
きのう　あさ　　　　　　　　　おも | | | |

明	明	bright, light		１	冂	日	日	日	明	明	明	
		あか（るい）　メイ			明るいへや　　明日　　明るい人							

あか　　　　　　　　あした　　あか

回	回	times, frequency		１	冂	冂	冋	回	回		
		まわ（る）　カイ			私の弟は一か月に十回ぐらいラーメンを食べます。						

かい

読めるようになった漢字
かんじ

春　夏　秋　冬　朝　朝ご飯　今朝　毎朝　昼ご飯　晩ご飯　今晩
　　　　　　　　　　　　はん　　　　　　　　　　　　はん　　　　はん

毎晩　午前　午後　二日前　三日後　名前　後　去年　昨年　昨日
　　　　　　　　　　　　　　　　　　な　　のち

一昨年　子供　元気　思う　思い出　明るい　明日　一回　二回
　　　　　　　　　　おも　で

三回　一週間　二度　時　今月　正月　先月　来月　中学　今度
　　　　　　　　　とき　　　　　　　　　　　　　　　　こんど

学期　教会　水族館　外国人　後ろ　半年　飛行機
がっき　きょうかい　すいぞくかん　がいこくじん　　はんとし　ひこうき

明けましておめでとうございます
あ

日本人の名前：川本　月本　中西　東山　古
なまえ　かわもと　つきもと　なかにし　ひがしやま　ふる

練習
れんしゅう

Read the following sentences.

1. 来年の春から夏まで日本にいます。

2. 冬の朝はとても寒くて、水が冷たかったです。

3. 夏は午前中はあまり暑くありませんが、午後はとても暑いです。

4. 昨日の晩、その子供は何時ごろ寝ましたか。

5. 去年の秋にきょうとに行きました。十月だったと思います。

6. おばあさんは明るくて、とても元気です。

7. 一年に二回、日本に帰ります。

8. 三年前に一度日本に行ったことがあります。その一か月後に
タイへ行きました。

9. 教会の後ろに何がありますか。

読む練習
れんしゅう

上手な読み方

Understanding the format of a postcard

Japanese postcards （葉書）are usually written vertically. In vertical writing, text is
はがき
read from right to left. The stamp is at the upper left corner of the front of the
card. Under the stamp, the sender's name and address are written. Write the sender's
zip code in the small boxes at the lower left corner. The addressee's address should
be written on the right side with the zip code in the boxes at the top of the card, and
his/her name should be in the center of the card. Use さま (様), a formal version of
さん , after the addressee's name.

On the back of the card, it is not necessary to write the name of the sender or
addressee. The card usually contains a short greeting phrase, a body, a short closing
phrase, and a date.

Seven-digit
postal code

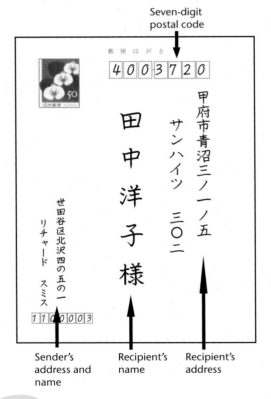

Sender's
address and
name

Recipient's
name

Recipient's
address

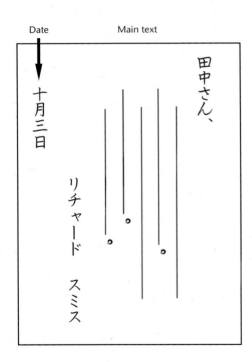

Date

Main text

練習
れんしゅう

The most important greeting card in Japan is probably the New Year's card
(ねんがじょう). New Year's cards are exchanged not only among friends and
relatives, but also among businesses, neighbors, students, and teachers. Look at the
following New Year's card and identify the sender's and addressee's address, name,
and zip code. Then identify the greeting phrases.

（New Year card, right image）

平成二十年元旦

今年もよろしくおねがいします。

明けまして
おめでとうございます

広島県西条市新町一八一八
ロバート・バンス

（Address card, left image）

50 NIPPON 年賀 2008

1234567

東京都新宿区西新宿三ー五ー十二

木下洋子様

葉書 （A postcard）
はがき

読む前に

A. しつもんに日本語でこたえて下さい。

1. 絵葉書 (*picture postcard*) をもらったことがありますか。
えはがき

2. いつ友達に絵葉書を書きますか。
ともだち　　えはがき

3. 絵葉書にはどんなことを書きますか。
えはがき

言葉のリスト
ことば

前略　　　　opening phrase
ぜんりゃく

ひっこす　　to move

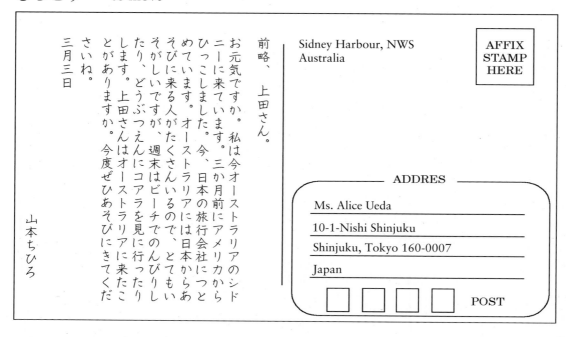

Sidney Harbour, NWS
Australia

AFFIX
STAMP
HERE

前略、上田さん。

お元気ですか。私は今オーストラリアのシドニーに来ています。三か月前にアメリカからひっこしました。今、日本の旅行会社につとめています。オーストラリアには日本からあそびに来る人がたくさんいるので、とてもいそがしいですが、週末はビーチでのんびりしたり、どうぶつえんにコアラを見に行ったりします。上田さんはオーストラリアに来たことがありますか。今度ぜひあそびにきてください。

三月三日

山本ちひろ

ADDRES

Ms. Alice Ueda

10-1-Nishi Shinjuku

Shinjuku, Tokyo 160-0007

Japan

POST

読んだ後で　　Comprehension

A. しつもんに日本語でこたえて下さい。
1. この葉書をもらった人はだれですか。
　　（はがき）
2. この葉書を書いた人はだれですか。
　　（はがき）
3. この人は四か月前どこにすんでいたと思いますか。
4. この人は今どこで何をしていますか。
5. この人はどうして葉書を書きましたか。
　　　　　　　　　（はがき）

B. In Japan, it is common to send greeting cards on New Year's day and in the middle of summer and winter. New Year's cards must be sent so that they will arrive on January 1. The post office has a pre-set period when people can send cards to have them delivered on New Year's day. New Year's cards go on sale in November, and those sold in the post office come with prizes ranging from stamp sheets to televisions. You can also use regular postcards, but you need to write 年賀 to indicate that it is a New Year's card.
　　　　　　　　　　（ねん が）

No New Year's card should be sent to a person who has lost an immediate family member or close relative during the past year. Instead, a winter greeting card (寒中見舞い) is sent in the middle of January.
　　　　　　　（かんちゅう み ま）

Summer greeting cards (暑中見舞い) are sent to friends and
　　　　　　　　　　（しょちゅう み ま）
acquaintances to inquire about the addressee's health in the summer heat and to tell news about yourself. Summer greeting cards sent after August 8 are called 残暑見舞い (*greetings in the lingering heat*) because this date
　　　　　（ざんしょ み ま）
indicates the beginning of autumn according to the old lunar calendar.

There are fixed expressions used in these cards. The following are some of the common expressions used in each type of card:

New Year's cards

Greeting phrases

> 明けましておめでとうございます。
> 　（あ）
> *Happy New Year*

> 新年おめでとうございます。
> （しんねん）
> *Happy New Year*

> 昨年は大変お世話になりありがとうございました。
> （さくねん　たいへん　せ わ）
> *Thank you for all your kind help throughout last year.*

> 今年もどうぞよろしくおねがいします。
> *I hope for your continuous favor this year.*

Winter greeting cards

Greeting phrases
> 寒中お見舞い申し上げます。
> （かんちゅう　み ま　もう あ）
> *Sending you midwinter greetings.*

Summer greeting cards

Greeting phrases

暑中お見舞い申し上げます。
しょちゅう　みま　もう　あ
Sending you midsummer greetings.

残暑お見舞い申し上げます。
ざんしょ　みま　もう　あ
Sending you late summer greetings.

1. Work with a partner. Read the following cards, and identify the type of each card, the sender, and the sender's recent news, if any.

2. Write summer and New Year's greeting cards to your friends following the examples on the previous page.

総合練習
そうごうれんしゅう

A. 私はだれですか

1. Work in a group of three or four. First, complete the following paragraph with your own information as in the example. Then, interview each other and write memos about other members in your group.

Example: 私の名前は<u>スーザン・ロス</u>です。私は<u>シカゴ</u>から来ました。
誕生日は<u>六月二十五日</u>です。私は子供の時は<u>しずかな子供</u>でした。<u>よく本を読んだり</u>、<u>おんがくを聞いたり</u>しました。<u>一か月に一度ピアノのレッスンに行きました</u>。<u>私はフランスに行った</u>ことがあります。<u>十五さいの</u>時でした。<u>フランスに友達がいた</u>からです。
だち

私の名前は＿＿＿＿＿＿＿＿＿です。私は＿＿＿＿＿＿＿＿＿から来ました。誕生日は＿＿＿＿＿＿＿です。私は子供の時
たんじょう
＿＿＿＿＿＿＿子供でした。＿＿＿＿＿＿＿＿＿＿たり、
＿＿＿＿＿＿＿＿＿＿たりしました。＿＿＿＿＿＿に
＿＿＿＿＿＿＿＿＿＿＿＿＿ました。
＿＿＿＿＿＿＿＿＿＿＿＿＿＿＿＿＿＿こと
があります。＿＿＿＿＿＿＿＿時でした。＿＿＿＿＿＿＿
＿＿＿＿＿＿＿＿からです。

Sample interview questions
Q: どこから来ましたか。
Q: 子供の時、どんな子供でしたか。
Q: 子供の時、どんなことをしましたか。
Q: どんなことをしたことがありますか。何さいの時でしたか。
どうしてしたんですか。

2. Work in a group. Each group chooses a person and describes the person, except for the name, to the entire class by using そうです for hearsay. The class will try to figure out which member of the group is being described.

Member 1: この人は子供の時、しずかな子供だったそうです。

Member 2: この人はフランスに行ったことがあるそうです。

Member 3: この人は十五さいの時にフランスに行ったことがあるそうです。

Member 4: この人は子供の時、本を読んだり、おんがくを聞いたりしたそうです。

Note that the person chosen to be described must still use そうです although he/she will be talking about himself/herself.

B. ロールプレイ

1. You are talking with your Japanese friend about your childhood. Describe what sort of things you did or didn't do.
2. Talk about the best vacation you ever had. What happened? Why was it so special?
3. You are attending a college reunion. Talk about what sort of things you did in college.

Whereas Enlish uses stress (or loudness) for accent, Japanese uses two relative pitches: high and low. Standard Japanese has the following rules.

1. The first mora (or syllable) and the second mora must have different pitches. Thus, a word always begins with either a low-high or a high-low combination.

2. Once the pitch goes low, it will never go up within a word.

3. For an N-mora word, there are N + 1 accent patterns. This becomes obvious when a particle follows a noun.

Common patterns

One-mora word

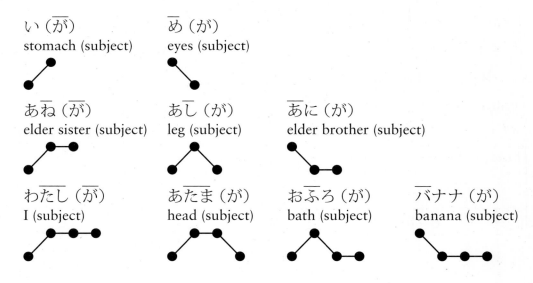

い (が̄)
stomach (subject)

め̄ (が)
eyes (subject)

あ̄ね (が̄)
elder sister (subject)

あし̄ (が)
leg (subject)

あ̄に (が)
elder brother (subject)

わた̄し̄ (が̄)
I (subject)

あ̄た̄ま (が)
head (subject)

おふ̄ろ (が)
bath (subject)

バ̄ナナ (が)
banana (subject)

APPENDIX B
VERB CONJUGATIONS

			Irregular Verb	Irregular Verb	る - verb	う - verb
Dictionary Form			くる (to come)	する (to do)	たべる (to eat)	いく (to go)
Plain	**Present**	**Affirmative**	くる	する	たべる	いく
		Negative	こない	しない	たべない	いかない
	Past	**Affirmative**	きた	した	たべた	いった
		Negative	こなかった	しなかった	たべなかった	いかなかった
Polite	**Present**	**Affirmative**	きます	します	たべます	いきます
		Negative	きません	しません	たべません	いきません
	Past	**Affirmative**	みました	しました	たべました	いきました
		Negative	きません でした	しません でした	たべません でした	いきません でした
Volitional	**Plain**		こよう	しよう	たべよう	いこう
	Polite		きましょう	しましょう	たべましょう	いきましょう
Potential	**Plain**		こられる	できる	たべられる	いける
	Polite		こられます	できます	たべられます	いけます
Conditional			くれば	すれば	たべれば	いけば
て - form			きて	して	たべて	いって

う - verb	う - verb	う - verb	う - verb	う - verb
およぐ (to swim)	かえる (to go home)	かく (to write)	のむ (to drink)	はなす (to talk)
およぐ	かえる	かく	のむ	はなす
およがない	かえらない	かかない	のまない	はなさない
およいだ	かえった	かいた	のんだ	はなした
およがなかった	かえらなかった	かかなかった	のまなかった	はなさなかった
およぎます	かえります	かきます	のみます	はなします
およぎません	かえりません	かきません	のみません	はなしません
およぎました	かえりました	かきました	のみました	はなしました
およぎません でした	かえりません でした	かきません でした	のみません でした	はなしません でした
およごう	かえろう	かこう	のもう	はなそう
およぎましょう	かえりましょう	かきましょう	のみましょう	はなしましょう
およげる	かえれる	かける	のめる	はなせる
およげます	かえれます	かけます	のめます	はなせます
およげば	かえれば	かけば	のめば	はなせば
およいで	かえって	かいて	のんだ	はなして

ADJECTIVE AND COPULA CONJUGATIONS

			い - adjective おおきい (big)	な - adjective しずか（な）(quiet)	Copula だ / です (be)
Plain	Present	Affirmative	おおきい	しずかだ	N だ
		Negative	おおきくない	しずかじゃない	N じゃない
	Past	Affirmative	おおきかった	しずかだった	N だった
		Negative	おおきくなかった	しずかじゃなかった	N じゃなかった
Polite	Present	Affirmative	おおきいです	しずかです	N です
		Negative	おおきくないです / おおきくありません	しずかじゃないです / しずかじゃありません	N じゃないです / N じゃありません
	Past	Affirmative	おおきかったです	しずかでした	N でした
		Negative	おおきくなかったです / おおきくありませんで した	しずかじゃなかったです / しずかじゃありませんで した	N じゃなかったです / N じゃありませんでした
		Prenominal	おおきい（だいがく）		
		Conditional	おおきければ		
		て - form	おおきくて		

APPENDIX D
COUNTERS AND TIME EXPRESSIONS

	General Counter ～つ	People ～にん	Bound Objects (book, magazine, etc.) ～さつ	Cylindrical Objects (pen, umbrella, etc.) ～ほん
	Common Counters			
1	ひとつ	ひとり	いっさつ	いっぽん
2	ふたつ	ふたり	にさつ	にほん
3	みっつ	さんにん	さんさつ	さんぼん
4	よっつ	よにん	よんさつ	よんほん
5	いつつ	ごにん	ごさつ	ごほん
6	むっつ	ろくにん	ろくさつ	ろっぽん
7	ななつ	しちにん	ななさつ	ななほん
8	やっつ	はちにん	はっさつ	はっぽん
9	ここのつ	くにん	きゅうさつ	きゅうほん
10	とお	じゅうにん	じゅっさつ じっさつ	じゅっぽん じっぽん
11	じゅういち	じゅういちにん	じゅういっさつ	じゅういっぽん
12	じゅうに	じゅうににん	じゅうにさつ	じゅうにほん

Specific Time			
Month 〜がつ	Day 〜にち	Time (o'clock) 〜じ	Time (minute) 〜ふん
1	いちがつ	ついたち	いちじ	いっぷん
2	にがつ	ふつか	にじ	にふん
3	さんがつ	みっか	さんじ	さんぷん
4	しがつ	よっか	よじ	よんぷん、よんふん
5	ごがつ	いつか	ごじ	ごふん
6	ろくがつ	むいか	ろくじ	ろっぷん
7	しちがつ	なのか	しちじ	ななふん、しちふん
8	はちがつ	ようか	はちじ	はっぷん、はちふん
9	くがつ	ここのか	くじ	きゅうぷん
10	じゅうがつ	とおか	じゅうじ	じゅっぷん、じっぷん
11	じゅういちがつ	じゅういちにち	じゅういちじ	じゅういっぷん
12	じゅうにがつ	じゅうににち	じゅうにじ	じゅうにふん
14		じゅうよっか (14)		
20		はつか (20)		
24		にじゅうよっか (24)		

Extent

	Year ~ねん	Month ~かげつ	Week ~しゅうかん	Day ~にち	Hour ~じかん
1	いちねん	いっかげつ	いっしゅうかん	いちにち	いちじかん
2	にねん	にかげつ	にしゅうかん	ふつか (かん)	にじかん
3	さんねん	さんかげつ	さんしゅうかん	みっか (かん)	さんじかん
4	よねん	よんかげつ	よんしゅうかん	よっか (かん)	よじかん
5	ごねん	ごかげつ	ごしゅうかん	いつか (かん)	ごじかん
6	ろくねん	ろっかげつ	ろくしゅうかん	むいか (かん)	ろくじかん
7	しちねん ななねん	ななかげつ	ななしゅうかん	なのか (かん)	しちじかん
8	はちねん	はちかげつ はっかげつ	はっしゅうかん	ようか (かん)	はちじかん
9	きゅうねん くねん	きゅうかげつ	きゅうしゅうかん	ここのか (かん)	くじかん
10	じゅうねん	じゅっかげつ じっかげつ	じゅっしゅうかん じっしゅうかん	とおか (かん)	じゅうじかん
11	じゅういちねん	じゅういっかげつ	じゅういっしゅうかん	じゅういちにち (かん)	じゅういちじかん
12	じゅうにねん	じゅうにかげつ	じゅうにしゅうかん	じゅうににち (かん)	じゅうにじかん
14				じゅうよっか (かん) (14)	
20				はつか (かん) (20)	
24				にじゅうよっか (かん) (24)	

APPENDIX E
DEMONSTRATIVE WORDS （こ そ あ ど）

	こ series	そ series	あ series	ど series
	Close to both speaker and listener	Closer to listener than to speaker; moderately away from both	Away from both speaker and listener	Interrogative
Adjective	この〜 (this 〜)	その〜 (that 〜)	あの〜 (that 〜)	どの〜 (which 〜)
Pronoun	これ (this thing)	それ (that thing)	あれ (that thing)	どれ (which thing)
Location	ここ (this place)	そこ (that place)	あそこ (that place)	どこ (where)
Direction	こちら (this way)*	そちら (that way)	あちら (that way)	どちら (which way)
Manner	こう (this way)	そう (that way)	ああ (that way)	どう (how)

* こちら can be used for "this person" (polite)

	Kanji		Kun-reading	On-reading	Examples
29	時	7	とき	ジ	一時、二時半、五時間べんきょうします。 いちじ、にじはん、ごじかん その時 とき
30	間	7	あいだ	カン	時間がありません。 じかん
31	分	7	わ（ける）・ わ（かる）	フン・ブン ・プン	二十分、分かりました。 にじゅっぷん、わ
32	半	7		ハン	毎日六時半におきます。 まいにちろくじはん
33	毎	7		マイ	毎週シカゴにいきます。毎日、毎月 まいしゅう　　　　　　まいにち　まいつき
34	年	7	とし	ネン	三年生、毎年 さんねんせい、まいとし
35	好	7	す（き）	コウ	テニスが好きです。 す
36	語	7	かた（る）	ゴ	日本語、フランス語ではなします。 にほんご　　　　　ご
37	高	7	たか（い）	コウ	古い高校、高い山 ふる　こうこう、たか
38	番	7	バン		やさいが一番好きです。 いちばん
39	方	7	かた	ホウ	サッカーの方がフットボールより好きです。 ほう　　　　　　　　　　　　　　　す
40	新	7	あたら（しい）	シン	新しいレストラン あたら
41	古	7	ふる（い）	コ	カラオケで古いうたをうたいます。 ふる
42	安	7	やす（い）	アン	今日はやさいが安いです。 やす
43	友	7	とも	ユウ	友達とかいものにいくのが好きです。 ともだち　　　　　　　　　　　す
44	一	8	ひと（つ）	イチ	一つ、一本、いぬが一匹います。 ひと、いっぽん、いっぴき
45	二	8	ふた（つ）	ニ	りんごが二つあります。二さつ、二本 ふた　　　　　　　　に　　　にほん
46	三	8	みっ（つ）	サン	けしゴムを三つかいました。　三本 みっ　　　　　　　　さんぼん
47	四	8	よ・よん・ よっ（つ）	シ	四つ、四時、ビールが四本あります。 よっ、よじ、よんほん
48	五	8	いつ（つ）	コ	五つ、ベルトが五本あります。 いつ、ごほん
49	六	8	むっ（つ）	ロク・ロッ	六つ、六時、えんぴつが六本あります。 むっ、ろくじ、ろっぽん
50	七	8	なな（つ）	シチ	七時、七本、オレンジが七つあります。 しちじ、ななほん、なな

	Kanji		Kun-reading	On-reading	Examples
51	八	8	やっ（つ）	ハチ・ハッ	八つ、八時、ペンが八本あります。 やっ　はちじ　　　　はっぽん
52	九	8	ここの（つ）	キュウ・ク	九つ、九時、バナナが九本あります。 ここの　くじ　　　　きゅうほん
53	十	8	とう	ジュウ・ジュッ	靴下が十あります。　十本、十時 くつした　とお　　　　じゅっぽん　じゅうじ
54	百	8		ヒャク・ビャク・ピャク	二百、三百、六百 にひゃく　さんびゃく　ろっぴゃく
55	千	8		セン・ゼン	二千、三千、八千、千円 にせん　さんぜん　はっせん　せんえん
56	万	8		マン	一万円、百万円 いちまんえん　ひゃくまんえん
57	円	8		エン	五十円、このセーターは、7800円です。 ごじゅうえん
58	店	8	みせ	テン	大きい店、店の人 みせ　みせ　ひと
59	行	9	い（く）	コウ	来年日本に行きます。 らいねん　　　い
60	来	9	く（る）	ライ	いつアメリカに来ますか。来週は来ない き　　　らいしゅう　こ
61	帰	9	かえ（る）	キ	たいてい七時にうちに帰ります。 しちじ　　　かえ
62	食	9	た（べる）	ショク	あさごはんを食べてください。学食 た　　　　　がくしょく
63	飲	9	の（む）	イン	ビールを二本飲みました。 の
64	見	9	み（る）	ケン	えいがを見に行きませんか。 み　い
65	聞	9	き（く）	ブン	インターネットでラジオを聞く、新聞 き　しんぶん
66	読	9	よ（む）	ドク	本を読むのが好きです。 よ
67	書	9	か（く）	ショ	てがみをあまり書きません。 か
68	話	9	はな（す）	ワ	友達と日本語で話すのが好きです。 だち　　　　はな

	Kanji		Kun-reading	On-reading	Examples
69	出	9	で（る）・で（かける）・だ（す）	シュッ	銀座に出かけます。 ぎんざ　で
70	会	9	あ（う）	カイ	人と会って、カフェで話をします。 あ　　　　　　　　　はなし
71	買	9	か（う）	バイ	買い物が好きです。 か　もの
72	起	9	お（きる）	キ	毎朝六時に起きます。 まいあさ　　　お
73	寝	9	ね（る）	シン	十二時ごろ寝ます。 ね
74	作	9	つく（る）	サク	ばんごはんはカレーを作りましょう。 つく
75	入	9	はい（る）・い（れる）	ニュウ	はこに入ります。店に入ります。 はい　　　　　　　はい
76	男	10	おとこ	ダン	女の人と男の子がいます。 おんな　　おとこ　こ
77	女	10	おんな	ジョ	山本さんは帽子をかぶった女の人です。 ぼうし　　　　　おんな
78	目	10	め	モク	目がわるいです。上から二番目です。 め　　　　　　　　　　　　　め
79	口	10	くち・ぐち	コウ	口が小さいです。　川口 くち　　　　　　　　　ぐち
80	耳	10	みみ	ジ	私は耳があまりよくありません。 みみ
81	足	10	あし	ソク	ジョンはせが高くて、足がながいです。 あし
82	手	10	て	シュ	手がきれいですね。テニスが上手です。 て　　　　　　　　　　　　　じょうず
83	父	10	ちち・とう	フ	父のなまえはジョンです。お父さん ちち　　　　　　　　　　　　とう
84	母	10	はは・かあ	ボ・モ	母のしごとは高校の先生です。お母さん はは　　　　　　　　　　　　　　かあ
85	姉	10	あね・ねえ	シ	姉は私より三さい上です。お姉さん あね　　　　　　　　　　　　ねえ
86	兄	10	あに・にい	ケイ・キョウ	兄が一人います。お兄さん　兄弟 あに　　　　　　　にい　　きょうだい
87	妹	10	いもうと	マイ	妹 はいません。 いもうと
88	弟	10	おとうと	ダイ	弟 は四時にアルバイトにいきます。兄弟 おとうと　　　　　　　　　　　　きょうだい
89	家	10	いえ・うち	か	父は七時ごろ家に帰ります。 ちち　　　　　　うち
90	族	10		ゾク	私の家は四人家族です。 うち　　　かぞく

	Kanji		Kun-reading	On-reading	Examples
91	両	10		リョウ	両親はニューヨークにすんでいます。 りょうしん
92	親	10	おや	シン	両親はアメリカが好きです。親切な人 りょうしん　　　　　　　　　　しんせつ
93	子	10	こ	シ	男の子が三人います。母のなまえは おとこ こ　　　　　　　　はは 「よし子」です。 こ
94	天	11		テン	明日の天気はいいでしょう。 あした てんき
95	気	11		キ	昨日は天気がよくありませんでした。 きのう てんき
96	雨	11	あめ	ウ	雨がしずかにふっています。 あめ
97	雪	11	ゆき	セツ	明日は大雪です。 あした おおゆき
98	風	11	かぜ	フウ	風がつよいです。台風が来ます。 かぜ　　　　　　たいふう
99	晴	11	は（れる）	セイ	ずっと晴れていて、雨がふりません。 は　　　　　　あめ
100	温	11	あたた（かい）	オン	先週は気温が35度まで上がりました。 きおん ど あ
101	度	11		ド	おふろの温度は42度ぐらいです。 おんど ど
102	東	11	ひがし	トウ	まちの東の方にこうえんがあります。 ひがし
103	西	11	にし	セイ	きょうとは東京の西にあります。 とうきょう にし
104	南	11	みなみ	ナン	南のうみはとてもきれいで温かいです。 みなみ　　　　　　　　　　　あたた
105	北	11	きた	ホク	ほっかいどうは日本の北にあります。 きた
106	寒	11	さむ（い）	カン	カナダのふゆは寒いです。 さむ
107	暑	11	あつ（い）	ショ	東京のなつはむし暑いです。 とうきょう あつ
108	多	11	おお（い）	タ	シンガポールは雨が多いです。 あめ おお
109	少	11	すく（ない）・ すこ（し）	ショウ	このまちは人が少ないです。 すく
110	冷	11	つめ（たい）	レイ	暑いから冷たいものを飲みましょう。 あつ つめ

	Kanji		Kun-reading	On-reading	Examples
111	春	12	はる	シュン	春は雨が多いです。 はる
112	夏	12	なつ	カ	日本の夏は暑いです。 なつ
113	秋	12	あき	シュウ	秋の山はとてもきれいです。 あき
114	冬	12	ふゆ	トウ	冬は寒いから、時々雪がふります。 ふゆ　　　　　ときどき
115	朝	12	あさ	チョウ	日曜日の朝、おそくまで寝るのが好き あさ です。
116	昼	12	ひる	チュウ	母が昼ごはんを作りました。 ひる
117	晩	12		バン	明日の晩ごはんは天ぷらです。 ばん
118	午	12		ゴ	月曜日の午後、両親と家族が来ます。 ご　ご 午前 ごぜん
119	前	12	まえ	ゼン	午前中にしゅくだいをします。中学の前 ごぜん　　　　　　　　　　　まえ 名前 なまえ
120	後	12	あと／うし（ろ） のち	ゴ	午後は暑かったです。一か月ぐらい後 ご　ご つくえの後ろ
121	去	12	さ（る）	キョ	去年南アメリカにいきますた。 きょねん
122	昨	12		サク	一昨年日本にいきました。昨日 おととし　　　　　　　　　きのう
123	供	12	とも／ども	キョウ	子供が二人います。 ども
124	元	12	もと	ゲン	父は元気です。元気なお母さん げんき　　げんき
125	思	12	おも（う）	シ	昨日の朝は風がつよかったと思います。 きのう　あさ　　　　　　　　　おも
126	明	12	あか（るい）	メイ	明るいへや、明日、明るい人 あか　　　あした　あか
127	回	12	まわ（る）	カイ	私の弟は一か月に十回ぐらいラーメン かい を食べます。

JAPANESE-ENGLISH GLOSSARY

This glossary contains all Japanese words that appear in the vocbulary list of each chapter. They are listed according to **gojuuon-jun** (Japanese alphabetical order). Each entry follows this format: word written in kana, word written in **kanji**, part of speech, English meaning, and chapter number where the word first appears. Abbreviations are identical to the labels used in each chapter vocabulary list.

adv.	adverb	*conj.*	conjunction	*q. word*	question word
い-*adj.*	い-adjective	*inter.*	interjection	*pref.*	prefix
な-*adj.*	な-adjective	*count.*	counter	*suf.*	suffix
う-*v.*	う-verb	*n.*	noun	*part.*	particle
る-*v.*	る-verb	*exp.*	expression	*cop. v.*	copula verb
irr. v.	irregular verb	*demo.*	demonstrative	*number*	number

あ

アイスクリーム　*n.* ice cream, 9

あがる (上がる)　う -*v.* to rise; to go up, 11

あかるい (明るい)　い -*adj.* cheerful (See Chapter 4 for "bright"), 10

あき (秋)　*n.* fall, autumn, 11

アクセサリー　*n.* accessories, 8

あけましておめでとうございます。(明けましておめでとうございます。)　*exp.* Happy
New Year, 12

あし (足)　*n.* leg, foot, 10

あたたかい (温かい)　い -*adj.* warm, 9

あたたかい (暖かい / 温かい)　い -*adj.* warm, 11

あたま (頭)　*n.* head, あたまがいい smart, intelligent, 10

あつい (熱い)　い -*adj.* hot (in temperature), 9

あつい (暑い / 熱い)　い -*adj.* hot, 11

あに (兄)　*n.* older brother (the speaker's), 10

あね (姉)　*n.* older sister (the speaker's), 10

あぶら (油 / 脂)　*n.* oil あぶらが　おおい fatty, oily, 9

あまい (甘い)　い -*adj.* sweet, 9

あめ (雨)　*n.* rain, rainy, 11

い

いいえ、そんなことはありません。　*exp.* No, that's not the case, 10

いいえ、まだまだです。　*exp.* No, I still have a long way to go, 10

いかが　q. word how (polite form of どう), 8

いくつ　q. word how many, 8

いくつ　q. word How old 〜 ? おいくつ　polite form of いくつ, 10

いくら　q. word how much (money), 8

イタリア　*n.* Italy, 9

いもうと (妹)　*n.* younger sister (the speaker's), 10

いもうとさん (妹さん)　*n.* younger sister (someone else's), 10

いや (な)　な -*adj.* unpleasant, 11

イヤリング　*n.* earring, 8

いらっしゃいませ。　　*exp.* Welcome, 8
いる (要る)　　う *-v.* to need something, 9
いれる (入れる)　　る *-v.* to put, 8

う

うた (歌)　　*n.* song, 7
うたう (歌う)　　う *-v.* to sing, 7
うでどけい (腕時計)　　*n.* wristwatch, 8
うどん　　*n.* Japanese wheat noodles, 9
うみ (海)　　*n.* ocean, sea, 12
うりば (売り場)　　*n.* department, section (of a store), 8

え

エアロビクス　　*n.* aerobics, 7
えーと　　*exp.* Well, Let's see. . . , 12
～えん (～円)　　*count.* counter for Japanese currency, 8

お

(お) さしみ (御刺身)　　*n.* sashimi (fillet of fresh raw fish, such as tuna) (usually used with お at the beginning), 9
(お) すし (御寿司)　　*n.* sushi (usually used with お at the beginning), 9
おいしい　　い *-adj.* delicious, good, tasty, 7
おおい (多い)　　い *-adj.* a lot, much, 9
おかあさん (お母さん)　　*n.* mother (someone else's), 10
おくさん (奥さん)　　*n.* wife (someone else's), 10
おこさん (お子さん)　　*n.* child (someone else's), 10
おじいさん (お祖父さん)　　*n.* grandfather (someone else's), 10
おちゃ (お茶)　　*n.* tea, green tea, 7
おとうさん (お父さん)　　*n.* father (someone else's), 10
おとうと (弟)　　*n.* younger brother (the speaker's), 10
おとうとさん (弟さん)　　*n.* younger brother (someone else's), 10
おとこ (男)　　*n.* male, おとこの人 man, 10
おととし (一昨年)　　*n.* the year before last year, two years ago, 12
おにいさん (お兄さん)　　*n.* older brother (someone else's), 10
おねえさん (お姉さん)　　*n.* older sister (someone else's), 10
おばあさん (お祖母さん)　　*n.* grandmother (someone else's), 10
おもいで (思い出)　　*n.* memories, 12
オレンジ　　*n.* orange, 7
おわる (終わる)　　う *-v.* to end, 7
おんな (女)　　*n.* female おんなの人 woman, おんなのこ girl, 10

か

～かい (～階)　　*count.* counter for floors of a building, 8
～かい (～回)　　*suf.* times, 12
がいこく (外国)　　*n.* foreign countries, 12
かいしゃいん (会社員)　　*n.* businessman, 10
かう (買う)　　う *-v.* to buy, 7

かお (顔)　　*n.* face, 10

〜かげつ (〜か月)　　*suf.* counter for month, 12

かける　　る *-v.* to put on (glasses), 10

かさ (傘)　　*n.* umbrella, 8

かぜ (風)　　*n.* wind, 11

かぞく (家族)　　*n.* family, the speaker's family, 10

〜かた (〜方)　　*suf.* person, polite form of 人 but cannot stand alone and needs a modifier いいかた (nice person), 10

かたい (固い)　　い *-adj.* hard, tough, 9

〜がつ (〜月)　　*suf.* month, 11

がっき (学期)　　*n.* semester, quarter いちがっき one semester はるがっき spring semester/ quarter, 12

かっこいい　　い *-adj.* good-looking, neat, 10

かぶき (歌舞伎)　　*n.* kabuki (Japanese traditional performing art), 12

かぶる　　う *-v.* ot put on (a hat, a cap), 10

かみ (髪)　　*n.* hair, 10

からい (辛い)　　い *-adj.* spicy, 9

カラオケ　　*n.* Karaoke, sing-along, 7

カレーライス　　*n.* curry and rice dish. An abbreviated form is カレー , 9

カロリー　　*n.* calorie, 9

かわいい (可愛い)　　い *-adj.* cute, adorable, 10

き

きおん (気温)　　*n.* air temperature, 11

きこう (気候)　　*n.* climate, 11

きせつ (季節)　　*n.* season, 11

きた (北)　　*n.* north, 11

きもの (着物)　　*n.* traditional Japanese clothes, kimono, 12

キャンプ　　*n.* camping, 12

きゅう (な)(急 (な))　　な *-adj.* sudden　　きゅうに　　suddenly, 11

きょうかい (教会)　　*n.* church, 12

きょうだい (兄弟)　　*n.* sibling, 10

きょねん (去年)　　*n.* last year, 11

きらい (な)(嫌い (な))　　な *-adj.* dislike, hate, 7

きる (着る)　　る *-v.* to put on (sweater, shirt, jacket), 10

く

くだもの (果物)　　*n.* fruit, 7

くち (口)　　*n.* mouth, 10

くつ (靴)　　*n.* shoes, 8

クッキー　　*n.* cookie, 9

くつした (靴下)　　*n.* socks, 8

くも (雲)　　*n.* cloud, 11

くもり (曇り)　　*n.* cloudy, 11

くもる (曇る)　　う *-v.* to become cloudy, 11

クラシック　　*n.* classical music, 7

クリスマス　*n.* Christmas, 12

け

ケーキ　*n.* cake, 9

けさ (今朝)　*n.* this morning, 11

けっこん (結婚)　*n.* marriage,　〜とけっこんする to marry 〜 , けっこんしている to be married, 10

けんか　*n.* fight, quarrel　けんかをする to fight, 12

こ

こ (子)　*n.* child, おとこのこ boy, おんなのこ girl, 10

〜ご (〜後)　*suf.* from 〜 , after 〜 (3 年ご three years from now), 12

ご〜 (御〜)　*pref.* polite prefix　ごちゅうもん, 9

こうちゃ (紅茶)　*n.* black tea, 7

コート　*n.* coat, 8

コーラ　*n.* cola, 7

ごかぞく (ご家族)　*n.* family (someone else's), 10

ごきょうだい (ご兄弟)　*n.* siblings (someone else's), 10

ごしゅじん (ご主人)　*n.* husband (someone else's), 10

こと　*n.* thing (intangible), 7

ことし (今年)　*n.* this year, 11

こども (子供)　*n.* child, 10

ゴルフ　*n.* golf, 7

こんげつ (今月)　*n.* this month, 12

さ

〜さい (〜歳 / 才)　*suf.* 〜 years old, 10

さいきん (最近)　*n.* recent, recently (it can be used as an adverb), 11

さかな (魚)　*n.* fish, 7

さがる (下がる)　う -*v.* to fall; to go down, 11

〜さつ (〜冊)　*count.* counter for bound objects (e.g. books, magazines), 8

さむい (寒い)　い -*adj.* cold, 11

サラダ　*n.* salad, 9

サンドイッチ　*n.* sandwich, 9

し

ジーンズ　*n.* jeans, 8

しょっぱい　い -*adj.* salty, 9

しかくい (四角い)　い -*adj.* square, 10

ジャケット　*n.* jacket, 8

ジャズ　*n.* jazz, 7

シャツ　*n.* shirt, 8

〜しゅうかん (〜週間)　*suf.* for 〜 weeks, 12

ジュース　*n.* juice, 7

しゅじん (主人)　*n.* husband (the speaker's), 10

しゅみ (趣味)　*n.* hobby, 7

しょう～ (小～)　*pref.* elementary, 小学生 elementary school student, 小学校 elementary school, 10

しょうがつ (正月)　*n.* the New Year often used with the polite prefix お，おしょうがつ，12

じょうず (な)(上手 (な))　な *-adj.* good at, skillful, 10

しょくじ (食事)　*n.* dining, 7

しょくじする (食事する)　*irr. v.* to dine, 7

しょくひん (食品)　*n.* food, 8

しる (知る)　う *-v.* to come to know, しっている to know, しらない don't know, 11

しんしふく (紳士服)　*n.* menswear, 8

じんじゃ (神社)　*n.* Shinto shrine, 12

しんせつ (な)(親切 (な))　な *-adj.* kind, 10

す

すいぞくかん (水族館)　*n.* aquarium, 12

スーツ　*n.* suit, 8

スープ　*n.* soup, 9

スカート　*n.* skirt, 8

すき (な)(好き (な))　な *-adj.* like, 7

スキー　*n.* skiing, ski, 7

すきでもきらいでもありません (好きでも嫌いでもありません。)　*exp.* I don't like or dislike it, 7

すくない (少ない)　い *-adj.* a little bit, 9

すこし (少し)　*adv.* a little, a few, 8

すずしい (涼しい)　い *-adj.* cool, 11

すっぱい (酸っぱい)　い *-adj.* sour, 9

ステーキ　*n.* steak, 9

ストッキング　*n.* stockings, pantyhose, 8

スパゲティ　*n.* spaghetti, 9

スポーツ　*n.* sport, 7

ズボン　*n.* trousers (primarily men's), 8

すむ (住む)　う *-v.* to reside, ～にすんでいる to live in ～, 10

する　*irr. v.* to put on (accessories), 10

せ

せ (背)　*n.* back (part of the body); height (of a person), 10

セーター　*n.* sweater, 8

セール　*n.* sale, 8

セット　*n.* a Western-style fixed menu, 9

せんげつ (先月)　*n.* last month, 12

ぜんぶで (全部で)　*exp.* all together, 8

そ

そば (蕎麦)　*n.* Japanese buckwheat noodles, 9

そふ (祖父)　*n.* grandfather (the speaker's), 10

そぼ (祖母)　*n.* grandmother (the speaker's), 10

それから   *conj.* and, in addition, then, 7

た

だい～ (大～)   *pref.* very much, 大すき like very much, 7

たいふう (台風)   *n.* typhoon, 11

たかい (高い)   い -*adj.* expensive (Chapter 4: high, tall), 7

たくさん   *adv.* a lot, many, much, 8

たとえば (例えば)   conj. for example, 7

たべもの (食べ物)   *n.* food, 7

たまご (卵 / 玉子)   *n.* egg, 7

たんじょうび (誕生日)   *n.* birthday, 8

ち

チーズ   *n.* cheese, 9

ちか (地下)   *n.* basement   ちかいっかい first basement floor, 8

チキン   *n.* chicken, 9

ちち (父)   *n.* father (the speaker's), 10

チャーハン   *n.* Chinese style fried rice, 9

ちゅう～ (中～)   *pref.* middle, 中学生 middle school student, 中学校 middle school/junior high school, 10

ちゅうがく (中学)   *n.* junior high school (shortened form of 中学校), 12

ちゅうかりょうり (中華料理)   *n.* Chinese cooking, 9

ちゅうもん (注文)   *n.* order, 9

ちゅうもんする (注文する)   *irr. v.* to order, 9

チョコレート   *n.* chocolate, 9

ちょっと   *adv.* a little, a few (more casual than すこし), 8

つ

～つ   *count.* general counter (Japanese origin number), 8

つくる (作る)   う -*v.* to make, 7

つづく (続く)   う -*v.* to continue, 11

つとめる (勤める)   る -*v.* to become employed, ～につとめている to be employed at, work for ～ , 10

つま (妻)   *n.* wife (of speaker), 10

つめたい (冷たい)   い -*adj.* cold, 9

つゆ (梅雨)   *n.* rainy season, 11

つよい (強い)   い -*adj.* strong, 11

つり (釣り)   *n.* fishing, 7

て

て (手)   *n.* hand, 10

T シャツ   *n.* T-shirt, 8

ていしょく (定食)   *n.* Japanese or Asian-styled dish set, 9

～ている   *aux. v.* resultant state, 10

デート   *n.* dating, 12

デートする   *irr. v.* to go out on a date, 12

デザート   *n.* dessert, 9

でも   conj. but, 7
てら (寺)   n. Buddhist temple, (often used as おてら), 12
てんき (天気)   n. weather, 11
てんきよほう (天気予報)   n. weather forecast, 11
てんぷら (天麩羅 / 天ぷら)   n. tempura (fish, shrimp, and vegetables battered and deep-fried), 9

と

〜ど (〜度)   suf. degree, 11
〜ど (〜度)   suf. times, 12
どうして   q. word why, 7
どうですか。   exp. How about 〜 ?, 7
どうぶつえん (動物園)   n. zoo, 12
トースト   n. toast, 9
とき (時)   n. when, at the time of 〜   (子供の時 when I was a child), 12
とし (年)   n. age; としうえ elder, older; とししした younger, 10
トマト   n. tomato, 7
ドライブ   n. driving (pleasure driving), 7
とる (撮る)   う -v. to take (a photograph), しゃしんを　とる , 7
とる (取る)   う -v. to take, get, 8
ドレス   n. dress, 8

な

なあ   part. A particle of exclamation to express desires or feelings without addressing anyone in particular. Used in casual speech, 12
ながい (長い)   い -adj. long, 10
なく (泣く)   う -v. to cry, 12
なつ (夏)   n. summer, 11
なんせい (南西)   n. southwest, 11
なんとう (南東)   n. southeast, 11

に

〜に　する   exp. to decide on 〜 , 9
にがい (苦い)   い -adj. bitter, 9
にく (肉)   n. meat, 7
にし (西)   n. west, 11
〜にち (〜日)   suf. day, 12
にわかあめ (にわか雨)   n. shower, 11
〜にん (〜人)   suf. 〜 people, 10
にんじん   n. carrot, 7

ね

ネクタイ   n. tie, 8
ネックレス   n. necklace, 8
〜ねん (〜年)   suf. specific year (2008 年), counter for year (十年), 12

の

のち (後)   *n.* after, 11
〜のち〜   *exp.* after　あめのちはれ sunny after rain, 11
のみもの (飲み物)   *n.* drinks, 7
のる (乗る)   う -*v.* to get on, to ride (ひこうきに　のる   get on a plane), 12

は

〜は　ありませんか。   *exp.* Do you have 〜 ? / Do you carry 〜 ? (lit, Isn't there 〜 ?), 8
ハイキング   *n.* hiking, 7
はく   う -*v.* to put on (skirt, pants, socks), 10
はくぶつかん (博物館)   *n.* museum, 12
はこ (箱)   *n.* box, 8
はじまる (始まる)   う -*v.* to begin, 7
はじめて (初めて)   *adv.* for the first time, 12
バスケットボール   *n.* basketball (abbreviated as バスケット or バスケ), 7
はな (鼻)   *n.* nose, 10
バナナ   *n.* banana, 7
はは (母)   *n.* mother (the speaker's), 10
はやい (早い)   い -*adj.* early, 11
はる (春)   *n.* spring, 11
はれ (晴れ)   *n.* sunny, 11
はれる (晴れる)   る -*v.* to become sunny, 11
バレンタインデー   *n.* St. Valentine's Day, 12
ハロウィン   *n.* Halloween, 12
パン   *n.* bread, 9
〜ばん (め)(〜番 (目))   *suf.* 〜 th (ordinal), 10
パンツ   *n.* (primarily women's) trousers, shorts, 8
はんとし (半年)   *n.* a half year, 12
ハンドバッグ   *n.* handbag, 8
ハンバーガー   *n.* hamburger, 9

ひ

ビーフ   *n.* beef, 9
ビール   *n.* beer, 7
ひがし (東)   *n.* east, 11
〜ひき (〜匹)   *count.* counter for fish and small four-legged animals, 8
ひくい (低い)   い -*adj.* low, カロリーがひくい low in calories, 9
ひこうき (飛行機)   *n.* airplane, 12
ピザ   *n.* pizza, 9
びじゅつかん (美術館)   *n.* art museum, 12
ヒップホップ   *n.* hip-hop music, 7
ひとりっこ (一人っ子)   *n.* only child, 10

ふ

ふく (服)   *n.* clothing, 8
ふく (吹く)   う -*v.* to blow, 11

ふじんふく (婦人服)　*n.* woman's clothing, 8
フットボール　*n.* (American) football (アメフト), 7
ふとる (太る)　う *-v.* to gain weight、ふとっている　to be fat, 10
ふゆ (冬)　*n.* winter, 11
フライドチキン　*n.* fried chicken, 9
ブラウス　*n.* blouse, 8
ふる (降る)　う *-v.* to fall, 11
プレゼント　*n.* present, 12
ブロンド (ブロンド)　*n.* blond, 10
ぶんぼうぐ (文房具)　*n.* stationery, 8

へ

ベルト　*n.* belt, 8

ほ

ほう (方)　*n.* direction, 11
ぼうし (帽子)　*n.* hat, cap, 8
ポーク　*n.* pork, 9
ほくせい (北西)　*n.* northwest, 11
ほくとう (北東)　*n.* northeast, 11
ほそながい (細長い)　い *-adj.* long/elongated, 10
ポップス　*n.* pop music, 7
〜ほん (〜本)　*count.* counter for long, cylindrical objects (e.g. pen, pencil, bottle), 8
ほんとうに / ほんとに (本当に)　*adv.* truly, really, indeed　ほんとに is more conversational
　　than ほんとうに , 11

ま

〜まい (〜枚)　*count.* counter for thin objects (e.g. paper, shirts, plates), 8
マイナス　*n.* minus, 11
〜まえ (〜前)　*suf.* 〜 ago　(一年まえ one year ago), 12
まつり (祭り)　*n.* festival (often used as おまつり), 12
まるい (丸い)　い *-adj.* round, 10
まんなか (真ん中)　*n.* center, middle, middle child, 10

み

みじかい (短い)　い *-adj.* short (length), 10
みず (水)　*n.* water, 7
みせ (店)　*n.* store, shop, 8
みせる (見せる)　る *-v.* to show, 8
みなみ (南)　*n.* south, 11
みみ (耳)　*n.* ear, 10
ミュージカル　*n.* musical, 12
ミルク　*n.* milk, 7

む

むしあつい (蒸し暑い)　い *-adj.* humid, 11

め

め（目） *n.* eye, 10
めがね（眼鏡） *n.* glasses, 10

も

もう *adv.* a little 〜 , 8
もっと *adv.* more, 7
もらう う -*v.* to receive, to get, 12

や

や *part.* and (when listing examples), 7
やきゅう（野球） *n.* baseball, 7
やさい（野菜） *n.* vegetable, 7
やさしい　ことばで　いってください。（やさしい　言葉で　言って下さい。） *exp.*
　　Please say it in easier words, 8
やすい（安い） い -*adj.* inexpensive, 7
やせる る -*v.* to lose weight, やせている to be thin, 10
やまのぼり（山登り） *n.* mountain climbing, 12
やわらかい（柔らかい） い -*adj.* soft , 9

ゆ

ゆうえんち（遊園地） *n.* amusement park, 12
ゆうがた（夕方） *n.* evening, 11
ゆき（雪） *n.* snow, snowy, 11
ゆびわ（指輪） *n.* ring, 8

よ

ようしょく（洋食） *n.* western style cuisine, 9
よる（夜） *n.* night, 11
よわい（弱い） い -*adj.* weak, 11

ら

ラーメン *n.* ramen, Chinese noodles in soup, 9
らいげつ（来月） *n.* next month, 12
ライス *n.* rice, 9
ラップ *n.* rap music, 7
ランチ *n.* lunch, luch set A-ランチ Lunch set A, 9
ランチ *n.* lunch, set lunch (Western style), 9

り

りょこう（旅行） *n.* traveling, 7
りんご *n.* apple, 7

れ

レタス *n.* lettuce, 7

ろ

ロック *n.* rock and roll, 7

わ

ワイン　*n.* wine, 7
わかる (分かる)　う -*v.* to understand,　日本語がわかる to understand Japanese, 10
わしょく (和食)　*n.* Japanese cuisine (にほんりょうり), 9
わるい (悪い)　い -*adj.* bad, 11

を

～を　おねがいします　 (～をお願いします)　*exp.* I would like to have ～ , 9
～を　ください　 (～を下さい)　*exp.* 8 Please give me ～ , 8

ENGLISH-JAPANESE GLOSSARY

A

a little ～　もう　*adv.*, 8
a little bit　すくない (少ない)　い -*adj.*, 9
a little, a few　すこし (少し)　*adv.*, 8
a little　ちょっと　*adv.*, 8
a lot, many, much　たくさん　*adv.*, 8
a lot, much　おおい (多い)　い -*adj.*, 9
accessories　アクセサリー　*n.*, 8
aerobics　エアロビクス　*n.*, 7
after　のち (後)　*n.*, 11
after　～のち～　*exp.*, 11
age　とし (年)　*n.*, 10
～ ago　(一年まえ one year ago)　～まえ (～前)　*suf.*, 12
air temperature　きおん (気温)　*n.*, 11
airplane　ひこうき (飛行機)　*n.*, 12
all together　ぜんぶで (全部で)　*exp.*, 8
amusement park　ゆうえんち (遊園地)　*n.*, 12
and (when listing examples)　や　*part.*, 7
and, in addition, then　それから　*conj.*, 7
apple　りんご　*n.*, 7
aquarium　すいぞくかん (水族館)　*n.*, 12
art museum　びじゅつかん (美術館)　*n.*, 12

B

back (part of the body); height (of a person)　せ (背)　*n.*, 10
bad　わるい (悪い)　い -*adj.*, 11
banana　バナナ　*n.*, 7
baseball　やきゅう (野球)　*n.*, 7
basement　ちか (地下)　*n.*, 8
basketball　バスケットボール　*n.*, 7
to become cloudy　くもる (曇る)　う -*v.*, 11
to become employed　つとめる (勤める)　る -*v.*, 10
to become sunny　はれる (晴れる)　る -*v.*, 11
beef　ビーフ　*n.*, 9
beer　ビール　*n.*, 7
to begin　はじまる (始まる)　う -*v.*, 7
belt　ベルト　*n.*, 8
birthday　たんじょうび (誕生日)　*n.*, 8
bitter　にがい (苦い)　い -*adj.*, 9
black tea　こうちゃ (紅茶)　*n.*, 7
blond　ブロンド (ブロンド)　*n.*, 10
blouse　ブラウス　*n.*, 8
to blow　ふく (吹く)　う -*v.*, 11

box　はこ（箱）　*n.*, 8
bread　パン　*n.*, 9
Buddhist temple (often used as おてら)　てら（寺）　*n.*, 12
businessman　かいしゃいん（会社員）　*n.*, 10
but　でも　*conj.*, 7
to buy　かう（買う）　う -*v.*, 7

C

cake　ケーキ　*n.*, 9
calorie　カロリー　*n.*, 9
camping　キャンプ　*n.*, 12
carrot　にんじん　*n.*, 7
center, middle, middle child　まんなか（真ん中）　*n.*, 10
cheerful　あかるい（明るい）　い -*adj.*, 10
cheese　チーズ　*n.*, 9
chicken　チキン　*n.*, 9
child　こども（子供）　*n.*, 10
child (someone else's)　おこさん（お子さん）　*n.*, 10
child　こ（子）　*n.*, 10
Chinese cooking　ちゅうかりょうり（中華料理）　*n.*, 9
Chinese style fried rice　チャーハン　*n.*, 9
chocolate　チョコレート　*n.*, 9
Christmas　クリスマス　*n.*, 12
church　きょうかい（教会）　*n.*, 12
classical music　クラシック　*n.*, 7
climate　きこう（気候）　*n.*, 11
clothing　ふく（服）　*n.*, 8
cloud　くも（雲）　*n.*, 11
cloudy　くもり（曇り）　*n.*, 11
coat　コート　*n.*, 8
cola　コーラ　*n.*, 7
cold　さむい（寒い）　い -*adj.*, 11
cold　つめたい（冷たい）　い -*adj.*, 9
to come to know　しる（知る）　う -*v.*, 11
cookie　クッキー　*n.*, 9
cool　すずしい（涼しい）　い -*adj.*, 11
counter for bound objects (e.g. books, magazines)　〜さつ（〜冊）　*count.*, 8
counter for fish and small four-legged animals　〜ひき（〜匹）　*count.*, 8
counter for floors of a building　〜かい（〜階）　*count.*, 8
counter for Japanese currency　〜えん（〜円）　*count.*, 8
counter for long, cylindrical objects (e.g. pen, pencil, bottle)　〜ほん（〜本）　*count.*, 8
counter for month　〜かげつ（〜か月）　*suf.*, 12
counter for thin objects (e.g. paper, shirts, plates)　〜まい（〜枚）　*count.*, 8
general counter (Japanese origin number)　〜つ　*count.*, 8
to cry　なく（泣く）　う -*v.*, 12
curry and rice dish　カレーライス　*n.*, 9

cute, adorable　かわいい (可愛い)　い -adj., 10

D

dating　デート　n., 12
day　〜にち (〜日)　suf., 12
to decide on　〜.　〜に　する　exp., 9
degree　〜ど (〜度)　suf., 11
delicious, good, tasty　おいしい　い -adj., 7
department　うりば (売り場)　n., 8
dessert　デザート　n., 9
to dine　しょくじする (食事する)　irr. v., 7
dining　しょくじ (食事)　n., 7
direction　ほう (方)　n., 11
dislike, hate　きらい (な)(嫌い (な))　な -adj., 7
Do you have 〜 ? / Do you carry 〜 ? (lit., Isn't there 〜 ?)　〜は　ありませんか。　exp., 8
dress　ドレス　n., 8
drinks　のみもの (飲み物)　n., 7
driving (pleasure driving)　ドライブ　n., 7

E

ear　みみ (耳)　n., 10
early　はやい (早い)　い -adj., 11
earring　イヤリング　n., 8
east　ひがし (東)　n., 11
egg　たまご (卵 / 玉子)　n., 7
elementary　しょう〜 (小〜)　pref., 10
to end　おわる (終わる)　う -v., 7
evening　ゆうがた (夕方)　n., 11
A particle of exclamation　なあ　part., 12
expensive (Chapter 4: high, tall)　たかい (高い)　い -adj., 7
eye　め (目)　n., 10

F

face　かお (顔)　n., 10
to fall　ふる (降る)　う -v., 11
fall, autumn　あき (秋)　n., 11
to fall; to go down　さがる (下がる)　う -v., 11
family (someone else's)　ごかぞく (ご家族)　n., 10
family, the speaker's family　かぞく (家族)　n., 10
father (someone else's)　おとうさん (お父さん)　n., 10
father (the speaker's)　ちち (父)　n., 10
female　おんな (女)　n., 10
festival (often used as おまつり)　まつり (祭り)　n., 12
fight, quarrel　けんか　n., 12
fish　さかな (魚)　n., 7
fishing　つり (釣り)　n., 7

food　しょくひん（食品）　*n.*, 8
food　たべもの（食べ物）　*n.*, 7
(American) football（アメフト）　フットボール　*n.*, 7
for 〜 weeks　〜しゅうかん（〜週間）　*suf.*, 12
for example　たとえば（例えば）　*conj.*, 7
for the first time　はじめて（初めて）　*adv.*, 12
foreign countries　がいこく（外国）　*n.*, 12
fried chicken　フライドチキン　*n.*, 9
from 〜, after 〜　〜ご（〜後）　*suf.*, 12
fruit　くだもの（果物）　*n.*, 7

G

to gain weight　ふとる（太る）　う -*v.*, 10
to get on, to ride　のる（乗る）　う -*v.*, 12
glasses　めがね（眼鏡）　*n.*, 10
to go out on a date　デートする　*irr. v.*, 12
golf　ゴルフ　*n.*, 7
good at, skillful　じょうず（な）（上手（な））　な -*adj.*, 10
good-looking, neat　かっこいい　い -*adj.*, 10
grandfather (someone else's)　おじいさん（お祖父さん）　*n.*, 10
grandfather (the speaker's)　そふ（祖父）　*n.*, 10
grandmother (someone else's)　おばあさん（お祖母さん）　*n.*, 10
grandmother (the speaker's)　そぼ（祖母）　*n.*, 10

H

hair　かみ（髪）　*n.*, 10
a half year　はんとし（半年）　*n.*, 12
Halloween　ハロウィン　*n.*, 12
hamburger　ハンバーガー　*n.*, 9
hand　て（手）　*n.*, 10
handbag　ハンドバッグ　*n.*, 8
Happy New Year　あけましておめでとうございます。（明けましておめでとうございます。）　*exp.*, 12
hard, tough　かたい（固い）　い -*adj.*, 9
hat, cap　ぼうし（帽子）　*n.*, 8
head　あたま（頭）　*n.*, 10
hiking　ハイキング　*n.*, 7
hip-hop music　ヒップホップ　*n.*, 7
hobby　しゅみ（趣味）　*n.*, 7
hot　あつい（暑い / 熱い）　い -*adj.*, 11
hot (in temperature)　あつい（熱い）　い -*adj.*, 9
how (polite form of どう)　いかが　*q. word*, 8
How about 〜?　どうですか。　*exp.*, 7
how many　いくつ　*q. word*, 8
how much (money)　いくら　*q. word*, 8
How old 〜?　いくつ　*q. word*, 10

humid　むしあつい (蒸し暑い)　い -adj., 11
husband (someone else's)　ごしゅじん (ご主人)　n., 10
husband (the speaker's)　しゅじん (主人)　n., 10

I

I don't like or dislike it.　すきでもきらいでもありません (好きでも嫌いでもありません。)
　　exp., 7
I would like to have ～.　～を　おねがいします (～をお願いします)　exp., 9
ice cream　アイスクリーム　n., 9
inexpensive　やすい (安い)　い -adj., 7
Italy　イタリア　n., 9

J

jacket　ジャケット　n., 8
Japanese buckwheat noodles　そば (蕎麦)　n., 9
Japanese cuisine (にほんりょうり)　わしょく (和食)　n., 9
Japanese or Asian-styled dish set　ていしょく (定食)　n., 9
Japanese wheat noodles　うどん　n., 9
jazz　ジャズ　n., 7
jeans　ジーンズ　n., 8
juice　ジュース　n., 7
junior high school (shortened form of 中学校)　ちゅうがく (中学)　n., 12

K

kabuki (Japanese traditional performing art)　かぶき (歌舞伎)　n., 12
Karaoke, sing-along　カラオケ　n., 7
kind　しんせつ (な)(親切 (な))　な -adj., 10

L

last month　せんげつ (先月)　n., 12
last year　きょねん (去年)　n., 11
leg, foot　あし (足)　n., 10
lettuce　レタス　n., 7
like　すき (な)(好き (な))　な -adj., 7
long　ながい (長い)　い -adj., 10
long/elongated　ほそながい (細長い)　い -adj., 10
to lose weight　やせる　る -v., 10
low　ひくい (低い)　い -adj., 9
lunch, luch set　ランチ　n., 9
lunch, set lunch (Western style)　ランチ　n., 9

M

to make　つくる (作る)　う -v., 7
male　おとこ (男)　n., 10
marriage　けっこん (結婚)　n., 10
meat　にく (肉)　n., 7
memories　おもいで (思い出)　n., 12

menswear   しんしふく (紳士服)   *n.*, 8
middle   ちゅう〜 (中〜)   *pref.*, 10
milk   ミルク   *n.*, 7
minus   マイナス   *n.*, 11
month   〜がつ (〜月)   *suf.*, 11
more   もっと   *adv.*, 7
mother (someone else's)   おかあさん (お母さん)   *n.*, 10
mother (the speaker's)   はは (母)   *n.*, 10
mountain climbing   やまのぼり (山登り)   *n.*, 12
mouth   くち (口)   *n.*, 10
museum   はくぶつかん (博物館)   *n.*, 12
musical   ミュージカル   *n.*, 12

N

necklace   ネックレス   *n.*, 8
to need something   いる (要る)   う -*v.*, 9
next month   らいげつ (来月)   *n.*, 12
night   よる (夜)   *n.*, 11
No, I still have a long way to go.   いいえ、まだまだです。   *exp.*, 10
No, that's not the case.   いいえ、そんなことはありません。   *exp.*, 10
north   きた (北)   *n.*, 11
northeast   ほくとう (北東)   *n.*, 11
northwest   ほくせい (北西)   *n.*, 11
nose   はな (鼻)   *n.*, 10

O

ocean, sea   うみ (海)   *n.*, 12
oil   あぶら (油 / 脂)   *n.*, 9
older brother (someone else's)   おにいさん (お兄さん)   *n.*, 10
older brother (the speaker's)   あに (兄)   *n.*, 10
older sister (someone else's)   おねえさん (お姉さん)   *n.*, 10
older sister (the speaker's)   あね (姉)   *n.*, 10
only child   ひとりっこ (一人っ子)   *n.*, 10
orange   オレンジ   *n.*, 7
order   ちゅうもん (注文)   *n.*, 9
to order   ちゅうもんする (注文する)   *irr. v.*, 9

P

〜 people   〜にん (〜人)   *suf.*, 10
person, polite form of 人   〜かた (〜方)   *suf.*, 10
pizza   ピザ   *n.*, 9
Please give me 〜.   〜を　ください (〜を下さい)   *exp.*, 8
Please say it in easier words.   やさしい　ことばで　いってください。(やさしい　言葉で　言って下さい。)   *exp.*, 8
polite prefix   ご〜 (御〜)   *pref.*, 9
pop music   ポップス   *n.*, 7

pork　ポーク　*n.*, 9
present　プレゼント　*n.*, 12
to put　いれる（入れる）　る -*v.*, 8
to put on (a hat, a cap)　かぶる　う -*v.*, 10
to put on (accessories)　する　irr-*v.*, 10
to put on (glasses)　かける　る -*v.*, 10
to put on (skirt, pants, socks)　はく　う -*v.*, 10
to put on (sweater, shirt, jacket)　きる（着る）　る -*v.*, 10

R

rain, rainy　あめ（雨）　*n.*, 11
rainy season　つゆ（梅雨）　*n.*, 11
ramen, Chinese noodles in soup　ラーメン　*n.*, 9
rap music　ラップ　*n.*, 7
to receive, to get　もらう　う -*v.*, 12
recent, recently　さいきん（最近）　*n.*, 11
to reside　すむ（住む）　う -*v.*, 10
resultant state　〜ている　aux. *v.*, 10
rice　ライス　*n.*, 9
ring　ゆびわ（指輪）　*n.*, 8
to rise; togo up　あがる（上がる）　う -*v.*, 11
rock and roll　ロック　*n.*, 7
round　まるい（丸い）　い -*adj.*, 10

S

salad　サラダ　*n.*, 9
sale　セール　*n.*, 8
salty　しょっぱい　い -*adj.*, 9
sandwich　サンドイッチ　*n.*, 9
sashimi　（お）さしみ（御刺身）　*n.*, 9
season　きせつ（季節）　*n.*, 11
semester, quarter　がっき（学期）　*n.*, 12
Shinto shrine　じんじゃ（神社）　*n.*, 12
shirt　シャツ　*n.*, 8
shoes　くつ（靴）　*n.*, 8
short (length)　みじかい（短い）　い -*adj.*, 10
to show　みせる（見せる）　る -*v.*, 8
shower　にわかあめ（にわか雨）　*n.*, 11
sibling　きょうだい（兄弟）　*n.*, 10
siblings (someone else's)　ごきょうだい（ご兄弟）　*n.*, 10
to sing　うたう（歌う）　う -*v.*, 7
skiing, ski　スキー　*n.*, 7
skirt　スカート　*n.*, 8
snow, snowy　ゆき（雪）　*n.*, 11
socks　くつした（靴下）　*n.*, 8
soft　やわらかい（柔らかい）　い -*adj.*, 9

song　うた（歌）　*n.*, 7

soup　スープ　*n.*, 9

sour　すっぱい（酸っぱい）　い -*adj.*, 9

south　みなみ（南）　*n.*, 11

southeast　なんとう（南東）　*n.*, 11

southwest　なんせい（南西）　*n.*, 11

spaghetti　スパゲティ　*n.*, 9

specific year (2008 年), counter for year（十年）　〜ねん（〜年）　*suf.*, 12

spicy　からい（辛い）　い -*adj.*, 9

sport　スポーツ　*n.*, 7

spring　はる（春）　*n.*, 11

square　しかくい（四角い）　い -*adj.*, 10

St. Valentine's Day　バレンタインデー　*n.*, 12

stationery　ぶんぼうぐ（文房具）　*n.*, 8

steak　ステーキ　*n.*, 9

stockings, pantyhose　ストッキング　*n.*, 8

store, shop　みせ（店）　*n.*, 8

strong　つよい（強い）　い -*adj.*, 11

sudden　きゅう（な）（急（な））　な -*adj.*, 11

suit　スーツ　*n.*, 8

summer　なつ（夏）　*n.*, 11

sunny　はれ（晴れ）　*n.*, 11

sushi (usually used with お at the beginning)　（お）すし（御寿司）　*n.*, 9

sweater　セーター　*n.*, 8

sweet　あまい（甘い）　い -*adj.*, 9

T

to take (a photograph), しゃしんを　とる　とる（撮る）　う -*v.*, 7

to take, get　とる（取る）　う -*v.*, 8

tea, green tea　おちゃ（お茶）　*n.*, 7

tempura (fish, shrimp, and vegetables battered and deep-fried)　てんぷら（天麩羅 / 天ぷら）　*n.*, 9

〜 th (ordinal)　〜ばん（め）（〜番（目））　*suf.*, 10

the New Year　しょうがつ（正月）　*n.*, 12

the year before last year, two years ago　おととし（一昨年）　*n.*, 12

thing (intangible)　こと　*n.*, 7

this month　こんげつ（今月）　*n.*, 12

this morning　けさ（今朝）　*n.*, 11

this year　ことし（今年）　*n.*, 11

tie　ネクタイ　*n.*, 8

times　〜ど（〜度）　*suf.*, 12

times　〜かい（〜回）　*suf.*, 12

to continue　つづく（続く）　う -*v.*, 11

toast　トースト　*n.*, 9

tomato　トマト　*n.*, 7

traditional Japanese clothes, kimono　きもの（着物）　*n.*, 12

traveling　りょこう（旅行）　*n.*, 7
trousers (primarily men's)　ズボン　*n.*, 8
(primarily women's) trousers, shorts　パンツ　*n.*, 8
truly, really, indeed　ほんとうに / ほんとに（本当に）　*adv.*, 11
T-shirt　Tシャツ　*n.*, 8
typhoon　たいふう（台風）　*n.*, 11

U

umbrella　かさ（傘）　*n.*, 8
to understand　わかる（分かる）　う-*v.*, 10
unpleasant　いや（な）　な-*adj.*, 11

V

vegetable　やさい（野菜）　*n.*, 7
very much, 大すき like very much　だい〜（大〜）　*pref.*, 7

W

warm　あたたかい（温かい）　い-*adj.*, 9
warm　あたたかい（暖かい / 温かい）　い-*adj.*, 11
water　みず（水）　*n.*, 7
weak　よわい（弱い）　い-*adj.*, 11
weather　てんき（天気）　*n.*, 11
weather forecast　てんきよほう（天気予報）　*n.*, 11
Welcome.　いらっしゃいませ。　*exp.*, 8
Well, Let's see...　えーと　*exp.*, 12
west　にし（西）　*n.*, 11
western style cuisine　ようしょく（洋食）　*n.*, 9
a Western-style fixed menu　セット　*n.*, 9
when, at the time of 〜　とき（時）　*n.*, 12
why　どうして　*q. word*, 7
wife (someone else's)　おくさん（奥さん）　*n.*, 10
wife (the speaker's)　つま（妻）　*n.*, 10
wind　かぜ（風）　*n.*, 11
wine　ワイン　*n.*, 7
winter　ふゆ（冬）　*n.*, 11
wristwatch　うでどけい（腕時計）　*n.*, 8

Y

〜 years old　〜さい（〜歳 / 才）　*suf.*, 10
younger brother (someone else's)　おとうとさん（弟さん）　*n.*, 10
younger brother (the speaker's)　おとうと（弟）　*n.*, 10
younger sister (someone else's)　いもうとさん（妹さん）　*n.*, 10
younger sister (the speaker's)　いもうと（妹）　*n.*, 10

Z

zoo　どうぶつえん（動物園）　*n.*, 12

INDEX